"We are living longer, but how might we [...] this question in her thoughtful and mult[...] group for well elders. Not surprisingly, bot[h] data support improvements for group mem[bers'] health, spirituality, and cognition. Weaving theories on aging, Buddhist philosophy, and physical and cognitive sciences, Martins provides texture and context for her research and offers an important prototype for working with the growing population of older adults and their unique experience."

—*Lucia McBee, Author,* Mindfulness-Based Elder Care

"This research work, groundbreaking in its execution, shows how mindfulness-based interventions with older people should be integrated into health promotion in order to foster active ageing. Mindfulness is established as a non-pharmacological treatment that allows practice to take the form of person-centred care. Carla's research shows how health treatment is more than merely clinical results. Her work makes us look upon ourselves to transform the mind and, incidentally, gives meaning to the new 21st-century geriatrics."

—*Domingo J. Quintana Hernández, Ph.D., Neuropsychologist and Associate Professor at the International University of La Rioja, Spain*

Mindfulness-Based
INTERVENTIONS
for Older Adults

of related interest

The Ethical Space of Mindfulness in Clinical Practice
An Exploratory Essay
Donald McCown
Foreword by Kenneth Gergen
ISBN 978 1 84905 909 1
eISBN 978 0 85700 510 6

Mindfulness-Based INTERVENTIONS *for Older Adults*

EVIDENCE FOR PRACTICE

Carla Martins, Ph.D.

Foreword by Shauna Shapiro, Ph.D.

Jessica Kingsley *Publishers*
London and Philadelphia

First published in 2014
by Jessica Kingsley Publishers
73 Collier Street
London N1 9BE, UK
and
400 Market Street, Suite 400
Philadelphia, PA 19106, USA

www.jkp.com

Copyright © Carla Martins 2014
Foreword copyright © Shauna Shapiro 2014

Front cover image source: iStockphoto®

All rights reserved. No part of this publication may be reproduced in any material form (including photocopying or storing it in any medium by electronic means and whether or not transiently or incidentally to some other use of this publication) without the written permission of the copyright owner except in accordance with the provisions of the Copyright, Designs and Patents Act 1988 or under the terms of a licence issued by the Copyright Licensing Agency Ltd, Saffron House, 6–10 Kirby Street, London EC1N 8TS. Applications for the copyright owner's written permission to reproduce any part of this publication should be addressed to the publisher.
Warning: The doing of an unauthorised act in relation to a copyright work may result in both a civil claim for damages and criminal prosecution.

Library of Congress Cataloging in Publication Data
A CIP catalog record for this book is available from the Library of Congress

British Library Cataloguing in Publication Data
A CIP catalogue record for this book is available from the British Library

ISBN 978 1 84905 487 4
eISBN 978 0 85700 880 0

Printed and bound in Great Britain

To all Beings everywhere

My great purpose is to Be
To Be what I truly am.
And to Be is the greatest beauty in me
The greatest beauty in you.
When I Am
I transcend limitations
My consciousness expands
I am awake.
When I Am
I become alive
In a timeless presence
That timelessness is now.
When I Am I find myself being conscious
Of the beauty of existence
Of being alone and never being lonely
Of losing myself and never being lost
Of dying and never being dead.
This is what I see in me
This is what I see in you
We are part of the same Life
We are One.

Carla Martins

Contents

Foreword by Shauna Shapiro, Ph.D. 13
ACKNOWLEDGEMENTS 15
PREFACE 17

Chapter 1 Mindfulness and MBSR 21
Meditation and mindfulness 21
Mindfulness-based stress reduction 22
Mindfulness and spirituality 24
MBSR and older adults 26
Mindfulness: psychological perspectives 29
Buddhist perspectives 34
Mindfulness and neuroplasticity 40
Older adults 42
Older adults and life meaning 51
Dying and death 53
Conclusion 60

Chapter 2 Methodology 65
Integral inquiry method 65
Mixed-method design and integral skills 66
Qualitative research methods 69
Quantitative research methods 72
Participants 74
Procedure 76

Chapter 3 Quantitative Results 81
Participants' characteristics 82
Sample: differences between CG and TG 83
Mindfulness 85

	Compassion	88
	Decentering	90
	Well-being	91
	Psychological symptoms	95
	Quality of life	98
	Physical health/symptoms	100
	Death perspectives	101
	Spirituality	102
	Neuropsychological performance	103
	Summary of quantitative results	107
Chapter 4	Qualitative Results	109
	Individual depictions	109
	Global results	152
	Summary of results	170
Chapter 5	Mixed-Methods Results	173
Chapter 6	Integral Results	177
	Change: openness versus resistance to change	177
	Wisdom	179
	Spiritual development	180
	Adaptation	182
Chapter 7	Discussion	183
	Interpretations and conceptualization of findings	183
	Delimitations and limitations	206
	Applications and implications of the study	207
	Summary and conclusions	209
APPENDIX 1	DESCRIPTION OF QUANTITATIVE MEASURES	211
APPENDIX 2	INTERVIEW PROTOCOL	224
APPENDIX 3	TREATMENT OF DATA	225
APPENDIX 4	MAAS STATISTICAL RESULTS	231
APPENDIX 5	FFMQ STATISTICAL RESULTS	235

Appendix 6	SCS Statistical Results. 240
Appendix 7	EQ Statistical Results 245
Appendix 8	SWLS Statistical Results. 248
Appendix 9	PANAS Statistical Results 249
Appendix 10	PWBS Statistical Results. 251
Appendix 11	POMS Statistical Results 255
Appendix 12	PSS Statistical Results. 259
Appendix 13	WHOQOL-BREF Statistical Results 260
Appendix 14	WHOQOL-100 Statistical Results 263
Appendix 15	SHCI Statistical Results 265
Appendix 16	Death Perspectives Statistical Results 266
Appendix 17	SWBQ Statistical Results 270
Appendix 18	Working Memory Index Statistical Results 273
Appendix 19	Processing Speed Index Statistical Results 275
Appendix 20	Memory Statistical Results. 277
	Glossary 279
	References 281
	Subject Index. 301
	Author Index. 302

List of Tables and Figures

Table 4.1	Participant ID Number 2: Themes and Dimensions. 115
Table 4.2	Participant ID Number 7: Themes and Dimensions. 121
Table 4.3	Participant ID Number 8: Themes and Dimensions. 128
Table 4.4	Participant ID Number 13: Themes and Dimensions 133
Table 4.5	Participant ID Number 14: Themes and Dimensions 140
Table 4.6	Participant ID Number 16: Themes and Dimensions 146
Table 4.7	Participant ID Number 18: Themes and Dimensions 151
Table 4.8	Mindfulness and Respective Dimensions: Examples of Significant Statements. 155
Table 4.9	Acceptance and Respective Dimensions: Examples of Significant Statements. 157

Table 4.10	Impermanence and Respective Dimension: Examples of Significant Statements	159
Table 4.11	Psychological Well-Being and Respective Dimensions: Examples of Significant Statements	160
Table 4.12	Physical Well-Being and Respective Dimensions: Examples of Significant Statements	161
Table 4.13	Perceptions of Aging and Respective Dimensions: Examples of Significant Statements	163
Table 4.14	Spirituality and Respective Dimensions: Examples of Significant Statements	164
Table 4.15	Social Interactions and Respective Dimensions: Examples of Significant Statements	167
Table 4.16	Cognitive Performance and Respective Dimensions: Examples of Significant Statements	168
Table 4.17	Daily Life and Respective Dimensions: Examples of Significant Statements	169
Table 4.18	Overall Experience: Examples of Significant Statements	169
Table 4.19	Core Themes, Secondary Themes, Dimensions, and Respective Frequencies	171
Table 5.1	Quantitative and Qualitative Results for the Different Dimensions	173
Figure 3.1	Decentering: Mean Scores for TG and CG at Assessment 1 and Assessment 2	90
Figure 3.2	SWLS: Mean Scores for TG and CG at Assessment 1 and Assessment 2	92
Figure 3.3	PANAS: Mean Difference Between Assessment 1 and Assessment 2 for TG and CG	93
Figure 3.4	PSS: Mean Scores for TG and CG at Assessment 1 and Assessment 2	97
Figure 3.5	SHCI: Mean Scores for TG and CG at Assessment 1 and Assessment 2	100
Figure 3.6	Free Recall: Mean Difference Between Assessment 1 and Assessment 2 for TG and CG	105
Figure 3.7	Trail Making: Mean Difference Between Assessment 1 and Assessment 2 for CG and TG	106
Figure 5.1	Mixed Results: MBSR for Older Adults	176

Foreword

In Western societies old age is often seen as a process of decline, loss of physical and cognitive abilities, loss of identity and social role in the world, and even loss of value and opportunity for growth. As a result, Western culture often seeks to deny or hide the changes that come with age, and devotes significant amounts of time and resources to remaining youthful. The inability to accept the natural process of aging prevents us from gaining the sacred wisdom and depth that are inherent in this universal and perennial process.

Part of healthy development and maturation is the recognition that aging does not only reflect loss and limitation, and can instead be viewed as moments of life filled with opportunities to learn, grow, adapt, and move towards greater awareness and wisdom. As we move towards old age we have the opportunity to define our experience with grace and acceptance instead of resistance and denial. Learning how to relate with an open curiosity to our aging body, the loss of professional roles, the loss of loved ones, the birth of new members in the family, is an essential part of the aging process.

Continuing our own personal development and understanding of our journey in this life is possible moment by moment. Learning never ends. Old age is a quest towards understanding who we are beyond the superficial appearances of existence and to learning to connect with our true self. Wise awareness, genuine compassion, and mindful presence are invaluable companions on our journey, offering valuable ways of relating to life as it changes moment by moment.

In this book, Carla Martins presents a brilliant and clear summary of the field of mindfulness as applied to older adults and how it might serve a complementary and holistic approach to augment physical and emotional well-being, stimulate cognitive performance and creativity, provide tools to deal with loss and daily life with more awareness, foster personal development, and serve as a means to dive deeper into understanding who we are as individual beings as we age. The book weaves together the rigor of clinical science and the wisdom of deep reflection to offer a text that will be of benefit to many—not only for those working with older adults, but for all those who seek to explore how mindfulness can change the way they relate to the aging process, moment by moment.

No matter how fast we run from it, we are all in a state of constant change, and right now in this moment, we are the youngest we will ever be. Learning to rest into the natural aging process with grace, open-heartedness, and curiosity offers the potential to transform individuals and our world.

Shauna Shapiro, Ph.D.
Co-Author, *Mindful Discipline* and
The Art and Science of Mindfulness

Acknowledgements

I would like to thank my dissertation Chair, Dr Mark McCaslin, and my dissertation committee, Dr Ruth Judy and Dr Shauna Shapiro, for their guidance and support during the completion of this study. I would also like to show my appreciation to Dr Ana Perez Chisti who also gave important contributions to the development of this research during its initial stages. My gratitude extends to all the instructors of Sofia University (formerly the Institute of Transpersonal Psychology) with whom I worked during the four years of my doctorate degree. To my cohort members, I'm deeply grateful and honored to have met you and to have shared this journey with you. Thank you for your support and love.

Thank you to the Foundation for Science and Technology (Fundação para a Ciência e a Tecnologia) in Portugal for awarding me a grant to complete the Ph.D. and conduct this research at Sofia University.

I am very honored and grateful to all participants who volunteered to participate in this study and without whom this research would not have been completed. In particular, I am very thankful for your interest, dedication, commitment, and presence throughout the duration of the study and also for sharing your wisdom and life experience with me. I have learned a lot with all of you in innumerable ways.

Thank you to all mindfulness and meditation teachers and researchers whose teachings and work I have encountered throughout the last two decades: Dr Jon Kabat-Zinn, Dr Shauna Shapiro, Dr Daniel Siegel, Dr Richard Davidson, Sharon Salzberg, Elana Rosenbaum, Florence Meleo-Meyer, Melissa Blake, Joan Halifax, Ram Dass, Echkart Tolle, Thich Nhat Hanh, Allan Wallace, Pema Chodron, Mooji, Amy Salzberg, Susan Kaiser Greenland, and many many others who served as an inspiration for my personal development and professional work in mindfulness.

Finally, I am deeply grateful for the support and love of my partner and family for their endless and unconditional love, support and encouragement throughout the process of completion of this study and book.

Preface

The secret of health for both mind and body is not to mourn for the past, nor to worry about the future, but to live the present moment wisely and earnestly.

Buddha

The intention of this work is to present a comprehensive and in-depth analysis of the effects on and experience of older adults during a mindfulness-based stress reduction (MBSR) program. This study investigated how MBSR affects well-being, psychological and physical health, neuropsychological performance, and spirituality in older adults.

MBSR is an eight-week program based on a rigorous and systematic practice of mindfulness techniques and yoga exercises and on the application of mindfulness and mindfulness principles in daily life (Kabat-Zinn, 1990). Mindfulness has been defined as a process of "paying attention in a particular way: on purpose, in the present moment, non-judgmentally" (Kabat-Zinn, 1994, p.4).

MBSR has been scientifically studied in a vast range of clinical and nonclinical groups. MBSR has been shown to be effective in reducing stress, alleviating suffering, improving quality of life, and fostering subjective and objective well-being (Didonna, 2009). Though there is a vast body of scientific literature on the clinical application of MBSR, studies developed with older adults did not show consistent results on the effectiveness of this intervention (Ernst *et al.*, 2008; McBee, 2008; Prewitt, 2000; Smith, 2006). Most studies were carried out with institutionalized elders and showed positive results in terms of physical and emotional well-being and improved ability to deal with stress (Ernst *et al.*, 2008; McBee, 2008). Studies developed with noninstitutionalized older adults involved patients with fibromyalgia (Prewitt, 2000) and chronic pain (Morone, Greco, and Weiner, 2008; Morone *et al.*, 2008) and revealed positive improvements in the ability to deal with pain. Another study looking at the effects of MBSR in older adults suffering from anxiety and depression provided mixed results showing positive changes in some individuals but no changes in others (Smith, 2006). However, these studies failed to address the impact of MBSR in terms of spiritual development, spiritual well-being, neuropsychological performance, and the interaction between these different dimensions in promoting individuals' well-being.

With the worldwide demographic changes of modern times, the number of older adults is increasing (U.S. Centers for Disease Control and Prevention, 2003). It is well known that the aging process and associated stress can diminish their quality of life and pose great emotional and physical challenges in their daily lives (Aldwin, Park, and Spiro, 2007). Aging is a natural process, a multidimensional phenomenon during which changes occur in different domains of individuals' lives that include physical, neurological, cognitive, social, psychological, and spiritual realms. These changes pose many challenges and interact, influencing individuals' personal experience of the process of aging and guiding individuals' personal adjustment, coping strategies, and attitudes towards the changes of this stage of life (Aldwin *et al.*, 2007).

Older adults face several challenges including physical ailments, disease, cognitive deterioration, and negative psychological states, or at least have to experience the inevitable challenges associated with changes that come with age (physical, emotional, social, cognitive, etc.). The need to intervene and help them live a better life is a concern of many, but the results are not always successful, possibly because most approaches and interventions for older adults focus on curing, which is often unrealistic and inappropriate (McBee, 2008). Elders often experience complex physical, psychological, and cognitive changes and/or limitations that require a multifaceted and holistic approach. Pharmacological treatments are not sufficient, especially in terms of managing pain, stress, and emotional distress (McBee, 2008). It is necessary to provide more holistic relief from the multiple losses and changes associated with the aging process and to teach elders to focus on and use their inner strengths and resources to live a more fulfilling and happy life (McBee, 2008). Focusing on ability rather than on disability is very important for successful aging (i.e., maintaining physical health, sustaining good cognitive functioning, and sustaining engagement in social and productive activities; Hupper, Baylis, and Kenerne, 2004).

Moreover, spiritual development is also a very important dimension in later life, often characterized by a search for meaning and relationships in the world (Erikson, 1980), and is based on a process of gerotranscendence characterized by a natural progression towards wisdom and maturation

(Tornstam, 2005). This inner journey that characterizes the late stage of life of some older adults is related to their well-being, health, and ability to cope with the experienced changes during this period of life (McFadden, 1995). Accordingly, it is important to integrate the spiritual dimension of individuals' development when providing support for their engagement in life and relief from these multiple changes and challenges. Transpersonal psychology has been defined as a field "concerned with the study of humanity's highest potential, and with the recognition, understanding, and realization of unitive, spiritual, and transcendent experiences" (Lajoie and Shapiro, 1992, p.91). It "encompasses the personal and the universal dimensions of life—body, heart, mind, and spirit, human and nonhuman, interbeing and ecological—a psychology open to our sacred place in the cosmos" (Caplan, Hartelius, and Rardin, 2003, p.150). This study aims to explore how the MBSR program can foster harmony in and among these personal and universal dimensions of elders' lives.

Mindfulness meditation is a transpersonal approach that fosters emotional transformation, personal growth, awareness of individuals as whole, and the integration and balance of the mind, body, and spirit (Walsh and Vaughan, 1993). It promotes a shift in awareness from the identification with the egocentric self to the transpersonal self's awakening of the full potential and healing possibilities within oneself (Walsh and Vaughan, 1993). Walsh and Vaughan (1993) referred to meditation as the "royal road to the transpersonal" (p.47). Mindfulness meditation allows meditators to see things with greater clarity and insight and to access the inner wisdom and healing strength to cultivate well-being in different levels of existence. Practitioners of mindfulness meditation become active in their own healing process as they learn to use their mind, their body, and the spiritual aspects of their existence to influence their healing process.

This study provided an understanding of how the MBSR program functioned as a holistic intervention for older adults and how it affected the different realms of their lives. It shed new light on the understanding of how MBSR can be used as a complementary intervention and nonpharmacological treatment for older adults in order to deal with the several changes that they experience during this period of life. This study also helped to identify specific ways in which the MBSR program needs to be adapted to address the special needs of older adults. Within the field of transpersonal psychology this study provided an in-depth understanding of how mindfulness practice fostered spiritual transformation in these older adults and how mindfulness as a spiritual practice provided them with new meanings and understandings about themselves, their lives, the aging process, and death. It expanded the understanding of transpersonal development in older adults and the interaction between physical health, psychological well-being, and spiritual transformation in promoting elders' well-being. Finally, it revealed the importance of adopting an holistic approach that takes into account the body, mind, and spirit of older adults in order to foster their integrity and health and to address the special needs of this age group.

My interest in this topic originated from my own experience in mindfulness practices and the MBSR program. For me mindfulness meditation is a wonderful tool to open the doors of my true sense of self and a practice that allows me to be present, to accept life changes with equanimity, to face suffering with courage and inner strength, to connect with my spiritual realm, to be in the world and connect with others, and to find meaning in each moment of my life. Mindfulness is a way of Being and a way of being present and open to life and the full potentialities of my existence. My experience as a student and instructor of the MBSR program has allowed me to have an experience of how this program can foster physical and psychological well-being, as well as individuals' growth and transformation regarding how they perceive and experience life. Moreover, my experience as a research clinical neuropsychologist involved in several clinical trials with Alzheimer's patients and older adult persons allowed me to sense a feeling of emptiness that some individuals experience in their lives and to perceive an empty look in their eyes which I believe means that they are hoping to find something more in life, something that is beyond words and beyond the conventional treatment or approach provided in most health care systems. This project is my attempt to find ways to provide these sentient beings with a glimpse of that "something," a sense of belonging, integration, and meaning in their lives: to provide an approach that would allow them to improve not only their body, brain, and mind, but also their beautiful spirit.

» Chapter 1 «

Mindfulness and MBSR

Meditation and mindfulness

> *Truth lies in the living present, in this moment, and must be discovered afresh in the present, in the eternal now.*
>
> Jiddu Krishnamurti[1]

The Sanskrit and Pali words for meditation in traditional Buddhism are *dhyāna* and *bhāvana*, which mean, respectively, mental cultivation or development (Olendzki, 2009). Sogyal Rinpoche (1993) stated that "meditation is bringing the mind home" (p.60); it is a practice that allows us to "introduce ourselves to that which we really are, our unchanging pure awareness, which underlies the whole of life and death" (p.60). It is a mental discipline by which one attempts to get beyond the conditioned, "thinking" mind into a deeper state of relaxation and awareness (Cahn and Polich, 2006).

Mindfulness is one of the main general types of meditation practices (Goleman, 1988). Mindfulness comes from the Pali word *sati* and the Sanskrit word *smirti*, which connotes awareness, attention, and remembering. Mindfulness has been described as the "heart of Buddhist meditation" (Nyanaponika, 1992, p.7) and refers to:

> (a) mindful awareness: an abiding presence or awareness, a deep knowing that manifests as freedom of mind (e.g., freedom from reflexive conditioning and delusion) and (b) mindful practice: the systematic practice of intentionally attending in an open, caring, and discerning way, which involves both knowing and shaping the mind. (Shapiro and Carlson, 2009, p.4)

---

1 J Krishnamurti Online (2014) Daily Quote Archive, available at www.jkrishnamurti.org/krishnamurti-teachings/daily-quote-archive.php, accessed on 14 May 2014.

Mindful awareness is a way of being and experiencing each moment of life in an open, receptive, and accepting way (Shapiro and Carlson, 2009) and mindful practice entails the development of skills that foment mindful awareness, including the ability to direct and sustain attention, nonreactivity, discernment, compassion, and recognition and disidentification with one's self (Shapiro and Carlson, 2009). It is a process of "paying attention in a particular way: on purpose, in the present moment, non-judgmentally" (Kabat-Zinn, 1994, p.4), a deliberate act of cultivating attention in the present moment and remembering to attend with persistent clarity to the object of the present experience (Olendzki, 2009). The object of present experience refers to any manifestation that arises at any given moment from the inner or the outer world, including thoughts, emotion, sensations, actions, sounds, or movement (Brown, Ryan, and Creswell, 2007). There are four foundations of mindfulness that can be used to practice mindfulness, including mindfulness of the body, of feeling (*vedanā*), of mind (*citta*), and of mental objects (*dhammas*) (Bucknell and Kang, 1997). Mindfulness involves 12 different attitudes: acceptance, nonjudgment, patience, nonstriving, trust, openness, letting go, gentleness, generosity, understanding, gratitude, and lovingkindness (Shapiro, Schwartz, and Bonner, 1998).

Mindfulness-based stress reduction

In recent years there has been an increasing dialogue between Eastern philosophy—especially Buddhism—and Western psychology and neuroscience (Mind and Life Institute) for the understanding of the nature of the human mind, alleviating human suffering, and healing and enhancing the human mind. These dialogues have led to the understanding that mindfulness meditation would be a very positive and beneficial practice in Western societies (e.g. Ekman, 2008; Goleman, 2003).

Accordingly, several programs have been developed integrating mindfulness meditation and psychological approaches in order to foster emotional and physical health. These programs are detached from any cultural or religious tradition, therefore allowing the application of mindfulness training in mental health and clinical settings (Didonna, 2009).

Jon Kabat-Zinn (1990) was the pioneer of this work, developing a program called mindfulness-based stress reduction (MBSR), designed to be used with nonclinical and clinical populations to address issues such as anxiety and chronic pain. The program uses several techniques, including the rigorous and systematic practice of mindfulness, yoga exercises, and group dialogues on themes associated with mindfulness practice, emotional development, and stress reduction, in order to teach individuals how to live fuller, healthier, and better-adapted lives.

Clinical and nonclinical applications of MBSR

The MBSR program has been shown to be an effective intervention in a wide range of clinical applications, resulting in significant improvements in health-related quality of life, reduction of physical symptoms, positive response to treatments and recovery, decreased psychological distress, improvements in objective and subjective well-being, increased ability to deal with stressful situations in daily life, increased ability to relax, increased energy levels, and improved self-esteem, among other measured outcomes (Didonna, 2009).

Several studies presented evidence of the efficacy of MBSR for treating several psychological disorders, such as anxiety and panic disorders (Kabat-Zinn, 1990; Miller, Fletcher, and Kabat-Zinn, 1995), eating disorders (Kristeller and Hallett, 1999; Wolever and Best, 2009), and trauma and post-traumatic stress disorder (Follette and Vijay, 2009). It was also shown that MBSR has very positive effects for treating physical complaints such as psoriasis (Kabat-Zinn *et al.*, 1998); chronic pain (Kabat-Zinn, 1982; Kabat-Zinn, Lipworth, and Burney, 1985); emotional and physical symptoms in individuals facing severe chronic diseases such as cancer (Carlson and Garland, 2005; Carlson *et al.*, 2009); multiple sclerosis (Mills and Allen, 2000); and fibromyalgia (Kaplan, Goldenberg, and Galvin-Nadeau, 1993).

In nonclinical populations, MBSR had significant effects on psychological symptoms, including reduction of intensity and frequency of negative emotions (Brown and Ryan, 2003; Chambers, Lo, and Allen, 2008); reduction in anxiety levels (Shapiro, Schwartz, and Bonner, 1998); improvement of general well-being (Didonna, 2009); and decreased negative self-focused attention (Murphy, 1995). The MBSR program also promoted improvements in the immune system in the general population (Davidson *et al.*, 2003); and quality of life of individuals who had suffered traumatic brain injuries (Bédard *et al.*, 2003).

Although these studies revealed very positive and promising effects of the MBSR intervention, a great number of these investigations suffered from significant methodological and conceptual limitations (e.g., small samples, pre-post designs with no control group, and advanced meditators rather than beginners; Baer, 2003), and most studies were based on quantitative methods, which provide a reductionist view of the participants' experience of mindfulness meditation. It is important not only to rely on quantitative studies but also to develop studies based on qualitative methodologies and to combine different assessment techniques and research methods to gather a broader and more complete analysis of the experience and effectiveness of the MBSR program (Baer, Walsh, and Lykins, 2009).

Mindfulness and spirituality

The word "spirituality" comes from the Latin root *spiritus*, which means breath or life, and *spiritulis*, which refers to a person of the spirit (Hill et al., 2000). Although there is a lack of consensus among definitions of spirituality because its concept overlaps with that of religion (Hill and Pargament, 2008; Wink and Dillon, 2008), spirituality is often associated with a search for meaning in life, a sense of community, an encounter with transcendence, as well as a search for the ultimate truth, respect and appreciation for the mystery of creation, self-growth, and transformation (Wink and Dillon, 2008; Wulff, 1996). "Spirituality" is used to refer to the personal, subjective experience of religion, and it is focused more on the existential and experiential side of an individual's internalized faith (Moberg, 2008).

Mindfulness is rooted in Buddhist philosophy and is often associated with spirituality and spiritual development. According to Buddhist traditions and Buddhist psychology, meditation is one of the spiritual practices that fosters the cultivation of a "receptive consciousness" (Brazier, 2003) in a practice during which the focus is not on the personal experience of the self but rather "towards the larger reality that contains it" (Andresen, 2000, p.18). Mindfulness is thought to enhance self-development by cultivating qualities such as self-confidence, inner strength, wholesome and positive mental states, presence of mind, and the development of the nonself (Brazier, 2003). The cultivation of nonself is based on the paradigm that individuals need to recognize their existential position in relationship to the world, their dependencies and conditioning, and the impermanent nature of their existence and of the environment (Brazier, 2003).

Selby (2003) considered that practicing meditation cultivates presence and awareness of the present moment and fosters the expansion of consciousness by allowing it to perceive the whole and the wholeness of being. This presence and awareness of the moment encourage spiritual peace, clarity, and awakening.

Moreover, meditation has been associated with several spiritual and religious practices. Most religions and spiritual philosophies (e.g., Buddhism, Christianity, Hinduism, Taoism, and Islam) integrate meditative practices in their routines (Siegel, 2007).

A number of studies have shown that religion and spirituality are positively associated with physical health (George, Ellison, and Larson, 2002; Powell, Shahabi, and Thoresen, 2003) and psychological well-being (Plante and Sherman, 2001). Nevertheless, almost no empirical studies have been developed on the relationship between spirituality and mindfulness.

MBSR and spirituality

Carmody *et al.* (2008) developed a study to assess the effects of the MBSR program on mindfulness and spirituality and to analyze the association between mindfulness, spirituality, and self-reported medical and psychological symptoms. The researchers found that, after completing the MBSR program, participants showed significant increases in mindfulness and spirituality scores, including increases in sense of inner meaning and peace as measured by the Toronto Mindfulness Scale, the Mindfulness Attention Awareness Scale, and the Functional Assessment of Chronic Illness Therapy–Spiritual Well-Being Scale. These increases were associated with reductions in medical and psychological symptoms as measured by the Medical Symptoms Checklist (MSCL) and the Hopkins Symptom Checklist 90, respectively. The researchers suggested that spirituality might be developed in a secular context and that the MBSR program might be an adequate context for individuals to develop spirituality outside of a religious context.

Similarly, MacKenzie *et al.* (2007), in a qualitative study with nine oncological patients and based on data from interviews and group discussions, found that participants in the MBSR program revealed a higher sense of spirituality. Researchers suggested that this high sense of spirituality was associated with the increased awareness "of the intricate interconnections among themselves, other individuals and eventually all aspects of nature through direct experience" (MacKenzie *et al.*, 2007, p.62). Conversely, Leigh, Bowen, and Marlatt (2005) examined the relationship between spirituality, mindfulness, and substance abuse in 196 undergraduate students who completed questionnaires on mindfulness and spirituality. Results revealed no correlations between mindfulness and spirituality.

Many studies have supported the benefits of the MBSR program and other mindfulness-based interventions in physical and psychological well-being (Grossman *et al.*, 2004), but very few examined the relationship between the mindfulness/MBSR program and spirituality. It is necessary to develop further controlled studies to identify and understand the association between particular types of mindfulness techniques and spirituality and their relationship with health and psychological well-being.

MBSR and older adults

There is a vast amount of scientific literature on the clinical applications of MBSR (Didonna, 2009). Nevertheless, only a few studies have been conducted with older adult groups.

Smith (2004) developed a study based on data from three MBSR courses conducted with older adults with anxiety disorders and/or chronic pain and three mindfulness-based cognitive therapy (MBCT) programs with older adults with major depressive episodes. Results from a thematic analysis revealed cognitive, emotional, physiological, psychological, and behavioral changes. However, this report is not clear about how the qualitative data were collected and analyzed, it does not look at the separate effects of MBCT and MBSR for older adults, and no information is presented on the number of participants involved in the study.

Smith (2006) conducted an MBSR program for six groups of elders with approximately 11 participants per group. All participants suffered from some kind of anxiety disorder and no cognitive impairment or psychosis. Some manifested additional physical conditions and/or depression. Anecdotal evidence revealed mixed results, with some participants showing benefits (e.g., participants with primary chronic pain and secondary anxiety and/or depression) while others did not report any improvement (e.g., participants with severe depression). The major limitation of this study is that results are not based on quantitative or qualitative analysis, but rather on anecdotal evidence.

Ernst *et al.* (2008) developed a quantitative study analyzing the effects of MBSR on the quality of life in nursing home residents. Twenty-two residents of a nursing home—16 females and 6 males, aged 72 to 98 years—were recruited for the study. Participants were screened for cognitive impairment using the Mini Mental State Examination (MMSE) and were enrolled if scores were above 17 (i.e., no dementia). Several measures were used pre and post the program to examine the effects of the MBSR program, including physical and mental health, quality of life, depression, cognitive performance, activities of daily living, and life satisfaction. Results revealed a significant increase in physical health and decrease in depression as compared with the control group. The major limitation of this study was that data from only nine participants were used in the analysis. Moreover, the researchers used the MMSE to assess individuals' cognitive performance, an instrument that has demonstrated ceiling effects when compared with more sensitive instruments that can detect mild cognitive impairment and not only dementia (Jager, Budge, and Clark, 2003).

Prewitt (2000) conducted a qualitative study examining the experiences during MBSR of ten older women with fibromyalgia, ranging in age from 48 to 74. The data were collected using three interviews (before the program, one month before the end of the program, and two to three months after the end of the program). Additional data were collected from journals kept by the participants during the program that included information related to the sessions and to home practice. Data also consisted of field notes from the eight classes kept by the investigator-observer. Narrative analysis of the data identified key themes, metaphors, and other expressive use of language that were then grouped into coding categories. Results revealed an increase in self-awareness and self-acceptance, recognition of the need to change habits and conditionings, and increased mindfulness of the negative effects of habits regarding physical well-being that contributed to pain and fatigue. Although this study was based on a small sample, the qualitative analysis used provided an in-depth and detailed understanding of the effects of the MBSR in older adult women with fibromyalgia.

Morone, Greco, and Weiner (2008) conducted a randomized study analyzing the effects of MBSR in a group of 37 older adults suffering from pain. Participants were randomized into a treatment group for the eight-week MBSR program and a wait-list control group. After completing the program, participants showed an increased level of acceptance of their limits and pain, increased activity, and improved physical function when compared with the control group. The major limitations of this study included the fact that the wait-list control group was an empty control group (i.e., did not participate in the MBSR program and did not do anything) and that their condition could have worsened because of the distress caused by waiting for the program to begin. Finally, both treatment group and the control group were not assessed during the eight weeks in terms of outside changes in therapy or treatment. The improvements observed in the treatment group may have resulted from other treatments.

Morone et al. (2008) developed a qualitative study based on narrative analysis of the daily journal entries of 27 older adults suffering from chronic pain who participated in an MBSR program and were required to journal about their experience during the program. Results showed that the MBSR program fostered the reduction of pain levels, because it was observed that participants started to perform tasks more mindfully, therefore becoming aware of when they needed to stop due to physical pain. Participants also revealed an increased level of insight regarding the emotional processes behind the increases in pain that they usually experienced. These observations were maintained at three-month follow-up. The qualitative methodology used in this study allowed an in-depth understanding of the experience of older adults with chronic pain that would not have been possible to assess if researchers had relied on quantitative methodologies. However, participants did not consistently turn in the weekly diaries, and diaries were open-ended rather than directing participants to comment on specific topics that could have captured themes associated with pain reduction.

McBee (2008) developed an eight- to ten-week mindfulness-based elder care program for use in nursing homes.[2] The program, adapted from the original MBSR program, allowed frail elders with significant physical and cognitive limitations to benefit from MBSR. She stated that nursing home residents showed an increase in their abilities to cope with the stresses of nursing home life, improved sense of well-being, and reduced pain (McBee, Westreich, and Likourezos, 2004). This program was also adapted for older adults in dementia care who had been provided with formal and informal caregivers, with positive results (McBee, 2009).

Other studies were conducted using mindfulness meditation and relaxation techniques that revealed positive results in terms of quality of life, well-being, and energy (Moye and Hanlon, 1996), physical and emotional well-being, reduction in agitation and behavioral problems, improved health-related quality of life, and reduced symptoms of depression in older adults living in nursing homes (Lindberg, 2005) and institutionalized older adults with dementia (Lantz, Buchalterm, and McBee, 1997). Studies

---

[2] For further information, please visit http://luciamcbee.com.

conducted with older adults with no cognitive impairment revealed that mindfulness and relaxation training reduced psychosocial stress and anxiety (Deberry, Davis, and Reinhard, 1989), increased restfulness and alertness, and decreased impatience (Alexander *et al.*, 1989).

Most investigations on the effects of MBSR in older adult groups looked at MBSR with older adults in nursing homes, and many revealed methodological limitations and poor controls (e.g., see Smith, 2004, 2006). These studies relied on either quantitative or qualitative data and none integrated both methods of investigation, which would have provided a broader and more complete analysis of the effectiveness of the program in older adults. Furthermore, no study has investigated the impact of MBSR in nonclinical older adult groups, in terms of cognitive performance and spirituality, and how improvements of different dimensions of elders' lives interact in promoting their well-being.

Mindfulness: psychological perspectives

Several cognitive and psychological processes have been suggested to explain the mechanisms behind mindfulness practice and its effectiveness in improving physical and psychological well-being and behavioral regulation (Chambers, Gullone, and Allen, 2009). These processes include those described as including mindfulness as a construct, a mode of awareness, a meditation practice, or a psychological process with behavioral correlates (Chambers *et al.*, 2009).

Self-regulation of attention, attitude, and intention

Bishop *et al.* (2004) suggest a two-component model of mindfulness. The first component involves the self-regulation of attention that entails "sustained attention, switching of attention, and the inhibition of elaborative processing" (Bishop *et al.*, 2004, p.233), and the second component involves the orientation of experience, which refers to the adoption of an attitude of investigation, curiosity, and acceptance of what the mind is experiencing in each moment. This investigative attitude allows individuals to gain insight into the process and nature of the mind and promotes the adoption of a decentering perspective in relation to thoughts and feelings. This decentering perspective means that thoughts and feelings are not seen as part of the individual's nature and reality, but rather as an impermanent and transient subjective manifestation (Segal, Williams, and Teasdale, 2002).

Shapiro *et al.* (2006) suggest a three-axiom model to explain how mindfulness works. They suggest that there are three basic axioms that constitute the core components and the basic building blocks of the practice out of which other mental states emerge: (a) intention, which refers to why one practices; (b) attention, meaning the ability to observe mental operations and information arising from moment to moment (i.e., sustained attention); and (c) attitude, which includes the qualities one brings to the practice, such as acceptance, openness, and kindness.

According to Shapiro *et al.* (2006) the interaction between these axioms is fundamental to understanding the different transformations that individuals experience through mindfulness practice. These interactions foster a shift in individuals' perspective on the contents of their consciousness (i.e., thoughts) such that practitioners no longer identify with thoughts and are able to observe moment-to-moment experience with greater clarity, objectivity, and detachment rather than being involved in the drama of mental processes. Individuals stop being the "subject" and become the "object" (Shapiro *et al.*, 2006, p.378) of their internal experience. This process is called *reperceiving*, which is defined as "a meta-mechanism of action, which overarches additional direct mechanisms that lead to change and positive outcome" (Shapiro *et al.*, 2006, p.377).

Shapiro *et al.* (2006) suggest that the interaction between the axioms fosters the development of four additional mechanisms, including (a) self-regulation, through which an individual's system maintains stability of its functions and adaptability to change; (b) values clarification, referring to the ability to go beyond the conditioned values of family, culture, and society and define what is true to oneself; (c) cognitive, emotional, and behavioral flexibility, which refers to a change in perspective about reality and allows less rigid responses to be experienced; and (d) exposure, which entails individuals' ability to observe emotions and sensations as an observer or witness of what is occurring in the present moment, thus allowing for more discernment and objectivity.

According to Shapiro and Schwartz (1999), intention and attention enhance the feedback loops of self-regulating mechanisms in order to create health. They suggest that the intention to cultivate attention in the present moment with a nonjudgmental, accepting, and open attitude allows individuals to connect with their body and mind, which leads to self-regulation, both emotional and behavioral, and, ultimately, to order and health.

Some theorists (Brown and Cordon, 2009; Varela and Depraz, 2003) suggest that cultivating attention in the present moment with a nonjudgmental, accepting, and open attitude is associated with emotional well-being, mindful emotional regulation, and behavioral regulation because mindfulness involves a disengagement from habitual automatized ways of evaluating reality (i.e., deautomatization), leading to a more balanced emotional state, a higher degree of veracity of perceptions, and better behavioral regulation.

Furthermore, a mindful processing of information involves a receptive and open mind—*beginner's mind* (Kabat-Zinn, 1990, p.35)—as the information that arises in each moment is intentionally observed without attachment to any particular point of view, interpretation, or outcome (Bishop, 2002; Kabat-Zinn, 1990). Individuals cultivate a nonreactive attitude towards the objects of observation and train to be present with the reality or phenomena being manifested from moment to moment. This present-moment awareness facilitates a more balanced and healthy regulation of individuals' actions by fostering more flexible and adaptive responses to events rather than by promoting the practice of engaging in automatized, habitual, and impulsive reactions (Brown *et al.*, 2007).

The concept of reperceiving suggested by Shapiro *et al.* (2006) has also been called *meta-awareness*. In mindfulness practice, as the practitioners become more experienced in observing their own mental processes (i.e., metacognitive awareness) with an attitude of detachment and acceptance, they become more able to observe the field of awareness in which the mental events occur (Kabat-Zinn, 1990). Practitioners are encouraged to sit with awareness of whatever arises in each passing moment without focusing on any particular object of attention, in a state called *choiceless awareness* (Kabat-Zinn, 1990). In this practice, the object of awareness is awareness itself—*meta-awareness* (Jordan, 2002). Krishnamurti (1998) called this process *attention without resistance* because practitioners become able to be aware of every movement of the mind without exclusion as they are not selecting and excluding any particular stimuli of attention. Whatever is present in the mind at any given moment is the object of attention. Objects of attention can be the breath, thoughts, sensations, or noises, as well as the silence and space in the mind. Chambers *et al.* (2009) suggest that the development of meta-awareness may "result in the recognition that 'mind' contains, but is not identical to, its contents…we are not our thoughts, feelings, or experiences" (p.563).

Acceptance

Acceptance comes from the Latin root *accipere*, which means to receive or take what is offered (Hayes, Strosahl, and Wilson, 1999). In a mindfulness context, it means "seeing things as they actually are in the present moment" (Kabat-Zinn, 1990, p.38) rather than trying to impose one's ideas about what one should be feeling, thinking, or experiencing. It "involves the abandonment of dysfunctional change of agendas and an active process of feeling feelings as feelings, thinking thoughts as thoughts, remembering memories as memories, and so on" (Hayes *et al.*, 1999, p.77).

Mindfulness practice enhances individuals' accepting of being with what is being experienced and observed in the present moment, defaulting to that state instead of to the mental tendency of desire or aversion (Brown *et al.*, 2007). Individuals tend to perceive and judge their experiences of situations, in relation to themselves, as either attractive or repulsive. Through experience (memories) and based on "cognitive appraisal of the significance of events for one's well-being" (Fenner, 1987, p.221) these tendencies lead to the development of like and dislike approaches, which automatically guide individuals' behavior. Through mindfulness practice, individuals learn to observe their mental processes with nonattachment, equanimity, and ease, and they learn to cultivate a state of "being" rather than "doing" that allows a greater openness and acceptance of the present-moment experience (Kabat-Zinn, 1990).

Mindful emotional regulation

Emotional regulation refers to the physiological, behavioral, and cognitive processes related to the generation of emotions and the ability to modulate the experience, expression, and management of emotions (Bridges, Denham, and Ganiban, 2004; Campos, Frankel, and Camras, 2004). There are two general types of emotional regulation: adaptive and maladaptive. Adaptive emotional regulation is when individuals are able to modulate between emotional states (positive and negative) and to reduce high levels of negativity, and maladaptive emotional regulation occurs when individuals lack sufficient flexibility to deal with the changes in the environment (Bridges *et al.*, 2004; Campos *et al.*, 2004).

Mindful attention allows individuals to distinguish between bodily sensations, feelings, thoughts, and actions; to understand their complex relationship to emotional states; and to observe and be aware of this dynamic interaction with discernment, acceptance, and nonjudgment

(Kabat-Zinn, 1990). Mindful emotional regulation facilitates an adaptive emotional regulation and healthy engagement with emotions (Hayes and Feldman, 2004), allowing individuals to observe and be aware of their experience of emotions with acceptance, nonjudgment, and openness, regardless of the intensity, content, or meaning of their experience instead of reacting to it either by suppression or experiential avoidance, impulsivity or passivity, or introspective strategies such as rumination or worry (Chambers *et al.*, 2009; Kabat-Zinn, 1990).

Mindful observation of emotions fosters the transformation of the emotional energy into a wholesome presence and allows a deeper understanding of life and true potentiality as a unique human being. Welwood (1985) stated:

> If I turn to face my own demons, they dissolve, revealing themselves to be my own living energy. Then I can begin to feel my tenderness, my vulnerability to life, which reminds me that what I really am is a living being who is exposed to the world, interdependent and connected with all other beings. (p.86)

Metacognitive awareness

Some theorists (Bishop, 2002; Bishop *et al.*, 2004; Teasdale *et al.*, 2002) have suggested that mindfulness may reflect a kind of metacognitive ability—*metacognitive awareness* or *metacognitive insight*—in which individuals develop the ability to observe their own mental processes (Bishop, 2002). Thoughts and feelings "are seen as passing events in the mind rather than as inherent aspects of self or as necessary valid reflections of reality" (Teasdale *et al.*, 2002, p.285). This process of decentering (Bishop *et al.*, 2004; Segal *et al.*, 2002) results in a cognitive diffusion, which refers to the ability to perceive thoughts as simply thoughts (rather than as binding realities) that one can alter in form, frequency, or situational sensivity (Blackledge, 2007; Masuda *et al.*, 2004). Cognitive diffusion increases the range and adaptability of responses to challenges (i.e., cognitive flexibility), which then allows individuals to consciously deal with challenges rather than automatically react to them (Hayes, 2003).

These processes of decentering, cognitive diffusion, and cognitive flexibility decrease the experiential avoidance of situations, foster the ability to explore present experiences nonreactively, discourage automatic reactions and habitual thought patterns, and increase the awareness of perceptual distortions that result from unexamined thoughts, feelings, and sensations that generate maladaptive behaviors (Brown *et al.*, 2007; Krasner, 2004). Metacognitive insight may also allow individuals to realize their true desires, needs, and values, thereby discouraging the mental tendency to be conditioned and controlled by internal and external conditions and allowing individuals to mindfully choose how to be and behave in the present moment (Brown *et al.*, 2007).

Increasing metacognitive awareness involves a change in an individual's relationship to mental events, thoughts, and feelings (Teasdale *et al.*, 2002) and promotes personal autonomy (Chambers *et al.*, 2009). Accepting and embracing moment-to-moment experience will transform individuals' need to change and control their experience, allowing the cultivation of more adaptive behaviors and psychological well-being (Chambers *et al.*, 2009).

Other cognitive and psychological mechanisms behind mindfulness include self-monitoring, self-control, self-acceptance, and self-understanding (Baer, 2003); enhancement of attention skills, including sustained attention and attention switching (Bishop, 2002); relaxation (Baer, 2003); inhibition of secondary elaborative processing thoughts, feelings, and sensations (Bishop *et al.*, 2004); and decrease in dysfunctional attitudes about the self (Ramel *et al.*, 2004).

In summary, mindfulness practice fosters the development of several psychological and cognitive mechanisms and processes that then allow individuals to develop more healthy and adaptive functioning and mechanisms to deal with the inner and outer world. These mechanisms allow individuals to maintain their well-being and open to a new dimension of awareness of themselves and the world.

Buddhist perspectives

Mindfulness has its roots in Buddhist traditional teachings, where it plays a central role in a spiritual life that is focused on the alleviation of suffering and the liberation of the mind (Thera, 1965). In order to understand Buddhist perspectives on the effects of mindfulness on individuals' well-being, some of the basic principles of Buddhism and Buddhist psychology are presented.

Buddhism and reality

According to Buddhist teachings, reality is divided into two general categories: *conventional reality* and *ultimate reality* (Boddhi, 2000). Conventional reality corresponds to concepts and everyday experiences in life. Buddhists believe that conventional reality does not exist as a reality separate from the individual experiencing it, because it results from mental constructions and conceptualizations of the world. It is a mere appearance or illusion (*maya*) and a projection of the mind's inner world. Ultimate reality refers to the direct realization of a nondualistic world of interconnected phenomena called *dhammas*. *Dhammas* are the final and irreducible components of existence (Boddhi, 2000). Ultimate reality includes consciousness or mind (*citta*), mental factors, matter, and nirvana (*nibbāna*). Consciousness is the awareness of phenomena. According to Buddhist teachings, human experience is based on moments of knowing objects (*cittas*) which are impermanent and in constant flux. Each *citta* arises simultaneously with multiple universal mental factors (*cetasikas*) including attention, one-pointedness, feeling, perception, and volition. These *cetasikas* are also called roots, and are the cause or reason for other mental states. There are six roots, divided into two groups. The unwholesome roots are greed or attachment, hatred or aversion, and delusion or ignorance, which lead to mental and physical suffering. The wholesome roots include nongreed, nonhatred, and nondelusion, roots that do not cause suffering and are founded in wisdom, lovingkindness, compassion, sympathy, and generosity (Boddhi, 2000). Nirvana (*nibbāna*) was defined by the Buddha as "a condition of freedom from bondage, torment, and suffering that results from seeing the true nature of the worldly condition of all things, and so being able to give up clinging to them" (Bhikkhu, 1997a). It is described as a release from suffering, ignorance, and selfishness and as an attainment of wisdom (*prajñā*) and compassion (*karunā*; Radhakrishnan and Moore, 1957).

The Four Noble Truths

Buddhist philosophy is based on the Four Noble Truths, which are not religious beliefs or principles of faith, but rather categories of experience and propositions to be experienced and verified in one's life (Batchelor, 1998). The Four Noble Truths reveal the reality of human suffering (*dukkha*), its causes, and how to achieve liberation from and understanding of life's difficulties (Brazier, 2003).

The First Noble Truth is called *dukkha*, which means suffering. It states that suffering and dissatisfaction are intricate components of life (Brazier, 2003) that lead individuals to experience pain, stress, sickness, and death. Buddhism does not see suffering as either good or bad but as an intrinsic and inseparable aspect of the reality of human life (Brazier, 2003). By acknowledging this predicament, Buddhism suggests that individuals need to accept the reality of suffering and attempt to lessen the influence of self-imposed sources of distress such as behavioral habits, cognitive tendencies, and afflictive emotional reactions (Neale, 2006).

The Second Noble Truth suggest that the root cause of suffering is ignorance (*avijjā*) in relation to the essence of self and phenomena and the impulses of attachment and aversion in relation to objects outside of one's being that arise due to the belief that phenomena are permanent, enduring, and fixed (Neale, 2006). Ignorance of the impermanence of experience (*anicca*) leads to attachment and aversion. Individuals tend to believe that objects, people, and states of mind are permanent, lasting, and separated identities, which belief results in a state of duality. This sense of separation between oneself, the object of experience, and the act of perception itself leads individuals to crave states of mind and things that bring them pleasurable feelings and to be repelled by aversive feelings. Aversive feelings, in turn, result in adverse affective conditionings, faulty cognitions, and tendencies to maladaptive behavior (Ekman *et al.*, 2005).

The illusion of separateness of oneself from others prevents an individual from recognizing her or his self as part of a larger field of reality (Welwood, 1985). An individual's identification with the object of self that is separate from others and with the idea of *me* feeds an inner state of I-ness and leads to the desire to protect the integrity of this I-self. Suffering is caused by emotional reactions such as desire, jealousy, anger, ignorance, and pride, and it is physical reactions that arise based on the desire to protect one's identity that lead to one's suffering (Brazier, 2003; Welwood, 1985). These reactions continuously feed the illusory emotional world of individuals and an incorrect understanding of the true reality (Brazier, 2003; Chambers *et al.*, 2009). Consequently, Buddhists believe that individuals do not experience reality as it truly is, but rather as a projection of mental states and an illusory view of self and others (Brazier, 2003).

The Third Noble Truth states that suffering can be eliminated because everything is impermanent (*anicca*) and in constant flux. If there is suffering, there is also cessation of suffering. Buddhism suggests that the mind is the cause of all suffering and has the ability to cease suffering and restore peace but that, for this to occur, it is essential that the conscious mind work towards eliminating negative cognitive tendencies, afflictive emotions, and unwholesome behaviors through behavioral discipline (*sila*), attentional control (*samadhi*), and reflective thinking (Neale, 2006).

The Fourth Noble Truth, also known as the Eightfold Path, suggests several ways through which suffering (*dukkha*) can be eliminated (Epstein, 1995). This path is also called The Middle Path and it can be practiced through three different stages: *sila* (ethical conduct), *samadhi* (attentional control), and *pañña* (wisdom; Hart, 1997). *Sila* allows individuals to lessen their attachments to pleasurable experiences and avoidance toward painful experiences. *Sila* involves the abstinence from all actions, all deeds, and all words that harm other people because, without these actions, the mind does not generate great agitation, craving, and aversion. *Sila* involves right speech, right action, and right livelihood. *Samadhi* is the practice of concentration and the practice of "developing the ability to consciously direct and control one's own mental processes" (Hart, 1997, p.58). It includes right effort, right mindfulness, and right concentration, which are skills used to counteract a regression towards psychological states of automaticity and mindlessness. Finally, *pañña* is translated as wisdom and is essential for liberation (nirvana). Wisdom is attained when the developed skills of awareness are used to purify investigation, analysis, and insight into the nature of the self and of phenomena. *Pañña* involves the practice of right thought and right understanding (Hart, 1997). In the Buddhist context, the term *right* does not entail a judgment of right or wrong, but rather to distinguish wholesome or unwholesome actions (Khong, 2009).

According to Buddhism right mindfulness (*satipatthāna*) is the first of the seven Factors of Enlightenment, which include mindfulness, investigation of the physical and mental phenomena (*dhamma-vicaya*), energy (*viriyā*), joy (*piti*), relaxation or tranquility of the body and mind (*passaddhi*), concentration (*samādhi*), and equanimity (*upekkhā*). Mindfulness is the basic factor necessary for the development of the other six Factors of Enlightenment (Thera, 1965). Moreover, mindfulness is also one of the five faculties (*indriyā*), the other four of which are confidence, energy, concentration, and wisdom. The development of mindfulness is essential for the development and balance of the other four faculties, in particular the balance between confidence (or faith) and wisdom (or reason), and between energy and concentration (or inner calm; Thera, 1965).

Buddhism suggests that, in mindfulness training, the mind begins by being trained in attention control known as bare attention, which "is the clear and single minded awareness of what actually happens to us and in us, at the successive moments of perception" (Thera, 1996, p.30). The practitioner observes whatever arises in the present moment with an open attitude, without reacting to the perceived phenomena "by deed, speech, or by mental comment, judgment or reflection" (Thera, 1965, p.30).

The practice of mindfulness is directed towards four objects, including the body, feelings, state of mind, and mental contents, which are known as the four "contemplations" (*anupassanā*) (Thera, 1965). The early stages of mindfulness practice involve only bare attention. When the practice becomes more advanced, mindfulness includes faculties of discursive thinking, investigation, decision making, information processing, contemplation, and analysis (Neale, 2006).

The concept of mindfulness (*sati*) is also associated with clear comprehension (*sampajañña*), which refers to one's reflective thoughts towards observed things and which come into play when a certain action is required. It is defined as "a regulative force of all our activities, bodily, verbal, and mental" (Thera, 1965, p.45). Clear comprehension means right knowledge (*ñāna*) or wisdom (*paññā*) based on right mindfulness (*sati*).

Mindfulness practice allows individuals to know the mind by observing the constant flux of thoughts and emotions providing important information about "the working of one's mind: the mechanisms of one's emotions and passions, the reliability of one's reasoning power, one's true and pretended motives, and many other aspects of mental life" (Thera, 1965, p.39). Individuals will realize the impermanent nature of the mind: "coming face to face with Change, as experienced vividly in our own body and mind, we have now started 'to see things as they really are'" (Thera, 1965, p.37).

Mindfulness promotes the process of shaping the mind (Thera, 1965). Individuals learn how to be present and fully aware of the present moment, with openness and acceptance, without trying to escape into thoughts about the present or the future that are merely reflections of consciousness (Thera, 1965). Mindfulness fosters the ability to disengage from habitual mental and emotional patterns of reaction towards outside and inner events. It allows the practitioner to learn to distinguish between the way things appear to the senses and the mental conceptualizations and projections one makes upon them. In this way the practitioner perceives what is presented to the senses, including her or his own mental states, with more clarity and discernment. All mental states are observed rather than mindlessly reacted to. Changes in the perception of the inner and outer realities result in changes in emotions, moods, and behavioral patterns, which changes, in turn, affect well-being and health (Ekman et al., 2005).

Mindfulness practice fosters the process of disidentification with the self that is rooted within emotional and mental patterns. This disidentification will allow individuals to see reality beyond their mental conditionings, face life adversities with equanimity and openness, and recognize their true and genuine nature (Ekman et al., 2005). Mindfulness allows individuals to recognize a self that is also impermanent and in the flow of moment-to-moment consciousness. The self becomes then, for that individual practitioner, not a separate identity that experiences reality, but rather a part of the reality being experienced. Liberation and happiness (*sukha*) are the results of realizing this selflessness and interconnection with all reality (Ekman et al., 2005).

Ultimately, mindfulness practice promotes the liberation of the mind through the realization of the truth and insight (*vipassāna*) into the Three Characteristics of existence: impermanence (*annicca*), suffering (*dukkha*), and impersonality/nonself (*anattā*) (Thera, 1965). The nature of insight is "to be free from desire, aversion, and delusion, and see clearly all things of the inner and outer world as 'bare phenomena' (*suddha-dhammā*), i.e., as impersonal processes" (p.44). Mindfulness brings the mind to a state of tranquility and awareness, a state of concentration, and insight (Thera, 1965).

According to Buddhism, through mindfulness meditation, unwholesome emotions and attitudes are subdued by the tranquility of the observing mind and wholesome mental states, including love, compassion, sympathetic joy, and equanimity are cultivated throughout the practice, which progression leads to happiness (*sukha*) and, ultimately, to the liberation of cyclic existence (Aronson, 1986). Mindfulness brings the practitioner back to the present moment and allows her or him to see life with more clarity and openness, to recognize and be aware of the beauty of the simplicity of life, to become more adaptable to the changes occurring in everyday life, to go beyond the extremes and opposites of life, to take responsibility for actions on a moment-to-moment basis, and to live in harmony and balance with the inner self and outer world (Thera, 1965).

Buddhist psychology suggests a metaphysical model underlying mindfulness practice that provides a deep understanding of the nature of life and universal experience, of human nature, of suffering, and of cessation of suffering. Buddhist psychology suggests that, ultimately, phenomena do not exist as a separate reality, that the notion of self prevents individuals from realizing the ultimate reality and experiencing happiness (Chambers *et al.*, 2009), and that mindfulness as a "way of being rather than doing" (Khong, 2009, p.122) can foster greater awareness of human existence and liberation (Khong, 2009).

The Buddhist approach incorporates a unified ontological-ontic dimension of mindfulness practice and the nature of Being. It looks at the fundamental nature of human beings, things, and phenomena (ontological dimension) and how these characteristics of Being are manifested in the ordinary, everyday world of beings (ontic dimension; Khong, 2009).

Mindfulness and neuroplasticity

Mindfulness meditation practice is a flexible and ongoing transformational process (Lutz, Dunne, and Davidson, 2007). With mindfulness meditation practice, an individual's process of emotions, attention, cognition, and introspection are always changing, developing, and adapting to the learning and to environmental input (Lutz *et al.*, 2007). As studies show (Davidson *et al.*, 2003; Lazar *et al.*, 2005) these changes occur not only at the emotional and psychological level but also at the level of the brain function and structure. This process of brain adaptation, structural change, and improved functioning resulting from experience is called brain plasticity, or neuroplasticity (Kempermann, 2006).

Lazar *et al.* (2005) found that in meditators there was an increased thickness in brain regions associated with attention, interoception, empathy, and sensory processing as compared with nonmeditators. The degree of thickness of these areas was associated with the length of time spent practicing mindfulness meditation. Differences were also found between the two groups in prefrontal cortical thickness, especially among older participants, suggesting that regular meditation practice may prevent age-related thinning of the prefrontal cortex. Lazar *et al.*'s study provided the first evidence of neural plasticity resulting from mindfulness practices, suggesting that "mindfulness practice might alter the very structures of our brains" (Siegel, 2007, p.104).

Similarly, Pagnoni and Cekic (2007) found that the regular practice of mindfulness meditation might have a neuro-protective effect in the aging brain associated with the prevention of a decrease of gray matter volume, particularly in the areas associated with attentional processing (e.g., the putamen). They suggested that these beneficial effects on the aging brain may possibly reduce the cognitive decline associated with normal aging.

Furthermore, Richard Davidson (as cited in Goleman, 2003) revealed that areas of the brain associated with emotions (frontal lobe, hippocampus, and amygdala) "are parts of the brain dramatically affected by the emotional environment in which we are raised, and by repeated experience" (p.189). He also suggested that mindfulness practices might be able to change neural connections in specific areas of the brain associated with attention and emotional regulation.

How exactly do these changes occur? During mindfulness practice attention is directed to a particular object, such as the breath. While attention is focused, certain brain areas and specific circuitry are activated that strengthen synaptic linkages in those areas and that might consequently increase synaptic densities in those regions (Lazar *et al.*, 2005; Siegel, 2007). The increase in synaptic density might account for the increased thickness in certain brain areas activated during meditation practices as shown by Lazar *et al.* (2005). These changes will be reflected not only in structural changes in the brain, but also in changes in brain function; mental experiences such as emotional balance and sense of well-being; bodily states, including immune system responses; response to stress; and in individuals' behaviors, such as a prevalence of equanimity and the presence of fewer automatic behavioral patterns in their daily lives (Siegel, 2007).

Garland and Gaylord (2009) state that such mindfulness-induced neuroplasticity is possibly mediated by changes in gene expression. They called this idea the *experience-dependent gene expression hypothesis*. Garland and Gaylord suggested that the mechanisms by which neurons secrete growth factors that activate gene translation in cell nuclei may change with mindful meditation practice, which results in the remodeling of synaptic connections.

Shah (2000) suggests that the continuous long-term practice of meditation can lead to qualitative and quantitative permanent changes in the nervous system. The continuous exposition to the same stimuli (e.g., observation of the breath) involves certain neurotransmitters and neuromodulators that may stimulate the development of latent neurons to develop center(s) which evolutionarily are higher than the present-day neo-cortex. The development of these new connections will affect the ability to think, rationalize, and react differently to sensory input. The higher centers of the brain activated during meditation will apply inhibitory control over the present-day neo-cortex and the present capacity of reasoning, thinking, willing, and feeling and will allows human beings to transcend the usual state of mind to achieve a greater awareness of existence and reality.

Older adults

Beautiful young people are accidents of nature, but beautiful old people are works of art.

Eleanor Roosevelt

Aging and conscious aging

The population of individuals aged 65 years and older is increasing worldwide (U.S. Centers for Disease Control and Prevention, 2003), posing many challenges for health care and social services. Research on older adults is increasingly concerned with investigaton of ways of promoting their well-being during this period of life and of defining practices or interventions that might help older adults cope with the inevitable changes they experience through the aging process (Birren and Schaie, 1996; Butler, Lewis, and Sunderland, 1991).

Aging is a multidimensional phenomenon that includes changes in different realms of individuals' existence. It is a process that is integral to human life, experienced individually and differently by each individual (King, 2004). Individuals experience physical, psychological, emotional, social, and spiritual changes as they begin their journey in late life.

As we are unique individuals, the experience of aging is heterogeneous and involves a multidimensional process. People have different psychological and cognitive abilities; different personalities; different social, cultural, economic, and educational backgrounds; different life experiences and ways of coping with change; and unique neural cognitive plasticity and neural reserve (Fernández-Ballesteros, 2006). All these factors, in combination with age as biological factor, account for how each human being ages (Lher, 1991).

In an attempt to understand individual differences in the aging process, several models and theories have been suggested to characterize successful aging (Baltes and Baltes, 1990; Cumming and Henry, 1961; Rowe and Kahn, 1997). These models share the basic notion that successful aging is characterized as maintaining good physical health, avoiding disease, sustaining good cognitive function, being actively engaged in social and productive activities, and being independent.

The Western concept of successful aging, although it currently attempts to move away from the negative outlook on aging, implies that successful aging has to be related with success, productivity, individuality, independence, wealth, health, and sociability. This array of characteristics clearly reflects the prevailing motivations common to Western societies of a fixation on productivity and success, and the low values assigned to death and aging, as well as how Western societies do not value the wisdom, self-knowledge, and experience of older adults (MacKinlay, 2001; Schachter-Shalomi, 1995). This limited concept of successful aging prevalent in the West suggests an adaptative approach as elders adjust to a life change and the losses associated with the aging process in order to remain as actively involved in the world and as productive as they were in the past (Moody, 2000).

A different approach to aging has been suggested with the concept of *conscious aging* (Moody, 2000). This concept has emerged during the first decade of the 21st century with the convergence of two historical movements: (a) the increase in the aging population in modern Western societies and (b) the emergence of humanistic and transpersonal psychology and lifespan developmental theories (Moody, 2000). Conscious aging is associated with a holistic path of spiritual development and increased wisdom during the later period of life (Moody, 2000; Robba, 2006). Conscious aging refers to a process in which elders bring awareness and mindfulness to the aging process. This awareness allows elders to recognize the positive aspects of aging and to "enhance knowledge of Self which ultimately leads to wisdom" (Robba, 2006, p.6). This holistic line of development in later life promotes a relationship with the world in terms of universal connection, loving service, self-knowledge, and individuation. Aging consciously is "accepting aging and learning from it" (Robba, 2006, p.8) and involves "becoming the person we were meant to be, in becoming more conscious of ourselves and of the cosmic mystery" (Moody, 2000, p.2)

Biological dimensions of aging

At the physical level several changes occur that alter appearance and may limit many body systems. These changes include decline in sensory systems, such as impairments in sight and the development of many visual disorders such as cataracts, glaucoma, and macular degeneration (Bond, Coleman, and Peace, 1993); limitations in hearing ability (Bond *et al.*, 1993); and reduced mobility caused by a decline in muscles and bones, thinning of the bones, and some disease processes such as osteoporosis and arthritis (Rusting, 1992). Changes also occur in the digestive, circulatory, endocrine, urinary, and immune systems (Gruenewald and Kemeny, 2007; Rusting, 1992). For many, these physical changes cause a reduction in body energy levels that affects daily life and has an impact on the psychosocial sphere of life (MacKinlay, 2001).

There is also evidence that neurological changes occur as individuals age, including the shrinkage of global brain volume or incidence of white matter lesions (Rabbitt *et al.*, 2008). Several studies (Breteler *et al.*, 1994; De Groot *et al.*, 2000; Rabbitt *et al.*, 2008) revealed that these neurological changes are associated with decline in both general and specific cognitive functioning, including general fluid intelligence, memory, speed of information processing, learning, and executive functioning.

The increasing challenges that older adults experience, in particular in relation to their body systems, cause feelings of fear such as fears of dependency, loss of control, suffering, increasing vulnerability to stressors, dementia, and death (Jewell, 2004; MacKinlay, 2001).

Psychosocial dimensions of aging

The social changes that occur in old age are associated with retirement and social isolation. Social isolation in some elders may be caused by the physical and cognitive changes and/or limitations that occur in old age (Bond *et al.*, 1993). Decrease in social engagement and increase in age may combine to impact physical health, cognitive functioning, and longevity (Gruenewald and Kemeny, 2007). Moreover, the quality of relationships impacts elders' health, including the levels of both their psychological and physiological well-being (Gruenewald and Kemeny, 2007).

Psychological problems that may develop for the aging include emotional distress, depression, and anxiety (McBee, 2006; Smith, 2006). Depression and anxiety in elders have been associated with high rates of physical disease comorbidity and disability. Furthermore, these mood states predict disability, morbidity, and mortality outcomes independently of elders' baseline disability and functioning status (Gruenewald and Kemeny, 2007). Research also shows that the level of their positive affective states and subjective well-being predict disease outcomes and mortality (Pressman and Cohen, 2005) and influence the likelihood of onset of certain diseases such as stroke (Ostir *et al.*, 2001).

Spiritual dimensions of aging

Developmental theorists have been trying to understand how spirituality manifests and changes in later life. In old age psychological and spiritual developments become blurred, as the main developmental issues in later life stages seem to fall into the search for meaning and relationships with the world (i.e., spirituality; Tornstam, 2005). Armstrong (2007) states that "old age brings with it access to a wider scope of being; to the collective unconscious of the psyche; to the transpersonal realms of human existence" (p.214).

From a Jungian perspective, old age is both the winter and the evening of one's life. During this period of life the goal lies in retaining and increasing one's personal wholeness and one's unity with the Self, inner events, inner environment, integration, and being. It involves a process of individuation, which is a process of becoming oneself (Brewi and Brennan, 1999).

Jung (1939a, 1971) believed that middle life and old age have specific developmental tasks that involve the consolidation of an integrated personality by integrating the conscious and unconscious parts of self. During mid-life there is a shift in the "center of attention and gravity from the ego to the Self" (Brewi and Brennan, 1999, p.57). These years are characterized by a call for "unity with the Self, unity with the cosmos, unity with the Kingdom of God" (Brewi and Brennan, 1999, p.58).

Jung (1939a, 1971) believed that, during mid-life crisis, as one is less involved with outward life and more involved with the inward life, less directed to the conscious and more directed to the unconscious, there is often an accelerated movement towards becoming the individual image of the transcendent that the person is meant to be (Brewi and Brennan, 1999). Old age is seen as an "'inner journey' a quest for the 'Self' to reintegrate the conscious, social mind with the unconscious in order to develop the whole personality" (Kelleher, 1992, p.26). It is the "birth to a life in which spirit is in the ascendancy and in which signals from within begin to be more important than the material values that governed life's first half" (Patton, 2006, p.305). It is a final stage in which individuals naturally progress towards individuation, wholeness, maturation, and wisdom (Patton, 2006). According to Jung (1971), individuation "means becoming an 'in-dividual', and, in so far as 'individuality' embraces our innermost, last, and incomparable uniqueness, it also implies becoming one's own self" (p.121). It is a process of "coming to selfhood" (p.122).

Jung (1971) identified this stage of development as both the winter of human life and the evening of life. During this stage spirituality and the transcendence of the conscious ego are the main focus in individuals' development. There is a need to turn inward and reconnect with aspects of the self that were silenced during the "morning" (p.17) of human life, when individuals' development focused on the "entrenchment in the outer world" (p.17), including the development of the individual's social role and social achievements. He noted this difference for that period of life: "but we cannot live the afternoon of life according to the programme of life's morning; for what was great in the morning will be little at evening, and what in the morning was true will at evening become a lie" (Jung, 1971, p.17).

Schachter-Shalomi (1995) suggested a new model of late-life development based on the concepts of *sage-ing* and *spiritual eldering* (Schachter-Shalomi, 1995, p.5) which were defined as "a process that enables older people to become spiritually radiant, physically vital, and socially responsible 'elders of the tribe'" (p.5). Schachter-Shalomi (1995) suggested that old age is a period for "spiritual unfoldment" (p.51), a period for evolution and growth in consciousness, for "a self-directed flowering of the spirit that unites all people" (p.39), and for direct and inner experience with the Divine. It is a period of self-transformation and inner reflection that allows elders to mindfully and consciously recognize the opportunity they have in this stage of life (Schachter-Shalomi, 1995). This stage of life can be viewed as an opportunity to learn and grow; to recognize the beauty of aging; to get in touch with their true nature and the meaning of life, death and mortality; to experience inner healing; and to be of service to humanity by leaving a legacy and passing on the wisdom of their life's experience (Schachter-Shalomi, 1995). Schachter-Shalomi (1995) state that "eldering implies that we take active responsibility for our destiny in old age, living by conscious choice, rather than social expectation" (p.39). Old age is also a period during which elders engage in *harvesting* their lives (Schachter-Shalomi, 1995). Harvesting is defined as "gathering the fruits of a lifetime's experience and enjoying them in old age" (Schachter-Shalomi, 1995, p.53). This task is perceived as a life-repair activity by which elders mindfully recognize their lifetime achievements, come to terms with personal issues that might poison their psychological well-being, and embrace the beauty and endless opportunities for growth that this period of life brings them. Harvesting tasks include (a) letting go of old grudges and coming to forgiveness so that bringing closure to painful issues of the past will allow elders to focus and to use their infinite energy in positive ways; (b) paying attention to intergenerational relationships so that elders can mentor younger generations and provide guidance in social communities; (c) recontextualizing difficult experiences of the past and finding here opportunities to grow; and (d) encountering one's mortality to learn "how to affirm the unity of life in death and death in life" (Schachter-Shalomi, 1995, p.91).

Based on this approach, Schachter-Shalomi (1995) developed several programs to foster spiritual eldering. He suggested some tools that can be used to promote conscious aging: meditation, contemplation, journaling, conscious breathing techniques, and art work. These tools allow elders to learn to mirror their true inner Self and bring that inner Self into their consciousness (Robba, 2006).

Erikson's (1980) model of psychosocial development proposed that in later life individuals go through the eighth challenge of life: *integrity versus despair*, during which a process of life review occurs. Old conflicts and issues are revisited from a different perspective in an effort to attain a sense of integrity and wisdom about the meaning of one's life that will increase self-esteem and life satisfaction (Verbraak, 2000). Failure to resolve these old conflicts will result in "despair," which "expresses the feeling that the time is short, too short for the attempt to start another life and to try out alternate roads of integrity" (Erikson, 1980, p.104).

More recently, Erikson (1997), based on her experience of aging and personality development during her eighties and nineties, suggested a new stage of identity development (the ninth stage), which is an extension and deepening of all the stages of life development called "gerotranscendence" (p.123). This stage is characterized by the development of an attitude of retreat and retirement from the world precipitated by the need to revisit all previous eight stages of development in order to resolve any unfinished conflicts. Erikson proposed that retreat from the world facilitated the development of spirituality.

Tornstam (2005) presented a theory on gerotranscendence that suggested that aging is a process of "natural progression towards maturation, and wisdom" (Tornstam, 1997, p.143), that "aging, or rather living, implies a process during which the degree of transcendence increases from young adulthood, and on" (p.39), that it is a lifelong and continuous process during which all experiences of earlier life are included. Gerotranscendence is a process that implies an integration of all life experiences (Tornstam, 2005) and that is characterized by a "shift in meta-perspective from a materialistic and rational vision to a more cosmic and transcendent one" (p.41) that does not imply disengagement or the withdrawal from society and social roles of adult life (Coleman, 1993) but rather a reorientation of life's perspective and experience towards a more spiritual understanding. The losses of late life are seen as opportunities for self-actualization and identity development, and for fostering the development of wisdom, individuals' self-knowledge, and empathy (Golub and Langer, 2007).

Levinson's (1978) theory of development in adulthood suggested that, during the *era or season* (p.18) of late adulthood (age 60 to death), individuals have a particular task to accomplish in order to achieve stability within this period of life. During this period individuals' task is based on a process of individuation that involves the experience of a period of crisis or despair as they confront the reality of their physical frailties and their mortality. As individuals approach their eighties, they start preparing for death. The late adulthood is to give meaning to life and death, and come to terms with self "knowing it and loving it reasonably well, and being ready to give it up" (p.39).

Reed (1991) developed a theory of self-transcendence based on research with older adults facing end-of-life issues. She suggested that spirituality at the end of life may provide direction towards personal transformation. Self-transcendence was defined as:

> The capacity to expand self-boundaries intrapersonally (towards greater awareness of one's philosophy, values, and dreams), interpersonally (to relate to others and one's environment), temporally (to integrate one's past and future in a way that has meaning for the present), and transpersonally (to connect with dimensions beyond the typically discernible world). (p.147)

Fowler (1981) suggested a model to describe the development of faith across lifespan. According to Fowler (1986) faith is associated with "the making, maintenance, and transformation of human meaning" (p.15) and is a "way of being, arising out of the way of seeing and knowing" (p.15). He suggested that the final stage of faith development—universalizing faith—is rare and only occurs in late life. This stage has been described as a selfless faith involving relinquishing and transcending of the self.

Another aspect of adult development is the development of consciousness. Within this context, transpersonal theories of human development have been suggested, including Wilber's (1980) structural-hierarchical paradigm, Washburn's (1988) dynamic-dialectical paradigm, and Ruumet's (1997) helical model of psychospiritual development.

These theories also suggested that transcendence is a fundamental and important aspect of human development.

The spiritual development that characterizes the last stage of life provides evidence of a continuous development in human life, a development that allows individuals to successfully adjust to the demands of the last stage of life. This pragmatic power of the self to develop, reorganize, and readjust in response to the various life circumstances allows older adults to retain a sense of self that is ageless—an identity that maintains its continuity and integrity, that transcends any physical, psychological, and social changes that arise with age. It also allows individuals to become more connected with their true inner nature, their inner self, and to understand the meaning of life, mortality, and death.

Studies have revealed that spirituality is associated with improved physical health (Koenig, McCullough, and Larson, 2001) and reduced risk of mortality and provides greater longevity (Moberg, 2008) and improved psychological well-being (Meisenhelder and Chandler, 2002; Wink and Dillon, 2008). These benefits arise from individuals' trust in and perceived support from a higher power and suggest that this trust may function as a coping mechanism for dealing with stress, physical limitations, and illnesses (Harvey, 2005), as well as with end-life issues (Reed, 1987, 1991). The sense of connection with a higher power fosters a greater sense of wholeness, as well as connectedness with themselves, others, and their own lives (Mckenzie *et al.*, 2000) and inspires hope for a positive future (Mckenzie *et al.*, 2000).

Aging and cultural differences

Cultural differences play an important role in the process of aging and how individuals experience this last period of their lives. According to social representations theory (Moscovici, 1988) the views that a given culture has towards aging constitute a shared cultural representation that includes values, ideas, and customs related to aging. This cultural representation is treated by members of that society as an established reality.

Evidence suggests that cultural values and beliefs influence the cross-cultural differences in perceptions of aging and aging attitudes. In Eastern cultures older adults have a powerful and respected role (Giles *et al.*, 2003; Ho, 1994; Levy and Langer, 1994; Sung, 2001) and are seen as a source of wisdom, knowledge, and experience (Ram Dass, 2000). In contrast, in Western cultures, wisdom is not valued and older adults are not respected for their knowledge and life experience (Ram Dass, 2000). In a society that values the external world and productivity, older adults are viewed very negatively (Giles *et al.*, 2003) and old people tend to be categorized into meaningful categories with distinct physical features, personality, and behavioral characteristics (i.e., as an expression of ageism; Butler, 1969). They are regarded as physically feeble, cognitively impaired, emotionally disturbed, financially deprived, and isolated from the world.

Confucian values of filial piety, hierarchical relations, and the practice of worship (Giles *et al.*, 2003), as well as the interdependent self-concept (Ashman, Shiomura, and Levy, 2006) that predominates in Asian cultures underlie the Asian attitudes towards older adults. These are suggested to promote positive views of aging and high esteem for older adults (Giles *et al.*, 2003). In contrast, Western cultures are youth-oriented (Giles *et al.*, 2003); emphasize independence, self-containment, and autonomy (Eyetsemitan, 2007); and hold a more independent self-concept in relation to the environment and others (Ashman *et al.*, 2006) that promotes a less positive societal view of aging than in Asian cultures.

Another factor behind these cultural differences is socioeconomic development (Löckenhoff *et al.*, 2009). Higher levels of economic development and industrialization have been associated with less positive attitudes and societal views of aging (Arnhoff, Leon, and Lorge, 1964). Changes in family structure, modernization, and Westernization of Asian societies may explain why some studies failed to find significant cross-cultural differences in aging attitudes between West and East societies (McCann *et al.*, 2004) and why there was reported an opposite direction of aging attitudes between Western and Eastern societies (Levy and Langer, 1994).

Studies (Ashman *et al.*, 2006; Levy, 2003; Levy *et al.*, 2000; Levy *et al.*, 2002, Gruenewald and Kemeny, 2007) have revealed that societal attitudes towards aging influence individuals' internalized age stereotypes and that perceptions of aging contribute to the development of self-stereotypes of aging which in turn have an impact on cognitive functioning, physical health, and psychological well-being of older adults. Self-stereotypes associated with ideas of decline and loss may cause older adults to focus on confirmatory facts and the dismissal of contradictory evidence of their aging concepts (Golub and Langer, 2007). Accordingly, studies (Levy *et al.*, 2000, 2002) have revealed that positive self-perception of aging (e.g., older adults remain useful and happy) increases longevity and reduces physical decline among older adults. In the line of the stereotype threat concept (Steele, 1997) it is also suggested that, when older adults believe that their physical and cognitive decline is certain, they might start exhibiting signs of this decline prematurely (Golub and Langer, 2007).

Summary

Physical, neurological, social, psychological, and spiritual changes interact, defining individuals' experiences of the process of aging, as well as guiding individuals' adjustment, coping strategies, and attitudes towards the changes of this stage of life. These changes do not always mean limitation or loss, but rather an adaptation to a new period of life. Elders move into a period of their life when they stop being "human *doers*" and begin being "human *beings*" (MacKinlay, 2001, p.21).

In late life there is an increasing interaction among the physical, psychosocial, and spiritual dimensions in promoting well-being and quality of life, and, although aging may be marked by physiological limitations "there remains potential for continued growth in the psychosocial and spiritual dimensions" (MacKinlay, 2001, p.12). In the midst of the changes in physical dimension, well-being tends to be related to the ability to transcend physical disabilities and chronic disease states (MacKinlay, 2001). MacKinlay (2001) states that "as the physical deteriorates, the spiritual may move further into transcending the physical disabilities, the fears, the physical limitations, the energy loss, the sensory loss" (p.151).

Accordingly, it is necessary to find holistic approaches to deal with these physical, psychological, neurological, and cognitive changes and their impact on elders' lives and approaches that can foster continued growth and development in late life, rather than focusing uniquely on pharmacological treatments.

Older adults and life meaning

He who has a Why to live can bear almost any How.

Nietzsche

The aging process is often perceived with fear. Individuals experience fear of retirement and loss of social role; fear of physical limitations, disease, cognitive deterioration, and senility; and fear of social isolation, dependency, loss of autonomy, and death (Eyetsemitan, 2007; Giles *et al.*, 2003; MacKinlay, 2001). In the midst of all the changes that occur in this period of life, many individuals experience a loss of meaning that causes an existential vacuum (MacKinlay, 2004) and a "crisis of meaning" (Missinne, 2004).

Viktor Frankl (2004a, 2004b) suggested that individuals have an intrinsic desire and motivation to give meaning to their lives. This search for meaning is the primary motivation in human life. Frankl (2004a) states that:

> For the meaning of life differs from man to man, from day to day and from hour to hour… One should not search for an abstract meaning of life. Everyone has his own specific vocation or mission in life to carry out a concrete assignment which demands fulfillment. Therein he cannot be replaced, nor can his life be repeated. Thus, everyone's task is as unique as is his opportunity to implement it… Each man is questioned by life; and he can only answer to life by answering for his own life; to life he can only respond by being responsible… The true meaning of life is to be discovered in the world rather than within man or his psyche. (pp.113–115)

Accordingly, a person can find meaning in life in what he does and creates in the world (creative values), in experiences he has in the world and with others (experiential values), and through the attitude he brings towards his or her experience of suffering (attitudinal values; Frankl, 2004a, 2004b).

According to a study developed by Missinne (2004), in old age, experiential and attitudinal values seem to be more important than creative values. Individuals tend to find meaning in their family, spiritual needs, good health, helping others, self-reliance, and suffering. Missinne (2004) states that:

> [The] meaning of life is also closely related with the meaning of suffering. Both are aspects of the same human reality. One aspect adds to the dimension of the others. Without suffering many people will never discover the meaning of their own life.

She states that old age is a "time for fulfillment," a time when individuals have the opportunity to achieve "meaningful conclusion of a life journey" (p.122).

MacKinlay (2001) suggested a developmental model of spirituality in old age based on a qualitative study using in-depth interviews with older adults designed to illustrate the components of spirituality in old age. According to this model, there are six major themes of spirituality in old age. The core theme in old age is a search for the ultimate meaning in life. A second theme is the way they respond to the ultimate meaning.

The other four themes include hope and fear, relationship and isolation, wisdom and final meaning, self-sufficiency and vulnerability. Each of these themes has a task to be accomplished, including identification of the source of ultimate meaning, finding appropriate ways to respond to the ultimate meaning, finding hope, finding intimacy with God and/or others, and transcending disabilities and loss, respectively. The goal of human beings is to achieve wholeness, which can only be experienced if each of the above tasks is accomplished. MacKinlay (2001) suggested that absolute wholeness may not be possible in this life, but the objective is to continue to grow spiritually until death. The outcome of spiritual wholeness is integrity and wisdom.

According to MacKinlay (2001) the ability to find one's individual and final meaning in life is understood as wisdom. MacKinlay (2001) uses the concept of wisdom in a spiritual context. Wisdom is recognized as an increasing ability to tolerate uncertainty and a deepening search for a meaning of life. It allows individuals to find meaning in life, to grow spiritually, to find meaning in being, to accept the inevitable losses of life, and to let go of things that are no longer important.

Dying and death

This existence of ours is as transient as autumn clouds.
To watch the birth and death of beings is like looking at the
movement of a dance.
A lifetime is like a flash of lightning in the sky,
Rushing by, like a torrent down a steep mountain.

Buddha

Death is a universal reality and an intrinsic part of life. From a sociological and anthropological perspective, death is a seen as a socially constructed phenomenon, as death and dying are experienced in different ways by individuals according to their cultural, personal, and religious background (Corless, Germino, and Pittman, 1994; Metzer, 1998). In Western cultures, fear and denial predominate among the ways in which people relate to death and face dying (Corless *et al.*, 1994; Kübler-Ross, 2009; Metzer 1998; Varela, 1997), while in the Eastern cultures, and particularly for Buddhists, people are less fearful of death and deal with this process with more serenity and peace (Mullin, 1998; Smith and Novak, 2003).

In the West, because of the advances of medicine, life expectancy has increased and the quality of life has improved; however, the focus on health has contributed to a more significant alienation of dying individuals (Strada, 2004). In the West, a majority of individuals die in hospitals and nursing homes without being surrounded by their family and loved ones (Field and Cassel, 1997; Kübler-Ross, 2009). Furthermore, in the West, a great deal of efforts are limited to pharmacological treatments to deal with physical symptoms and pain associated with dying process and to allow individuals to have a *good death*, which was defined as dying "free from avoidable distress and suffering for patients, families, and caregivers; in general accord with patients' families' wishes; and reasonably consistent with clinical, cultural, and ethic standards" (Field and Cassel, 1997, p.95), but less attention is directed to spiritual care of the dying.

Western cultures place such great emphasis on the importance of the values of eternal beauty, success, and material possessions that individuals live their daily lives as if death and illness are not normal realities in the process of life (Varela, 1997). Individuals become attached to material entities (i.e., people and possessions) and live in the illusion that possessions can give stability, safety, and happiness (Varela, 1997). There is a collective denial of impermanence, change, suffering, and death (Strada, 2004). Ultimately we all know life is impermanent, "but we tend to live 'as if' we will never die" (Strada, 2004, p.129). We live "in a false belief in continuity and permanence. When we live like that, we become, as Dudjom Rinpoche said, unconscious, living corpses" (Sogyal Rinpoche, 1993, p.17).

Chuang Tzu (in Sogyal Rinpoche, 1993) stated that:

> The birth of a man is the birth of sorrow. The longer he lives the more stupid he becomes, because his anxiety to avoid unavoidable death becomes more and more acute. What bitterness! He lives for what is always out of reach! His thirst for survival in the future makes him incapable of living in the present. (p.17)

The basic principles associated with the Four Noble Truths of Buddhism, which include suffering, ignorance of impermanence and separateness, *karma* (i.e., the natural law of cause and effect, so that whatever we do has an effect on others and ultimately on ourselves), and *samsāra* (i.e., the endless cycles of births, deaths, and rebirths), are incorporated in Buddhist practices such as meditation. Practitioners of Buddhist meditation learn to integrate these principles into their daily lives (Sogyal Rinpoche, 1993). According to Buddhist teachings, all things are impermanent, including our dreams, desires, hopes, and fears, and nothing can "resist the universal supremacy of death" (Radhakrishnan and Moore, 1957, p.272):

> Life is a stream of becoming. There is nothing permanent in the empirical self. One thing is dependent on another. This is the law of dependent origination (*pratityasamutpāda*). Even the self is a composite of *samjña* (perception), *vedanā* (feeling), *samskāras* (volitional dispositions), *vijñāna* (intelligence), and *rupa* (form). All these forms change according to the law of *karma*. (Radhakrishnan and Moore, 1957, p.272)

In Buddhist practices awareness of the reality of impermanence, the inevitability of death and dying, are fundamental, and, in this tradition, consistent support is given throughout the dying process (Sogyal Rinpoche, 1993). In Buddhism birth and death can be found at the macro and micro level—at the cosmic level, and in the individual person. Long (1975) stated the principle in this way:

> Neither human beings neither the universe itself experiences wither an absolute beginning or an absolute end. When this same drama is viewed as the microlevel in terms of seconds and fractions of seconds rather than years or aeons, birth and death are discovered to occur simultaneously in each instant of time. The human is nothing more than a conglomeration of "aggregates" (i.e., body, sensations, perceptions, mental formations, and consciousness) which, taken together form the mind-body organism engaged in the process of coming-to-being and passing-away in every moment. (p.65)

Moreover, in Buddhism there are several teachings concerning death, "how to live toward death," and "how to die well" (Long, 1975, p.69), so that individuals who follow the Buddhist teachings can learn how to cultivate a state of mind that will promote either a "good rebirth" (Long, 1975, p.69) or the liberation from the cycle of rebirth and death (Long, 1975). Buddhism also has several meditation practices focused on impermanence (e.g., mindfulness meditation on breath—*ānāpānā-sati*, bodily sensations, etc.), suffering (e.g., *tonglen* meditation), and recollection of death that consists of reflecting on our own mortality in order to foster proper living and reduce death anxiety when it approaches (Bhikkhu, 1997b; Sogyal Rinpoche, 1993).

In Buddhism, the belief is that spiritual care and preparation for death is a lifetime process in which to develop a felt sense of impermanence, and that it is only by developing a deep knowledge and understanding of life and death that we can live a meaningful life and experience a peaceful death (Long, 1975; Strada, 2004). Moreover, in Buddhist practice, the person is accompanied during the process of dying, wherein spiritual practices (e.g., *phowa*, which means the transference of consciousness) are used to help the dying person to maintain a peaceful state of mind (Long, 1975; Sogyal Rinpoche, 1993). After the death of the physical body, the spiritual guidance continues in order to guide the dead person's consciousness through the different *bardos* (i.e., intermediate stages between death and rebirth) and the next reincarnation (Sogyal Rinpoche, 1993).

In the West, Buddhism influenced some approaches towards the dying (e.g., Karuna Hospice Services in Australia,[3] San Francisco Zen Hospice Project,[4] Amara Association for Dignity in Life and Death in Portugal[5]) and many theorists (Byock, 1996; Imara, 1975; Singh, 1998; Yalom, 1980, 1985) conceptualize death as an opportunity for growth and psychospiritual transformation.

The experiences associated with dying are very challenging and most of the time involve the awareness of the proximity of death and need for finding psychological, physical, and spiritual resources to support and deal with this process. This involves finding meaning and purpose in life as death approaches (Strada, 2004). For some, the experience of dying is associated with great pain and alienation; and some individuals in the midst of this suffering experience powerful spiritual and personal connection when faced with their impending death (Byock, 1996; Yalom, 1980).

Yalom (1980) considered that death is one of the ultimate concerns of human beings and that anxiety regarding death is one of the most primitive causes of anxiety experienced by individuals. He continued to suggest that this anxiety of death is projected into other aspects of life. Based on his work with cancer patients, he suggested that the greatest fear individuals have is to experience loneliness when they are facing imminent death (Yalom, 1985). He also observed that, when individuals have to confront death and the reality of their own mortality, the experience of deep crisis fosters emotional growth and greater appreciation for life.

Byock (1996) suggested a developmental model in which dying is conceptualized as a stage in the human life-cycle, just as are childhood, adulthood, and old age. Dying is an integral and important part of life.

---

3   For more information please visit www.karuna.org.au.
4   For more information please visit www.zenhospice.org/1%20_about_zhp/about_zen_mission.htm.
5   For more information please visit www.amara.pt.

It is a period of opportunity to find meaning in life, "to develop a sense of completion, satisfaction, and even a sense of mastery within areas of life that are of subjective import to the person" (p.247). Suffering is seen as inherent to major life transition stages and as an opportunity to grow. Frankl (2004a) suggested that suffering ceases to be suffering when individuals find meaning in suffering, and that, "in accepting this challenge to suffer bravely, life has a meaning up to the last moment, and it retains this meaning literally to the end" (p.118). He also suggested that "death as a temporal outward limitation does not cancel the meaning of life but rather is the very factor that constitutes its meaning, so the inner limits only add to the meaning of man's life" (p.79).

Byock (1996) suggested that individuals who grow during their dying "are those who express satisfaction in the direction of personal change that occurred in response to progressive stresses of disabling illness, and for whom an enhanced subjective sense of self emerges during the process" (p.248). In these cases dying is seen as a stage of "growing on" (p.249). Dying is an opportunity to grow, to accept one's life and imperfection, to review life, to find meaning and transcend suffering, and to embody a "sense of renewed (at times enhanced) meaning and sense of completion, at times even fulfillment" (p.251).

Singh (1998) conceptualized that death is a psychospiritual transformation that involves three stages. The first stage is *chaos*, which encompasses Kübler-Ross's (2009) five stages of dying, including denial and isolation, anger, bargaining, depression, and acceptance, and a process of understanding and detaching from a separate sense of self. The second stage is *surrender*, which involves the recognition and awareness of one's inherent spiritual essence. The last stage is *transcendence*, which involves a process of deep spiritual integration.

Death attitudes in old age

Research on the death attitudes of older adults and their fears and anxieties about their own mortality has revealed mixed results. Some studies showed a linear increase in death anxiety with advancing age (Madnawat and Kachhawa, 2007; McMordie and Kumar, 1984; Schumaker, Warren, and Groth-Marnat, 1991), others showed a linear decrease (Keller, Sherry, and Piotrowski, 1984), and others a curvilinear relation with death anxiety ascending to a peak of death anxiety in middle age (Gesser, Wong, and Reker, 1987) and stabilizing in later life (Fortner and Neimeyer, 1999). A recent study showed that older adults in their mid-seventies experienced less fear of dying than did younger older adults in their sixties (Wink and Scott, 2005).

Fortner, Neimeyer, and Rybarczyk (2000) conducted a meta-analysis of several published and unpublished studies of death anxiety in older adults. They reported that higher levels of death anxiety in older adults were related to lower levels of ego integrity (i.e., Erikson's [1980] concept of ego integrity). Death anxiety was associated with more physical and psychological problems, and it was higher in institutionalized individuals than in older adults living independently. Age, gender, and religiosity were not associated with death anxiety in the old age population. Results revealed that death anxiety declines from middle age to old age and stabilizes during the final decades of life. Fortner *et al.* (2000) suggested that this might be associated with the idea that individuals move towards greater acceptance of their past and, consequently, of their mortality (Erikson, 1997, 1980; Levinson, 1978), an increased focus on the "here and now," greater tolerance of ambiguity and uncertainty as a result of life experience, and the tendency to become more introspective and focused on their inner journey (Brewi and Brennan, 1999).

Ethnicity was shown to be associated with death anxiety and fear of death in older adult Caucasian participants displaying higher levels of death anxiety than did African American participants (Depaola *et al.*, 2003). Moreover, personal anxiety about one's own aging and negative attitudes of others towards older adults were associated with death anxiety in older adults (Depaola *et al.*, 2003).

These mixed results led scholars to suggest that death anxiety response patterns are a function of the population examined in each particular study rather than a general characteristic of older adults (Wagner and Lorion, 1984) and that death anxiety is a multidimensional phenomenon with different groups of participants (Gesser *et al.*, 1987; Neimeyer, 1997–1998). Accordingly, studies should rely on multidimensional measures in order to achieve a better understanding of the association between death anxiety and older adults' attitudes towards death (Depaola *et al.*, 2003).

Grief and bereavement in old age

Bereavement has been defined as "the objective situation of having lost someone significant, a category that includes parents, siblings, partners, and friends" (Hansson and Stroebe, 2007, p.10). Grief has been defined as "a primarily emotional (affective) reaction to the loss of a loved one through death" (Hansson and Stroebe, 2007, p.13) and grieving is "the process of coping with bereavement" (Hansson and Stroebe, 2007, p.13).

In old age, individuals experience more episodes of bereavement and might be exposed to a cumulative negative effect of loss of loved ones because there is a heightened risk for multiple and sequential loss of loved ones and friends. Generally, bereavement is associated with a considerable grief reaction that might be experienced over a period of months or years after the loss (Hansson and Stroebe, 2007).

Individuals might experience nonclinical consequences of bereavement on different levels such as loneliness, personal functioning, personal control, social functioning, coping, and social participation and clinical consequences such as depression, anxiety, traumatic grief, suicide, and mortality (Hansson and Stroebe, 2007). They might experience feelings of guilt, frustration, and identity crisis (Kumar, 2010). Research (Hansson and Stroebe, 2007) showed that in old age individuals exhibit a heterogeneous experience and response to bereavement depending on gender, age, circumstances and time of death, emotional closeness, caregiving conditions, physical and emotional health, coping strategies, economic resources, interpersonal resources, and culture.

Summary

Research shows that death anxiety, grief, and bereavement in old age are a heterogeneous experience and a multidimensional phenomenon in which many variables seem to come into play to determine how individuals experience the death of others and perceive the proximity of their own death. Some elders experiencing death anxiety often have to experience the loss of significant others (e.g., husband or wife, family, friends, etc.), and the process of grief and bereavement can be very difficult and cause clinical and nonclinical consequences for the grieving older person (Hansson and Stroebe, 2007, Kumar, 2010). Accordingly, it is important to understand in which ways individuals can be prepared and supported during these experiences in order to cope positively with the reality of their own death and the deaths of others.

Herman Feifel (as cited in Fortner *et al.*, 2000) suggested that:

> The way we conceptualize death may influence the way in which we engage in our lives. In particular, how we anticipate our future death—with fear, equanimity, or eagerness—may shape the way we live and experience the present. (p.95)

It is also possible that, by shaping the way we understand the present moment and reality (i.e., by understanding the reality of impermanence of everything in life), individuals can change the way they perceive death. As the Zen master Dōgen (as cited in Long, 1975) stated:

> To find release you must begin to regard life and death as identical to Nirvāna, neither loathing the former nor coveting the latter. It is fallacious to think that you simply can move from birth to death. Birth, from the Buddhist point of view, is a temporary point between the preceding and succeeding; hence it can be called "birthlessness." The same holds for death and deathlessness. In life there is nothing more than life, in death nothing more than death: we are born and dying at every moment. (p.70)

Mindfulness practice is dedicated to the contemplative practice of deeply looking into the nature of the self and reality by bringing attention to the present moment. It contemplates the interrelated nature of body and mind; subject and object; self, other and the world (Jyoti, 2010). By acknowledging change, impermanence, uncertainty, and suffering as intrinsic and integral parts of human existence, elders may change the way they perceive death and experience the loss of others and allow themselves to accept their past, their present, and their mortality, thus promoting a higher sense of self-integrity rather than despair (Kumar, 2010).

Ram Dass (2000) stated that:

> Having come to realize that we are more than the body and mind—and more than their combined self-image, the Ego—we can begin to view dying and death through quite different eyes. We are no longer quite so afraid of our own thoughts and feelings, however disturbing they may be. In learning to step outside the Ego into Soul consciousness, we know that we are more than our thoughts and feelings and the mind that experiences them. We are Souls, and as such we come to the mystery of dying and death without quite the same level of fear and dread. (p.147)

Conclusion

Aging is a dynamic and complex process. It involves challenges in physical, psychological, and spiritual dimensions of individuals' lives. In spite of the general concept that age involves losses such as losses of physical autonomy, psychological well-being, social role, and meaning, it is apparent that, despite the increasing physical limitations that arise with age, individuals experience in that time of life an opportunity to grow and flourish, to find meaning in their lives that goes beyond the physical limitations of their body and the temporal limitation of their lives.

How can an MBSR program foster elders' growing, flourishing, and dynamic transformation process? How can mindfulness practice promote elders' wholeness and integrity? Can these practices promote elders' well-being, psychological and physical health, neuropsychological performance, and spiritual development? These are the questions this study seeks to answer.

One of the key learning principles of MBSR is that, as long as we are breathing, there is more right with us than wrong. This understanding can greatly help elders to cultivate awareness and focus on their strengths rather than relying solely on the changes and limitations that arise with the aging process (McBee, 2008). Focusing on changes and limitations can cause emotional distress, loss of motivation, and isolation. Smith (2006) stated that focusing on people's abilities rather than on their limitations "empowers participants by combating the double stigmatization that many experience as both mental health patients and as old people" (p.194). Mindfulness programs might help older adults cultivate acceptance towards the constant changes and losses they face during the aging process, face their physical changes with a new perspective (e.g., more awareness and acceptance), and cultivate new behavioral and cognitive coping responses towards these changes.

Moreover, mindfulness fosters a process of disidentification (reperceiving) in which individuals gradually learn to stop seeing themselves as their body, mind, and emotions, and the things that they have lost throughout life and connect with a sense of self that goes beyond the limited boundaries of the ego. Individuals learn to stop identifying themselves with their limitations and losses, embrace life as it manifests, and connect with their transcending self. Vaughan (1977) described self-transcendence "as acceptance which is comparable to faith in that it implies a willingness to live out one's destiny and take responsibility for one's life" (p.277).

Depression is a very common mental health problem among older adults in the United States and Europe (Smith, 2006) and has been associated with loneliness, cognitive impairment, physical limitations, health issues, and loss of social status and role (Chew-Graham, Baldwin, and Burns, 2008). Moreover, anxiety is also a frequent problem in older adults due to declining health, multiple changes that arise, and others' ageism (Smith, 2006). MBSR was shown to be effective in secondary depression and anxiety; therefore, it is a promising intervention to alleviate these symptoms (Kabat-Zinn *et al.*, 1992; Miller *et al.*, 1995) and to foster positive emotions in older adults.

The cultivation of positive emotions and emotional balance is very important in old age, as it has been shown that elders who do so have a propensity to focus on positive emotions in ways that sustain health in late life and promote optimal functioning and a high quality of life (Davis *et al.*, 2007). The MBSR program can present elders with tools that can be used to cultivate positive emotions and emotional balance, which, in turn, will foster physical health and quality of life.

Mindfulness practice might also allow older adults to recognize age self-stereotypes they may hold and to cultivate positive emotions towards their aging process, consequently having an effect upon their physical and psychological well-being. The MBSR component of applying mindfulness principles and mindful presence in interrelationships with others may allow older adults to distance themselves (i.e., observe with equanimity) from possible ageism attitudes and stereotypes others may hold in relation to aging.

Mindfulness practices involve awareness of the impermanence of reality. This understanding might foster elders' understanding of the impermanence of life, promote a more positive attitude and acceptance towards death (their own and that of others), and reduce the anxiety and fear of death. Through mindfulness practice, elders can change how they relate to death and enhance their appreciation of everyday life (Lief, 2001). By acknowledging and accepting mortality, they might reduce death anxiety and fear, thereby fostering a more positive psychological well-being for themselves as older adults.

Older adults studied often showed deficits in processing skills because of the reduced processing efficiency in working memory, inhibitory deficits (McDowd, 1997), loss of efficiency in suppression mechanisms (Palladino and DeBeni, 1999), decline in processing speed and attention resources (Craik, 1999), and decline in distraction control (Darowski *et al.*, 2008). Mindfulness practice and an MBSR program involve the training of attention and of the inhibitory skills to suppress automatic cognitive operations. Several studies have shown that mindfulness practices improve attention in practitioners (Treadway and Lazar, 2009) and working memory functioning (Chambers *et al.*, 2008). Accordingly, older adults might improve their attention and inhibitory processing (e.g., of automatized thoughts and distraction stimuli) skills by practicing mindfulness, which in turn will improve their cognitive processing abilities. These changes might be paralleled with structural changes in the brain as a result of brain plasticity. Modern theorists believe that cognition can be repaired and retrained in elders and the brain can regrow brain areas and take over new areas to compensate for damage and synaptic losses (Begley, 2007).

MBSR has been associated with increases in a sense of meaning and peace, which, in turn, were associated with reductions in medical and psychological symptoms (Carmody *et al.*, 2008) and with an increased awareness "of the intricate interconnections among themselves, other individuals and eventually all aspects of nature through direct experience" (MacKenzie *et al.*, 2007, p.62). These results revealed that spirituality might be developed in a secular context and that the MBSR program might be an adequate context in which individuals could develop spirituality outside of a religious context. Accordingly, MBSR may offer a means for older adults to reconnect with spiritual practices and be provided with new meanings and understandings of life and the aging process, which, in turn, might promote physical health and psychological well-being.

Mindfulness is a holistic intervention that can improve the quality of life of older adults in various ways. It might help elders cultivate a sense of well-being, connection with their lives, willingness to live, and an acceptance towards the process of death and dying. It might provide means of cultivating emotional and physical balance in a period of their lives filled with stresses related to the aging process. By facilitating mindful aging, individuals can realize what it means to continue to grow and develop during late life. Limitations are not seen as losses but as opportunities to develop adaptations and grow in the face of life's restrictions. This focus on continued growth and change throughout lifespan may have positive implications in elders' quality of life and experience of aging (Golub and Langer, 2007).

» Chapter 2 «

Methodology

As was discussed in the previous chapter, mindfulness practice has been scientifically investigated in several clinical and nonclinical populations. Results revealed that the practice of mindfulness is associated with reduced stress, improved quality of life, and increased objective and subjective well-being in a vast range of clinical and nonclinical groups (Didonna, 2009).

The primary research question of this study was: what are the effects and lived experiences of the MBSR program for older adults in terms of psychological well-being, subjective well-being, physical health, neuropsychological performance, and spirituality? This randomized controlled trial attempted to understand how MBSR could provide a holistic intervention for older adults groups.

Integral inquiry method

The integral inquiry approach was developed by Braud (1998) and is based on the assumption that scientific research needs to rest on an expanded view of conventional science and scientific methods. Conventional research methods are mainly based on quantitative and experimental methods. These methodological approaches may offer the greatest confidence in conclusions, but they "sacrifice depth of understanding and lose knowledge of the contexts, complexities, and richness of what is being studied" (Braud, 1998, p.37). Nonconventional research methods use qualitative methods that allow the researcher to explore with great depth the phenomenon being studied and provide "an appreciation of the complex dynamic, and often subtle ways in which events and experiences come together and play themselves out in the lives of particular individuals" (Braud, 1998, p.41). In integral inquiry both quantitative and qualitative methods of research are honored and used as complementary tools to investigate particular research questions (Braud, 1998).

Mixed-method design and integral skills

This study used a mixed-method design (Creswell, 2009) and an integral inquiry approach because the aim of this investigation was to obtain a multidimensional understanding of the effects and the lived experience of the MBSR program in older adults in terms of psychological well-being, physical health, neuropsychological performance, and spirituality.

Qualitative and quantitative data were collected, integrated, and connected in order to interpret the effects and the lived experience of the MBSR program in older adults. Quantitative data were collected in order to examine the relationship between mindfulness, well-being, psychological symptoms, physical health, neuropsychological performance, and spirituality before and after participating in the MBSR program. Qualitative data allowed a rich, complete, and in-depth exploration of the lived experience of the MBSR program in older adults in terms of their perceptions of aging, psychological well-being, physical health, cognitive performance, and spiritual development. Adding a qualitative component to the study provided an advantage for studying meditative states because it presented an opportunity for an in-depth exploration of participants' experiences and the meaning of these experiences (Braud and Anderson, 1998).

The mixed-method design was selected because this study sought to converge, corroborate, and correspond results from different methods (i.e., using triangulation) and to extend the range of inquiry by using different methods for different inquiry components (Creswell, 2011). The quantitative component looked at treatment outcome (TO) and the qualitative component looked at the lived experiences of participants during the MBSR program. The mixed-method design allowed me to overcome the limitation of quantitative methods of investigation that tend to be reductionist in their attempt to quantify and control isolated variables and generalize findings (Creswell, 2009).

This study employed convergent parallel mixed-method design as quantitative and qualitative data were gathered concurrently in the study and both data sets were equally prioritized during analysis. Furthermore, quantitative and qualitative strands were kept independent during the analysis and then mixed during the overall interpretation (Creswell, 2011). This method was used in order "to obtain different but complementary data on the same topic" (Morse as cited in Creswell, 2011, p.77).

The integration of both quantitative and qualitative data allowed a broader and more complete understanding of the phenomena and increased the overall strength of the study (Creswell, 2009). As stated by Braud and Anderson (1998), "the world of human beings and their experiences is multileveled and complex, and to provide a faithful account of that world, research approaches must be correspondingly multifaceted and pluralistic" (p.256).

Braud and Anderson (1998) suggested several integral skills to be applied in a wide variety of research methods and approaches, including intention, visual and auditory skills, playing, quieting and slowing down, kinesthetic and proprioceptive skills, direct knowing and intuition, and unconscious process and materials, among others. Some of the integral skills that were used throughout the various stages and procedures of this study included intention, compassion, slowing down, mindfulness, auditory and visual skills, proprioceptive skills, and intuition. These skills are described in more detail below.

Toms and Toms (1998) stated that:

> [Intention] is a force that has the power to manifest what you want to happen. This occurs through consciousness by focusing on a specific overarching purpose…there is a letting-go of expectation or attaining results even though the intention remains and the focus of energy stays on the present…your concentration is on whatever you are doing in the moment. (pp.113–114)

Accordingly, at each different stage of the research, I set different intentions that guided and directed her attention and presence (e.g., intention to find the appropriate participants for the study, intention to be mindfully present during the study intervention, etc.).

The word *compassion* comes from two words in Latin: *com* that means *with*, and *pati* that means *suffer*. Therefore, literally, the word means *to suffer with*. Compassion encompasses love, empathy, kindness, awareness, discernment, acceptance for others and self, and having a knowing that comes from one's heart. These are all intermeshed and are difficult to treat as independent qualities. They all serve a way of direct knowing and how we experience the objective and subjective reality around us (Martins, 2008).

Compassion can be applied throughout the research process and in the researcher's presence and motivation to explore the subjective and objective dimensions of human experience and awareness. It is essential to love what one is aiming to study in order to explore it with kindness and sympathy. This compassionate knowing directs the way the researcher asks questions, establishes the hypothesis, searches for literature, develops instruments of assessment, conducts the study, works, analyzes the data, develops theories, and communicates findings to the target audience (Martins, 2008).

In this study, this compassionate knowing directed my attitude, presence, and actions when I defined the research questions and the hypothesis and searched for the relevant literature and instruments used for the quantitative assessment, as well as designed the interview protocol, directed the way the study was conducted and data were analyzed, and chose how the findings were communicated. Bringing a compassionate heart to the topic of research arose from my intention to give voice and expression to my own personal experience of the phenomenon being studied, and a desire to expand this experience by studying the experience of other individuals. This compassion and resonance allowed me to explore deep and subtle meanings and to awaken subtle and intuitive approaches that enabled me to experience the study in my own body, heart, and senses. The senses spoke for themselves, providing information and understanding of the phenomenon being analyzed, through auditory and visual skills (e.g., inner voice, imagery, and dreams), mindful presence, and many other skills that allowed me to perceive subtle forms of knowing. With a compassionate presence, I was in service of a higher purpose for humanity. I gave myself completely to the investigation, feeling an interconnectedness with all individuals involved in the experience, and sharing this experience with participants. Compassionate presence allowed me to form compassionate intentions for the main purpose of the investigation and the various stages of the study. Moreover, a presence with compassion allowed me to ask meaningful questions about the study, not only because of my own personal experience of the phenomena being analyzed, but also based on a compassionate and loving intention to access deeper and richer understandings of the phenomena in other individuals and to discover how this practice can foster awareness and a more full and balanced life (Martins, 2008).

Slowing down means "to grow quiet and listen; to stop thinking, stop moving, almost stop breathing; to create stillness in which, like mice in a deserted house, capacities and awareness too wayward and too fugitive for everyday use may delicately emerge" (McGlashan, 1988, p.156). Slowing down allowed me to direct my attention to whatever was happening in the present moment and to become mindfully aware of it. The present-moment experience is not static; it is impermanent and always moving. I followed this flow of experience, bringing my attention to become aware of what I was listening to in the inner and outer world, feeling in my body, and finding in the thoughts in my mind, and then sensing the interconnectedness between everything in the world and the underlying oneness of life. It involved an attention "without resistance" (Krishnamurti, 1998, p.137), allowing everything that was arising in each present moment and being aware of this movement in all the perceptions of the senses and the heart. This flowing awareness of experience allowed me to observe and obtain information and understanding of the phenomena being studied through subtle forms of knowing, such as auditory skills (e.g., mindfully listening to outer and inner sounds and the "inner voice"), visual skills (e.g., mindfully observing images arising in the mind and bringing awareness to images arising from the "inner vision" [Vaughan, 1998, p.189]), proprioception skills (i.e., mindfully observing the sensory impression arising from within and from the surface of the body), and mindfully recognizing mental, emotional, bodily, and spiritually based intuition (Vaughan, 1998).

Qualitative research methods

Heuristic research was used during preparation, collection, and analysis of the qualitative data. I used heuristic methods to inform my personal inquiry into the lived experience of the MBSR program and its effects in elders' lives.

Heuristic research is a qualitative method developed by Clark Moustakas (1990) that focuses on "a search for the discovery of meaning and essence in significant human experience. It requires a subjective process of reflecting, exploring, sifting, and elucidating the nature of the phenomenon under investigation" (Douglass and Moustakas, 1985, p.40). Heuristic research is "concerned with meanings, not measurements; with essence, not appearance; with quality, not quantity; with experience, not behavior" (Douglass and Moustakas, 1985, p.42). The objective is not to prove or disprove something but to discover and offer a deep understanding of the phenomenon as it is experienced by individuals. In the process of heuristic research, the researcher is "creating a story that portrays the qualities, meanings, and essences of universally unique experiences" (Moustakas, 1990, p.13). In heuristic research the involvement of the researcher is explicitly acknowledged and "the self of the researcher is present throughout the process and, while understanding the phenomenon with increasing depth, the researcher also experiences growing self-awareness and self-knowledge…it incorporates creative self-processes and self-discoveries" (p.9).

Some of the heuristic tools that were used in this study include self-dialogue, tacit-knowing, intuition, indwelling, and focusing. These methods will be described below.

Self-dialogue involved dialoguing and becoming one with the question of the investigation in order to allow the phenomenon to speak to my own experience. In order to understand the experience of phenomenon studied, I needed to understand how I experience it myself. Moustakas (1990) stated that "one must begin with oneself. One's own self-discoveries, awareness, and understandings are the initial steps of the process" (p.16).

Tacit knowing refers to an implicit knowledge within oneself. This was summarized by Polanyi (1983) as "the fact that we can know more than we can tell" (p.4). Moustakas (1990) stated it in this way:

> Such knowledge is possible through a tacit capacity that allows one to sense the unity or wholeness of something from an understanding of the individual qualities or parts. Knowledge of the trunk, branches, buds, flowers, leaves, colors, textures, sounds, shape, size—and other parts—ultimately may enable a sense of the treeness of a tree, and its wholeness as well. (p.21)

Intuition acted as a bridge from the tacit knowledge to a more explicit and observable dimension of knowledge. Intuition allowed me to observe factors, make inferences, and understand a phenomenon by using an "internal capacity" (Moustakas, 1990, p.23) that "makes immediate knowledge possible without the intervening steps of logic or reasoning" (Moustakas, 1990, p.23). In heuristic research the researcher uses intuition to make changes in method, procedure, direction, and understanding in order to achieve an in-depth understanding of the essential meaning of the phenomenon (Moustakas, 1990).

Indwelling was used as a tool to access tacit knowing and intuition. It refers to a concentrated attention to and awareness of the topic of inquiry in order to appreciate the parts and wholeness of the phenomenon and deeply understand the nature or meaning of the phenomenon of human experience being studied. Moustakas (1990) stated that this process is "conscious and deliberate, yet it is not linear or logical. It follows clues wherever they appear; one dwells inside them and expands their meanings and associations until fundamental insight is achieved" (p.24).

Focusing refers to a process during which the researcher clears an inward space for thoughts and feelings to surface that were not present in the conscious dimension. It is "an inner attention, a staying with, a sustained process of systematically contacting the more central meanings of an experience" (Moustakas, 1990, p.25). Focusing allowed me to discern main themes associated with the phenomenon of inquiry, thoughts and feelings, and cognitive knowledge that include meanings and perceptions that reflect internal changes of the researcher (Moustakas, 1990).

The heuristic inquiry involved various phases including initial engagement, immersion in the research question, illumination, explication, and creative synthesis. The phase of initial engagement was associated with my inner search and self-dialogue to determine the main research question of the study. The questions investigated were: How do elders experience the MBSR program in their mind, body, and spirit? How do elders experience themselves during the program? What is the experience of feeling connected with the present moment? How do elders experience life during the MBSR program? The main question was: What is the lived experience of the MBSR program in older adults? The phases of immersion, incubation, illumination, explication, and creative synthesis were used throughout the study to answer the questions of this investigation.

In the immersion phase I lived the questions of this investigation to daily life: being present in every moment to the experience of my life allowed me to connect with the meaning of mindfulness living. Every situation where the topic was present (e.g., MBSR sessions, personal meditation practice, personal life situations where mindfulness was consciously used, conversations about the topic, and interviews with the participants) were opportunities for me to understand the phenomenon. During the incubation phase I moved away and isolated myself from the topic under investigation. Conscious and direct attention was no longer given to the question or to situations where raw material could arise. By distancing myself from the question under investigation I allowed the inner tacit knowledge to grow and reach its full potentiality and intuition to bring further and deeper understandings of the phenomenon that were not present at the level of immediate awareness. By being open and receptive to what was naturally occurring in this silent process of incubation, I found that illumination occurred. I was able to access the understandings that developed during the incubation phase and allowed the tacit knowledge and intuition to reach conscious awareness, providing a more creative understanding of the topic. Many times, insights happened when I was involved in activities in nature or during meditation practices. Often, these insights manifested as images and/or as a felt sense in my whole body. A few times, these were presented in dreams that had a clear meaning. These provided a clearer understanding of the essence and meaning of the phenomenon being studied and sometimes presented information that modified what had been previously understood or revealed hidden meanings. After themes arose from the illumination phase, I used focusing, indwelling, self-searching, and self-disclosure to be aware of my own awareness, feelings, thoughts, beliefs, and judgments that could be obscuring my understanding of the topic and projected in the understandings that had been achieved at that stage. This explication phase allowed me to make inner space and time to focus my attention on aspects of the topics that were still hidden. This process allowed me to achieve the main core themes of the investigation and the associated details that allowed an understanding of the topic as a whole. Finally, the creative synthesis stage involved the presentation of the understandings that answered the research questions, which arose from the illumination and explication phases.

In anthropological and social studies, researchers refer to two different kinds of data concerning human behavior and two different kinds of fieldwork done and viewpoints obtained, two kinds of each of those that are designated as *emic* or *etic* (Creswell, 2007; Harris, 1976). An emic account is a description of behavior that comes from a person within the culture, while etic account is a description presented by an observer. As I did not belong to the age group being explored in this study, the heuristic inquiry was based on my personal views and experience of the MBSR program, and provided an outsider's perspective of participants' experience of the MBSR program (etic account) rather than an insider's perspective (emic) (Creswell, 2007; Harris, 1976).

Quantitative research methods

In order to assess participants' degree of mindfulness and the relationship between this dimension and well-being, psychological symptoms, physical health, neuropsychological performance, and spirituality, several quantitative measures were used before and after the intervention program. These scales included the Mindfulness Attention Awareness Scale (MAAS), the Five Facet Mindfulness Questionnaire (FFMQ), the Self-Compassion Scale (SCS), the Experiences Questionnaire (EQ), the Satisfaction With Life Scale (SWLS), the Positive and Negative Affect Schedule (PANAS), the Psychological Well-Being Scale (PWBS), the Profile of Mood States-Short Form (POMS-SF), the Perceived Stress Scale (PSS), the World Health Organization Quality of Life-BREF

(WHOQOL-BREF), the Death Perspectives Scale (DPS), the Subjective Health Complaint Inventory (SHCI), the physical and spiritual domains of the WHOQOL-100 assessment instrument, the Spiritual Well-Being Questionnaire (SWBQ), two indexes of the Portuguese version of the Wechsler Adult Intelligence Scale (WAIS) III, and the Trail Making A and B Test (TMT). All the selected scales used were validated and/or translated to Portuguese from Portugal. These pre- and post-assessments allowed me to measure the effects of the MBSR in study participants.

Mindfulness was assessed using the MAAS (Brown and Ryan, 2003) and the FFMQ (Baer *et al.*, 2006). The MAAS assessed the general tendency to be attentive and aware of present-moment experience in daily life and the FFMQ assessed five facets of mindfulness, including observing, describing, acting with awareness, being nonjudging of inner experience, and nonreactivity to inner experience (Baer *et al.*, 2006). The SCS (Neff, 2003) and the EQ (Fresco *et al.*, 2007) were used to assess self-compassion and reperceiving, respectively.

Well-being was assessed using measures to evaluate subjective well-being (SWB) and psychological well-being (PWB). SWB was assessed using the SWLS (Diener *et al.*, 1985; Simões, 1992) that measured the cognitive component of SWB and the PANAS (Watson, Clark, and Tellegen, 1988; Galinha and Pais Ribeiro, 2005) that evaluated the emotional component of SWB. PWB was assessed using the PWBS (Ryff and Keynes, 1995) using the Portuguese version translated by Silva in 2004 (unpublished).

Psychological symptoms were assessed using the POMS-SF (Shacham, 1983; Viana, De Almeida, and Santos, 2001) that measured six mood factors: tension/anxiety, depression/dejection, anger/hostility, vigor/activity, fatigue/inertia, and confusion/bewilderment. *Stress* was assessed using the PSS (Cohen, Kamarck, and Mermelstein, 1983; Pais Ribeiro and Marques, 2009) and the WHOQOL-BREF (Skevington, Lotfy, and O'Connell, 2004; Vaz Serra *et al.*, 2006) instrument was used to evaluate participants' *quality of life*.

Death perspectives were assessed using the DPS (Barros-Oliveira and Neto, 2004; Spilka *et al.*, 1977). This scale assessed death from eight different perspectives: death as pain and loneliness, death as afterlife or reward, indifference towards death, death as unknown, death as forsaking dependents plus guilt, death as courage, death as failure, and death as a natural end (Spilka *et al.*, 1977).

Physical health/symptoms was assessed using the SHCI (Alves and Figueiras, 2008, Eriksen, Ihlebaek, and Ursin, 1999) and the physical domain (Domain 1) of the WHOQOL-100 assessment instrument (Canavarro *et al.*, 2009; WHOQOL Group, 1998) that evaluated pain and discomfort, energy and fatigue, and sleep and rest.

Spirituality was assessed using the spirituality domain (Domain 6) of the WHOQOL-100 assessment instrument (Canavarro *et al.*, 2009; WHOQOL Group, 1998) and the SWBQ (Gomez and Fisher, 2003; Gouveia, Marques, and Pais Ribeiro, 2009). The SWBQ assessed SWB in four domains: personal, communal, environmental, and transcendental spiritual well-being.

Neuropsychological performance was assessed using two indexes of the Portuguese version of the WAIS III (Barreto, Moreira, and Ferreira, 2008), including (a) the working memory index that includes the arithmetic and digit span subtests that will assess working memory (i.e., the system involved in temporal storage and manipulation of the information required for complex cognitive tasks such as language, comprehension, reasoning, and learning, a system that stores and processes information and is subdivided into three systems, including the central executive that resembles attention, the visuospatial sketch pad that stores and rehearses speech-based information, and the phonological loop that holds information in phonological form; Baddeley, 1992; Eysenck and Keane, 1995); and (b) the processing speed index that includes the digit symbol coding and incidental learning in a pairing of subtests to assess processing speed and memory (Strauss, Sherman, and Spreen, 2006). The TMT (Army Individual Test Battery, 1944) was used to measure attention, executive functions, and motor speed.

All the selected scales used are validated to the Portuguese population, apart from the PWBS, which has been translated into Portuguese in a version from Portugal (Silva, 2004, unpublished) and the Montreal Cognitive Assessment (MOCA), which was officially translated to Portuguese (Simões *et al.*, 2007) and validated for the Portuguese Population (Freitas *et al.*, 2010). These measures are described in detail in Appendix 1.

Participants

A sample of 24 participants was recruited, including both men and women aged 65 and over, to participate in the study. Twelve participants were randomly assigned to a treatment group (TG) that participated in the eight-week MBSR program or to a control group (CG) who did not participate in the MBSR during the study but were on a waiting list to participate in the MBSR after the study ended. Participants included in the study were selected based on the following inclusion criteria: no cognitive impairment, no recent diagnosis of chronic illness, no terminal illness or clinical diagnosis of depression or anxiety, no mobility difficulties, no previous regular experience in meditation and yoga practices, willingness to participate in an eight-week MBSR program with a 90-minute session once per week and a full day (six to seven hours) session between the sixth and seventh week of the program. Participants were not accepted in the study if they lived in nursing homes.

Participants were recruited from the general population through advertisements via emails, mail, and distribution of flyers; talks and distribution of flyers at Third Age Universities; word of mouth; and referrals from psychologists. I gave presentation talks on MBSR at Portuguese Third Age Universities.

Individuals interested in participating in the study were asked to respond by telephone or email and were scheduled for a screening telephone appointment, at a convenient time for me and the respondent. The screening telephone appointment was the first part of the screening process during which I asked a series of questions from the screening questionnaire to determine age, gender, and physical and mental health conditions already diagnosed by their physician. Potential participants were asked a few questions to determine whether they had had any previous regular experience of meditation and yoga, and to determine their willingness to comply with program participation requirements. This screening questionnaire evaluated whether participants fitted the inclusion criteria (as listed above, apart from the cognitive performance criterion). If the respondent was eligible for the study, he was scheduled for an in-person cognitive screening (i.e., the second part of the screening process) at my clinical office, at a convenient time arranged by me and the respondent, to assess her or his cognitive performance. I used a cognitive screening test, the MOCA (Nasreddine et al., 2005) to screen for cognitive performance. The respondents who fitted the inclusion criteria were informed that they had been accepted into the study and were given detailed information about the study, including the aim and duration of the study; the required commitment during the MBSR program in terms of number of sessions, practice, and completion of exercises between sessions; assessment interviews before and after the program; and the location where the MBSR program was to be conducted. The respondents who were interested in participating and able to commit to the full duration of the study scheduled the initial pre-MBSR assessment.

Procedure

The selected participants had an initial assessment, at my clinical office, before the beginning of the MBSR program. This initial assessment began by providing participants with an overview about the aim and structure of the study and a description of my personal interest in the topic. Participants were given the consent form to read, ask any questions, and sign. I made every effort to make sure that participants understood the study and that the information was clearly comprehended.

After signing the consent form, participants were given: (a) a personal and medical questionnaire with questions related to demographic information, socioeconomic status, religious background, medical history, general health state, and medication; and (b) the psychological and neuropsychological tests described above. After completing the questionnaires and assessments, participants were informed whether they were assigned to the TG or the CG. Participants that were assigned to the TG were given an information sheet with the dates and times of each MBSR session and the address of the location where the MBSR sessions were taking place. The initial assessment lasted approximately 60 to 70 minutes.

The eight-week MBSR program was taught by myself at a meditation center in Porto, Portugal. During the eight weekly sessions and the one intensive day of the MBSR program, participants were presented different mindfulness practices and were invited to practice during each session. After each mindfulness practice, participants were invited to share their experience and make sense of what did or did not happen during the practice and of any particular difficulty they might have experienced. They were encouraged to honor and affirm their own experience in their own terms, speaking first in pairs and then sharing to the whole group. While participants shared their experience with the whole group, I was careful and mindful to honor and accept each participant's experience and statement and to provide support in relation to any difficulty or insecurity they might be experiencing. This allowed an environment of cooperative inquiry into the process being experienced by participants during the program.

Several topics were presented and discussed during each session related to mindfulness practices, mindfulness principles, the application of mindfulness in daily life, and understanding the role of mindfulness in stressful situations, stressful communications, emotional difficulties, and mindful eating. After the presentation and discussion of each defined topic, participants had space and time to share any questions or doubts that might have arisen during discussions. At the end of each session, participants were given information about the meditations they needed to practice during the week and the activities they needed to complete for the next session.

Between the sixth and seventh session, participants had an intensive silent session that lasted five hours. This was two hours less than had been initially expected, because I had observed that the weekly two-hour session had sometimes been physically demanding for participants. So the final session was rescheduled to only five hours, and took place with interspersed sitting, standing, and lying down meditation practices. During this intensive day, participants were presented with and guided through several mindfulness practices and a yoga sequence, in silence. Before the session finished, participants had time and space to share their experiences and challenges with the whole group and to ask any questions related to the practices. Again, I was mindful to honor and accept each participant's experience and provided support when difficulties and challenges were shared.

At the end of the first session, participants were given a manual that contained exercises and information related to the course and a log sheet on which they kept a record of when and for how long they had meditated during the week, along with any observations pertaining to their daily experience while meditating and/or practicing yoga. Every two weeks participants were given an audio CD containing the different guided mindfulness practices and yoga sequences presented and practiced during sessions. There were four CDs in total: (a) CD1 Body Scan Meditation (lying down meditation), (b) CD2 Yoga Sequence A (sitting postures), (c) CD3 Sitting Meditation, and (d) CD4 Yoga Sequence B (standing postures). Each audio CD was approximately 45 minutes in duration. Participants were invited to practice mindfulness meditation every day with the CDs. All the CDs had been audio-recorded by myself. I have had professional training from the Center for Mindfulness at the University of Massachusetts to be an instructor of the MBSR program and have four years of practice as an MBSR instructor. All the sessions, practices, and CDs had been developed according to the protocol presented by the Center for Mindfulness in Medicine, Health Care, and Society of the University of Massachusetts Medical School when I completed the training program for teaching MBSR, to ensure the safety of participants through sessions and home practices.

At the beginning of each session, participants were asked to share, in pairs and then with the whole group, their experiences of the mindfulness and/or yoga practices they had completed at home. This allowed participants to reflect upon and share possible difficulties and challenges they had experienced during the practices and the impact of the practices in their daily lives and well-being.

At the end of the last MBSR session, participants were asked to schedule the final assessment with me at a date and time of mutual convenience and were reminded to bring to the final assessment the log sheet on which they had kept the record of their daily practices. Participants were asked to determine a date for the final assessment to be scheduled during the first two to three weeks after the end of the program. After the final assessments, seven participants were selected for an interview based on the meditation practice they had completed according to the instructions during the MBSR program and on life events that might have influenced the effects of the program in their lives. The interview was scheduled at a date and time of mutual convenience between Weeks 4 and 6 after the end of the program. Individuals assigned to the CG were assessed within three months following the first assessment with the same psychological and neuropsychological tests completed in the beginning of the study.

The final assessment started by providing participants with an overview about the aim and structure of the assessment. They were asked to present their log sheet on which they had kept a record of when and for how long they had meditated during the week and any observations pertaining to their daily experience while meditating and/or practicing yoga. The assessment consisted of a short questionnaire administered to determine any major life events or health issues that had occurred during the eight weeks of the program that might have influenced their psychological and physical health, well-being, and neuropsychological performance. Participants were also assessed using the same psychological and neuropsychological tests completed at the initial interview, which administration lasted approximately 60 to 70 minutes. After reviewing information on the rate of compliance in terms of regularity of practice and presence in program sessions and changes in life events and health status, I contacted the seven selected participants for the second and final post-intervention assessment. Participants were invited for the interview if they had a high rate of practice and presence in program sessions and if they had experienced none or a minimal amount of life events (e.g., death of a loved one, reconciliation with a family member, illness, etc.), and none or minimal changes in medication since the first assessment.

Participants were contacted by phone to arrange a date and time of mutual convenience for the second final assessment.

This final meeting consisted of a semi-structured interview on the impact of the MBSR on elders' experiences of aging, physical and psychological well-being, and spirituality. The semi-structured interview used a general template of questions (Appendix 2) to direct the interviews, and the use of follow-up questions allowed flexibility to each particular participant, in order for me to more fully develop and understand themes presented by the interviewee. This allowed more in-depth questions about particular themes presented by the interviewee. The approximate duration of the interview was 60 to 90 minutes. All interviews were tape-recorded and, for confidentiality reasons, each participant was given a code number that was used to identify the tapes of each participant's interview. I transcribed the tape-recorded interviews using the code numbers to label the tapes for participant identification.

Before beginning the interview, I invited participants to spend ten minutes in a formal meditation. While guiding this meditation, I invited participants to create an intention to be present during the interview with openness and receptivity to their own process of sharing their experience and to allow this experience to come from their inner being and heart center. The interviewee was invited to mindfully express his or her experience and to observe any nonverbal experiences that might occur during the interview, including emotions, bodily reactions, sensations, and feelings, in the same way in which he had been practicing during the MBSR program, and to try to express these nonverbal aspects as fully and richly as possible. At this point I informed the participant that the interview would be audio-recorded in the manner in which they had been informed that it would and had agreed to in the beginning of the study.

During the interview, I cultivated an open and compassionate presence, to promote an environment of cooperative inquiry. Verbal and nonverbal feedback was provided when appropriate to motivate and facilitate the interviewee's expression. Whenever participants seemed to be having difficulties expressing their experience, I prompted them to use metaphors or images to explain them. I took notes of the nonverbal responses of the interviewee, such as change in tone of voice and expressive movements. I was also mindful of the felt sense experienced throughout the interview, in order to be aware of any additional questions that should be asked with the intention to further understand participants' unique experience.

At the end of the interview and the final assessment, I asked the participants how they were feeling and whether they needed to share any further information, then expressed appreciation for their time given to participation throughout the study.

During the intervention process, I had kept a journal with information pertaining to integral aspects of participants' process and of her own transformative process and understanding of the topic being studied. I kept this journal from the beginning of the study through data collection and intervention, keeping a record therein of a personal immersion in the research question of the study. Each entry of the information recorded in the journal was dated. All the information was written with a mindful and contemplative attitude. The methods of heuristic inquiry described earlier, including self-dialogue, tacit knowing, intuition, and indwelling, as well as mindfulness meditation practices, were used by me throughout the process of data collection, data analysis, and personal journal documentation. Details on treatment of both quantitative and qualitative data are presented in Appendix 3.

» Chapter 3 «

Quantitative Results

This section presents participants' characteristics and the quantitative analysis and findings of this study. Descriptive statistics were computed in the Statistical Program for Social Sciences (SPSS) to assess the frequency distribution of observed values and relevant statistics for the quantitative values. A *t*-test was computed in order to assess the significance of differences between mean values observed for both groups for dichotomous variables. When the assumption of normality was verified, the parametric *t*-test was computed; when it was not verified, the correspondent Mann–Whitney *U* was computed.

A paired *t*-test was computed to evaluate the differences between quantitative variables in two distinct moments (i.e., Assessment 1 and Assessment 2) in the control group (CG) and treatment group (TG) and separately in each dependent variable (DV). When the assumption of normality was verified, the parametric paired *t*-test was used, otherwise the correspondent nonparametric test (i.e., the Wilcoxon sign test) was computed.

A variable *delta* was created by calculating the difference between Assessment 2 and Assessment 1 and was used to statistically analyze the mean value of variation of scores in order to assess the evolution of the TG and CG in the various dependent variables. Correlation coefficients using the *delta* variable were computed to assess the correlation between practice (formal and informal) and number of sessions attended and observed variations in the various dependent variables between pre- and post-intervention in the treatment group. Regression analysis was computed to determine the causal effect between participants' changes in results of mindful awareness scales and the number of sessions attended, number of days practiced per week with the CDs, and completion of the experiential exercises. Correlation coefficients using the *delta* variable were computed to assess the relation between decentering, mindfulness, and acceptance and the relation between each of these variables and measures of psychological and physical symptoms, well-being, quality of life, and spiritual well-being. A MANOVA was computed to assess whether changes in mindfulness, acceptance, and decentering mediated changes in measures of psychological and physical symptoms, well-being, quality of life, and spiritual well-being.

Formal practice was measured from the percentage of home practice completed by participants with the CDs provided during the MBSR program. Informal practice was measured from the percentage of compliance with informal practices requested to be completed at home between sessions, such as mindful eating and completion of mindful exercises from the manual given at the beginning of the MBSR program. This data were gathered from the home practice record sheet that participants were given at the beginning of the program. All participants completed the home practice record sheet during the program and returned it to me at the end of the program.

Please refer to the tables in the appendices, which present the study's relevant quantitative data. Results are presented according to the different dimensions being measured and the associated instruments presenting the relevant computed statistics outlined above.

Participants' characteristics

The sample of this study comprised 24 participants equally divided into control group (CG) and treatment group (TG) (i.e., 12 participants in each group). Ages ranged between 65 and 73 years old, with a mean of 72 years old, and the majority of the observed values were obtained for those between 65 and 73 years old. The sample contained 63 percent female participants and 37 percent male participants. The vast majority of the participants were married (75 percent), 13 percent were widowed, 8 percent were single, and 4 percent (one case) were living with a partner.

The educational background of participants were as follows: 38 percent of the participants completed high school, 29 percent had a graduate degree, 17 percent had nine years of school, 8 percent had six years of school, and another 8 percent had five years of school. All participants in the sample were from the middle social class. The sample included 92 percent Catholic, 4 percent (one case) reporting spirituality, and another case (4 percent) reporting no religion.

In terms of health status at Assessment 1 (i.e., pre-intervention) the most frequent situation for chronic illness was none in 30 percent of the sample; hypertension occurred in 17 percent of the sample, high blood pressure in 13 percent, and high cholesterol in 13 percent. There was one participant (4 percent) with diabetes and hepatitis C, one participant (4 percent) with hypotension, one participant (4 percent) with Parkinsonism, another (4 percent) with diabetes and hypertension, and one participant (4 percent) with a heart condition. The most frequent situation for medication was none in 30 percent of the sample; hypertension occurred in 25 percent of the sample, and high blood pressure and cholesterol both occurred in 17 percent of the sample. Other medications observed were correspondent with the chronic illness described above.

At Assessment 2 (i.e., post-intervention), 25 percent of participants reported new illness, including one who had had heart surgery, and 75 percent of participants reported that they did not have a new illness. In terms of new medication, 16 percent started new medication and 84 percent did not start any new medication. No participant had experienced a significant life event, as those were defined by the study's parameters, between the first and second assessments.

In terms of daily practice, 54 percent of participants (50 percent from the CG and 4 percent from the TG) did not practice with the CDs provided at all. The other 46 percent of participants (all from the TG) showed a great variation in terms of daily practice with the CDs, with percentages of daily use ranging between 9 percent and 100 percent and the most frequent values ocurring at between 86 percent and 90 percent. In the sample, 58 percent of the participants (12 from the CG and two from the TG) had no daily informal practice. The rest of the sample varied in terms of compliance with daily informal practice, with values ranging between 20 percent and 100 percent, and the most frequent values occurring between 70 and 100 percent. In terms of number of sessions attended, 50 percent (i.e., the CG) did not attend any session and, among participants from the TG, results revealed that values for attendance varied from 55 percent to 100 percent, the most frequent values occurring at between 90 percent and 100 percent. The TG showed mean values of 57 percent in daily practice with the CDs, 59 percent for daily informal practice, and 92 percent in terms of sessions attended.

Sample: differences between CG and TG

To ensure the homogeneity between the CG and the TG, a t-test was computed to observe significant differences between the two groups. Results revealed that, in terms of age, the two groups were not significantly different ($t(22) = 1.52$, $p = .14$), with a mean (M) of 73.5 and standard deviation (*SD*) of 5.55 for the CG and a $M = 70.50$ and $SD = 4.011$ for the TG.

In the sample, the CG had more females ($n = 8$) than did the TG ($n = 7$) and the CG had fewer males ($n = 4$) than did the TG ($n = 5$), but the differences were not statistically significant: $\chi^2(1) = .18, p = .67$. In terms of civil status, the CG had more married participants and the TG had more participants who were single, widowed, and living with partner, but the differences were not statistically significant: $\chi^2(3) = 4.22, p = .29$.

The educational background of the CG and the TG was significantly different: $\chi^2(4) = 10.29, p = .02$. The CG had more participants with five and six years of school and who had completed high school, while the TG had more participants with nine years of education and with a graduate degree.

In the sample, all participants in the TG and CG belonged to the middle class, so no statistical test was performed to compare differences between groups. In terms of religion, all participants in the CG were Catholic. The TG counted several Catholic participants ($n = 10$), one with no religion, and one whose religion was designated as Spirituality (i.e., it included several philosophical perspectives such as Buddhism, Hinduism, etc.).

In terms of chronic illness and medication at Assessment 1, the differences were not statistically significant between the two groups. For chronic illness $\chi^2(11) = 12.33, p = .37$ and for medication $\chi^2(11)$ 12.33, $p = 0.37$. At Assessment 2, the TG had more new illness cases ($n = 5$) compared with the CG ($n = 1$), but differences were not statistically significant: $\chi^2(3) = 5.27, p = 0.08$. The CG also revealed fewer cases of taking new medication ($n = 1$) compared to the TG ($n = 3$), but, again, differences were not statistically significant: $\chi^2(2) = 2.47, p = .32$. No participant had a significant life event during the study, so no statistical test was computed to assess group differences in that regard.

The CG and the TG had similar statistics resulting from the screening test (MOCA). The mean value of MOCA was similar for the CG (M = 26.5, $SD = .67$) and TG ($M = 26.58, SD = .67$), and the differences were not statistically significant: $U = 66.5, p = .72$. According to the results, the two groups were well balanced as concerned results from the screening.

Mindfulness

Mindfulness was assessed using the MAAS (Brown and Ryan, 2003) and the FFMQ (Baer et al., 2006).

MAAS

The CG and TG showed similar scores at Assessment 1 and differences were not significant between the groups (Appendix 4, Table A4.1). At Assessment 2 the CG had a slight decrease while the TG showed an increase in MAAS score and the observed differences were statistically significant for TG and CG (Appendix 4, Table A4.1). Looking at the effects of the MBSR program on MAAS scores pre- and post-intervention it was verified that in the CG, MAAS mean scores decreased from Assessment 1 to Assessment 2 and the differences were statistically significant (Appendix 4, Table A4.2). The TG showed an increase in mean scores from Assessment 1 to Assessment 2 and the differences were also statistically significant (see Appendix 4, Table A4.2).

A statistical *t*-test was computed to measure the variations from pre- to post-intervention as between CG and TG on MAAS scores using the *delta* variable computed for this DV. Results showed that the mean value variation of MAAS scores was higher for the TG than for the CG and the differences were statistically different (see Appendix 4, Table A4.3). These results revealed that the participation in the MBSR program significantly affected participants' scores on MAAS.

The observed changes in MAAS scores in the TG were positively correlated with daily practice with CDs, daily informal practice, and number of sessions attended (see Appendix 4, Table A4.4). Regression analysis showed that only daily informal practice was significant to explain the variation in MAAS scores in the TG (see Appendix 4, Table A4.5).

Correlations between MAAS and other measures of the training process (i.e., acceptance and decentering) revealed that the mean variation value of MAAS was significantly correlated with that of FFMQ, SCS, and the EQ. At Assessment 1 no significant correlations were found between these variables, but at Assessment 2 correlations were significant between MAAS and FFMQ and SCS. No significant correlation was found between MAAS and the EQ (see Appendix 4, Table A4.6).

MAAS mean variation value scores were significantly correlated with mean variation values of SWLS, PANAS positive affect (PA), PANAS negative affect (NA), PWBS, PSS, POMS, and WHOQOL-BREF, including the physical, psychological, social relations, and environmental domains. Correlations were also significant for the WHOQOL-100 physical and spiritual domains, for SHCI, and for SWBQ. In terms of the mean value variation of the neuropsychological measures, the MAAS *delta* was significantly correlated with direct digits, arithmetic, digit symbol coding, digit symbol incident, and free recall. These results suggested that changes in mindfulness process were related to the changes observed in well-being, psychological and physical symptoms, quality of life, spiritual well-being, and some measures of neuropsychological performance (see Appendix 4, Table A4.6).

In order to assess whether changes in the MAAS mediated changes in other scales measuring well-being, psychological and physical symptoms, quality of life, and spiritual well-being, a MANOVA was computed using data from *delta* variables. Results revealed that, for the global model, variation in PANAS PA and NA, PSS, POMS, SHCI, and the WHOQOL-BREF psychological, physical, social interactions, and environmental dimensions, as well as with WHOQOL-100 physical and spiritual dimensions, showed a significant relationship with the factor MAAS. An increase in mean variation of MAAS induced a significant increase in all referred variations variables apart from those of the POMS, PSS, and SHCI. For POMS, PSS, and SHCI, an increase in MAAS scores induced a significant decrease in the variation of these variables (see Appendix 4, Table A4.7).

FFMQ

At Assessment 1 FFMQ scores were lower for the CG than for the TG and differences were statistically significant. In the CG, FFMQ scores showed a slight decrease at Assessment 2, while the TG showed an increase at Assessment 2 and differences were statistically significant (see Appendix 5, Table A5.1).

The parametric *t*-test was computed to look at the differences between CG and TG's FFMQ global score and subscales (i.e., dimensions) scores at Assessment 1 and Assessment 2. At Assessment 1, the FFMQ global score and subscale observation results were significantly higher for TG than for CG, and the subscales descriptions—act with awareness, nonjudgment, nonreaction—produced no significant differences as between CG and TG. At Assessment 2, the mean value of the FFMQ global score and scores of subscales—observation, description, act with awareness, nonjudgment, and nonreaction—were higher for TG than for CG, and differences were statistically significant. The statistical analysis for FFMQ dimensions, including observation, description, act with awareness, nonjudgment, and nonreaction revealed that at Assessment 1 mean differences between CG and TG were not significant across dimensions with the exception of observation (see Appendix 5, Table A5.2).

A paired *t*-test was computed to look at differences between pre- and post-intervention in the CG and TG, separately. Results revealed that the FFMQ global score and subscales' scores showed no significant differences for the CG, with the exception of the subscale of observation, which decreased significantly. The FFMQ global score and subscales' scores increased significantly for the TG, with the exception of the subscale of description, which increased with no statistical significance. Therefore, the MBSR improved the results of the FFMQ in the TG (see Appendix 5, Table A5.3).

A statistical *t*-test was computed to analyze the mean value variations of the CG and TG as between pre- and post-intervention using the variable *delta* created. Results revealed that variations were significantly higher for the TG in the FFMQ global score and subscales' scores, therefore suggesting the efficacy of the MBSR program in increasing mindfulness as measured by this scale (see Appendix 5, Table A5.4).

In the TG, correlations between the three levels of practice that included daily practice with CDs, daily informal practice, and attended sessions significantly impacted the observed changes in FFMQ global score and score of different dimensions. The daily practice with CDs was significantly correlated with improvements and the daily informal practice correlated with the subscales of act with awareness and nonreaction. Table A5.7 presents the results of the correlation statistics.

The FFMQ global score was analyzed using regression analysis in relation to the three levels of participation variables: daily practice with CDs, daily informal practice, and number of sessions attended, which, taken together, represented the independent variable (IV). Only the daily informal practice result was significant enough to explain the variation in FFMQ scores. More information regarding coefficients is presented in Appendix 5, Table A5.6.

Correlations between *delta* FFMQ (global score) and the *delta* SCS, *delta* FFMQ, and *delta* EQ revealed that the mean variation values of FFMQ were significantly correlated with MAAS results, SCS, and EQ. The FFMQ mean variation value scores were significantly correlated with mean variation values of SWLS, PANAS PA, PANAS NA, PWBS,

PSS, POMS, WHOQOL-BREF including the physical, psychological and environmental domains. Correlations were also significant for the WHOQOL-100 spiritual domain, but not significant for the physical domain. Correlations were significant between FFMQ and SHCI and SWBQ. In terms of the mean value variation of the neuropsychological measures, FFMQ *delta* was significantly correlated with direct digits, digit symbol coding, digit symbol incident, and free recall (see Appendix 5, Table A5.7). These results suggested that changes in mindfulness process were related to the changes observed in well-being, psychological and physical symptoms, quality of life, spiritual well-being, and some measures of neuropsychological performance.

In order to assess whether changes in the FFMQ (global score) mediated changes in other scales measuring well-being, psychological and physical symptoms, quality of life, and spiritual well-being, a MANOVA was computed using data from *delta* variables. Results revealed that, for the global model, variation in POMS, WHOQOL-BREF physical dimension, and SHCI showed a significant relationship with the factor FFMQ. An increase in mean variation of FFMQ induced a significant increase in all referred variations variables, apart from the POMS and SHCI. For POMS and SHCI, an increase in FFMQ induced a significant decrease in the variation of these variables (see Appendix 5, Table A5.8).

Compassion

Compassion was assessed using the SCS (Neff, 2003). At Assessment 1 SCS scores were lower for the CG and higher for the TG. The CG scores showed a slight decrease at Assessment 2 while the TG showed an increase at Assessment 2. Results revealed that the SCS global result was not statistically different as between the TG and the CG, at Assessment 1 (see Appendix 6, Table A6.1).

The same was observed in all subscales of the SCS, with the exception of reverse scores: self-kindness, self-judgment, common humanity, isolation, and mindfulness. Accordingly, at Assessment 1, the dimension of subscale reverse scores was the only dimension that showed significant differences between the CG and the TG.

At Assessment 2, results revealed that the SCS global score was statistically different as between the TG and the CG. The same was observed in all subscales of the SCS, with the exception of reverse scores: self-kindness, self-judgment, common humanity, and mindfulness. Accordingly, at Assessment 2, the SCS global score and all subscales' scores showed significant differences between results for the CG and the TG (see Appendix 6, Table A6.2).

A paired *t*-test was computed to look at the mean difference in SCS as between pre- and post-intervention in the CG and TG, separately. The SCS subscales scores showed no significant differences for CG and the global score of the SCS scale results decreased significantly. The SCS global scale and the subscales of self-kindness, self-judgment, common humanity, mindfulness, along with the reverse scores results increased significantly in the TG. The subscale of isolation did not reveal significant changes. Overall, it was concluded that the MBSR program improved the results in the TG (see Appendix 6, Table A6.3).

A statistical *t*-test was computed to analyze the mean value variations of the CG and TG as between pre- and post-intervention in the SCS and subscales. Variations in the SCS global score and the subscales of self-kindness, self-judgment, common humanity, as well as the reverse scores were significantly higher for the TG when compared with the CG. The isolation and mindfulness subscales' variations showed no significant difference as between the TG and the CG (see Appendix 6, Table A6.4).

Correlations between SCS and other measures of the training process (i.e., mindfulness and decentering) revealed that the mean variation value of SCS was significantly correlated with MAAS, FFMQ, and EQ. SCS's mean variation value scores were significantly correlated with mean variation values of SWLS, PANAS PA, PANAS NA, PWBS, PSS, POMS, and WHOQOL-BREF in the physical, psychological, and environmental domains. Correlations were also significant for the WHOQOL-100 spiritual domain, SHCI and SWBQ. In terms of the mean value variation of the neuropsychological measures, MAAS *delta* was significantly correlated with direct digits, arithmetic, digit symbol incident, and free recall. These results suggested that changes in self-compassion process were related to the changes observed in well-being, psychological and physical symptoms, quality of life, spiritual well-being, and some measures of neuropsychological performance (see Appendix 6, Table A6.5).

In order to assess whether changes in the SCS mediated changes in other scales measuring well-being, psychological and physical symptoms, quality of life, and spiritual well-being, a MANOVA was computed using data from *delta* variables. Results revealed that, for the global model, variation in SWLS, PANAS PA, PWBQ, POMS, and SWBQ showed a significant relationship with the factor SCS (Appendix 6, Table A6.6). An increase in mean variation of SCS induced a significant increase in all referred variations variables apart from the POMS. For POMS an increase in SCS induced a significant decrease in the variation of these variables.

Correlations of the level of participation that included daily practice with CDs, daily informal practice, and attended sessions with SCS scores were computed. Results suggest only that the subscale of isolation was related with informal practices and the dimension self-judgment with the number of sessions attended. All other correlation did not reach significance levels (see Appendix 6, Table A6.7).

Decentering

The EQ (Fresco *et al.*, 2007) was used to assess decentering data. At Assessment 1 SCS scores were lower for the CG and higher for the TG, but differences were not statistically significant. The CG scores showed a slight decrease at Assessment 2, while the TG showed an increase at Assessment 2 and differences were statistically significant (see Figure 3.1 and Appendix 7, Table A7.1).

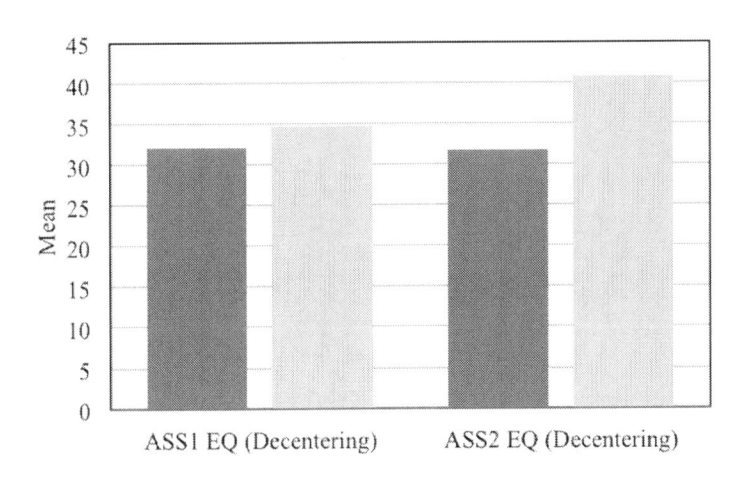

FIGURE 3.1 DECENTERING: MEAN SCORES FOR TG AND CG AT ASSESSMENT 1 AND ASSESSMENT 2

Paired *t*-test results showed that mean differences between Assessment 1 and Assessment 2 were not statistically different for the CG, but were significantly different for the TG (see Appendix 7, Table A7.2). Finally, a statistical *t*-test was computed to analyze the mean value variations of the CG and TG between pre- and post-intervention. Results showed that the mean variation of decentering score was significantly higher in the TG when compared with the CG, thus suggesting that the participation in the MBSR program had increased decentering scores in participants of the TG (see Appendix 7, Table A7.3).

Correlations between EQ and other measures of training process (i.e., acceptance and mindfulness) revealed that the mean variation value of EQ was significantly correlated with MAAS, FFMQ, and SCS. EQ mean variation value scores were significantly correlated with mean variation values of SWLS, PANAS PA, PANAS NA, PWBS, PSS, POMS, and WHOQOL-BREF, including the physical, psychological, and environmental domains. Correlations were also significant for the WHOQOL-100 spiritual domain, SHCI and SWBQ. In terms of the mean value variation of the neuropsychological measures, EQ *delta* was significantly correlated with direct digits, digit symbol coding, digit symbol incident, and free recall. These results suggested that changes in decentering were related with the changes observed in well-being, psychological and physical symptoms, quality of life, spiritual well-being, and some measures of neuropsychological performance (see Appendix 7, Table A7.4).

In order to assess whether changes in the EQ mediated changes in other scales assessing well-being, psychological and physical symptoms, quality of life, and spiritual well-being, a MANOVA was computed using data from *delta* variables. Results revealed that, for the global model, variation in SWLS, PANAS PA and NA, PWBQ, PSS, POMS, SHCI, WHOQOL-BREF in the dimension environment, and WHOQOL-100 in the dimension physical showed a significant relationship with the factor EQ (see Appendix 7, Table A7.5). An increase in mean variation of EQ induced a significant increase in all referred variations variables apart from the SHCI, PSS, and POMS. For these three scales, an increase in EQ induced a significant decrease in the variation of these variables.

Correlations between the level of participation that included daily practice with CDs, daily informal practice, and attended sessions revealed that decentering was positively correlated with daily informal practice and number of sessions attended (see Appendix 7, Table A7.6).

Well-being

Well-being was assessed using measures to evaluate subjective well-being (SWB) and psychological well-being (PWB). SWB was assessed using the SWLS (Diener *et al.*, 1985; Simões, 1992) that measured the cognitive component of SWB and the PANAS (Watson *et al.*, 1988; Galinha and Pais Ribeiro, 2005), which evaluated the emotional component of SWB. PWB was assessed using the PWBS (Ryff and Keynes, 1995; Portuguese version translated by Silva, 2004).

SWLS

At Assessment 1 SWLS scores were higher for the CG and lower for the TG, but differences were not statistically significant. The CG scores showed a slight decrease at Assessment 2, while the TG showed an increase at Assessment 2. Differences between the TG and CG were not statistically significant (see Figure 3.2 and Appendix 8, Table A8.1).

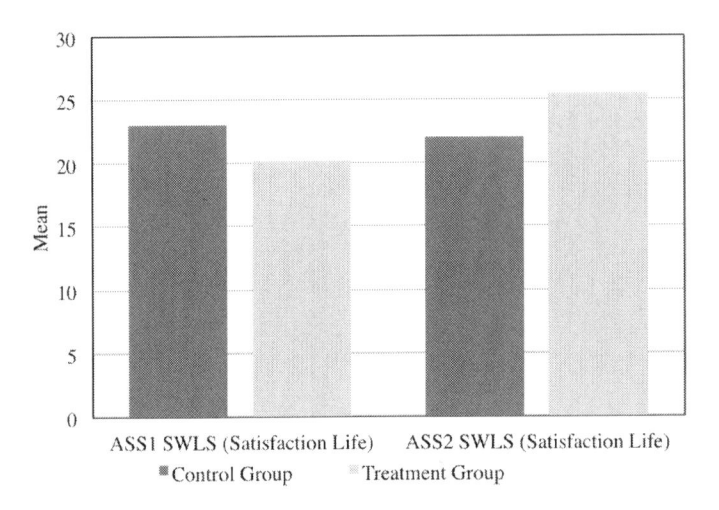

FIGURE 3.2 SWLS: MEAN SCORES FOR TG AND CG AT ASSESSMENT 1 AND ASSESSMENT 2

Paired *t*-test results showed that mean differences as between Assessment 1 and Assessment 2 were not statistically significant for the CG, but were significantly different for the TG (see Appendix 8, Table A8.2). Finally, a statistical *t*-test was computed to analyze the mean value variations of the CG and TG as between pre- and post-intervention using the *delta* variable created. Results showed that the mean variation of the SWLS score was significantly higher in the TG when compared with the CG. These statistical results reflected that the participation in the MBSR program improved participants' satisfaction with life (see Appendix 8, Table A8.3).

Correlations between the level of participation that included daily practice with CDs, daily informal practice, and attended sessions showed that SWLS was not correlated with daily practice with CDs, daily informal practice and number of sessions attended (Appendix 8, Table A8.4).

PANAS

At Assessment 1 positive affect (PA) scores were lower for the CG and higher for the TG and differences between the two groups were statistically significant. The CG scores showed a slight decrease at Assessment 2, while the TG showed an increase at Assessment 2 and differences between the two groups were statistically significant. At Assessment 1 negative affect (NA) scores were lower for the CG and higher for the TG, and differences were not significant between the two groups. At Assessment 2, the CG showed an increase in NA scores, while the TG showed a decrease in scores, but differences between the groups were not significant (see Appendix 9, Table A9.1).

Paired *t*-test results showed that mean differences as between Assessment 1 and Assessment 2 for PA were not statistically significant for the CG, but were significantly different for the TG. The mean differences between Assessment 1 and Assessment 2 for the NA were statistically significant for the CG and for the TG (see Figure 3.3 and Appendix 9, Table A9.2).

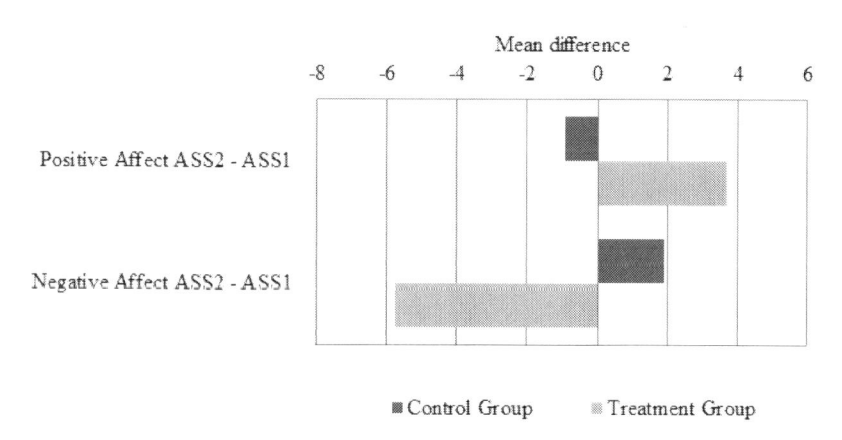

FIGURE 3.3 PANAS: MEAN DIFFERENCE BETWEEN ASSESSMENT 1 AND ASSESSMENT 2 FOR TG AND CG

Finally, a statistical *t*-test was computed to analyze the mean value variations of the CG and TG between pre- and post-intervention using the *delta* variable created for PANAS. Results showed that the mean variation of PA scores was significantly higher in the TG when compared with the CG. The mean variation of NA scores was significantly higher for the TG than the CG. According to the statistical results presented, it is concluded that the participation in the MBSR program decreased NA and increased PA in the TG's participants (see Appendix 9, Table A9.3).

Correlations between the level of participation that included daily practice with CDs, daily informal practice, and attended sessions showed that PA was positively correlated with daily practice with CDs and not related with daily informal practice and number of sessions attended. NA was not correlated with any of the three levels of practice: daily practice with CDs, daily informal practice, and number of sessions attended (see Appendix 9, Table A9.4).

PWBS

At Assessment 1 PWBS scores were higher for the TG and lower for the CG but differences were not statistically different. The TG scores showed an increase at Assessment 2 while the CG showed a decrease at Assessment 2 and differences between the two groups was statistically significant (see Appendix 10, Table A10.1).

Paired *t*-test results showed that mean differences of PWBS scores between Assessment 1 and Assessment 2 were statistically different for the CG, revealing that the scores decreased significantly from Assessment 1 to Assessment 2. The TG also showed statistically significant mean differences between Assessment 1 and Assessment 2 indicating that there was a significant improvement in psychological well-being among participants of the TG who completed the MBSR program (see Appendix 10, Table A10.2). Finally, a statistical *t*-test was computed to analyze the mean value variations of the CG and TG between pre- and post-intervention using the *delta* variable created. Results showed that the mean variation of PWBS score was significantly higher for the TG when compared with the CG (see Appendix 10, Table A10.3).

Statistical analysis was also computed for the PWBS subscales that included autonomy, environmental mastery, personal growth, relations with others, purpose in life, and self-acceptance. A *t*-test was computed to analyze the differences between TG and CG at Assessment 1 and Assessment 2 (see Appendix 10, Table A10.4).

Paired *t*-test results showed that mean differences of PWB subscales results revealed that in the CG there was no significant difference in any of the subscales between Assessment 1 and Assessment 2, while for the TG there were significant differences in all subscales, with the exception of environmental mastery (see Appendix 10, Table A10.5).

Finally, a statistical *t*-test was computed to analyze the mean value variations of the CG and TG as between pre- and post-intervention using the *delta* variable created. All PWBS subscales showed statistical significance in terms of mean variation scores as between TG and CG. TG showed a higher mean variation (i.e., increase in psychological well-being) in all subscales (see Appendix 10, Table A10.6). The statistical analysis conducted for PWBS revealed that the MBSR program improved the psychological well-being of participants of the TG. This was evident in the PWBS global score and subscales of autonomy, environmental mastery, personal growth, relations with others, and self-acceptance.

Correlations between the level of participation that included daily practice with CDs, daily informal practice, and attended sessions showed that the dimension of environmental mastery was in the PWBS positively correlated with daily practice with CDs and daily informal practice was positively correlated with the dimension of personal growth in the PWBS. All other dimensions were not related with levels of practice (see Appendix 10, Table A10.7).

Psychological symptoms

Psychological symptoms were assessed using the POMS-SF (Shacham, 1983; Viana *et al.*, 2001), which measured six mood factors: tension/anxiety, depression/dejection, anger/hostility, vigor/activity, fatigue/inertia, and confusion/bewilderment. Stress was assessed using the PSS (Cohen *et al.*, 1983; Pais Ribeiro and Marques, 2009).

POMS

At Assessment 1 POMS scores were higher (i.e., indicating more psychological symptoms or mood disturbance) for the TG and lower for the CG but differences were not statistically different. The CG scores showed an increase at Assessment 2, while the TG showed a decrease (i.e., indicating less psychological symptoms or mood disturbance) at Assessment 2 and differences between the two groups were statistically significant (see Appendix 11, Table A11.1).

Paired *t*-test results showed that mean differences of POMS scores between Assessment 1 and Assessment 2 were statistically different for the CG, which revealed that they showed a significant increase in mood symptoms. The TG also showed statistically significant mean differences between Assessment 1 and Assessment 2 meaning that there was a significant improvement in mood symptoms among participants of the TG who completed the MBSR program (see Appendix 11, Table A11.2). Finally, a statistical *t*-test was computed to analyze the mean value variations of the CG and TG as between pre- and post-intervention, using the *delta* variable created. Results showed that the mean variation of the POMS score was significantly lower (i.e., indicating less presence of mood symptoms) for the TG when compared with the CG (see Appendix 11, Table A11.3).

Statistical analysis was also computed for the POMS subscales that included tension, depression, hostility, vigor, fatigue, and confusion. A *t*-test was computed to analyze the differences between TG and CG at Assessment 1 and Assessment 2. Results revealed that at Assessment 1 the TG had higher mean scores for tension, depression, hostility, fatigue, and confusion than did the CG and that the subscale vigor was similar in both groups. Differences were not statistically significant. At Assessment 2 the TG showed lower mean scores on the subscales of tension and fatigue, and differences were statistically significant. The mean values for the subscales of depression, hostility, fatigue, and confusion were also lower for the TG than for the CG, but differences were not statistically different (see Appendix 11, Table A11.4).

Paired *t*-test results showed that mean differences of the POMS global score as between Assessment 1 and Assessment 2 were statistically different for the CG and were also significantly different for the TG. Looking at the subscales results revealed that in the CG there was a significant difference in the tension, depression, vigor, and fatigue subscales, while for the TG there was a significant differences in tension, depression, hostility, vigor, fatigue, and confusion (see Appendix 11, Table A11.5).

Finally, a statistical *t*-test was computed to analyze the mean value variations of the CG and TG as between pre- and post-intervention using the *delta* variable created. Results showed that the mean variation of POMS score was significantly higher in the TG when compared with the CG. All POMS subscales also showed some statistical significance in terms of mean variation scores as between TG and CG. TG showed a lower mean variation (i.e., a decrease in psychological symptoms) in all scales, with the exception of vigor, which had a higher mean variation (i.e., an increase in vigor; see Appendix 11, Table A11.6).

Correlations between the level of participation that included daily practice with CDs, daily informal practice, and attended sessions showed significant negative correlations between daily practice with CDs and the subscales of tension and confusion. Significant negative correlations were also found between daily informal practice and the subscales of tension and depression. Significant positive correlations were found between daily practice with CDs and vigor and between daily informal practice and vigor (see Appendix 11, Table A11.7).

PSS

At Assessment 1 PSS scores were higher for the CG and lower for the TG but differences were not statistically different. The CG scores showed a slight decrease at Assessment 2, while the TG showed a more pronounced decrease at Assessment 2. Differences between the two groups were statistically significant (see Figure 3.4 and Appendix 12, Table A12.1).

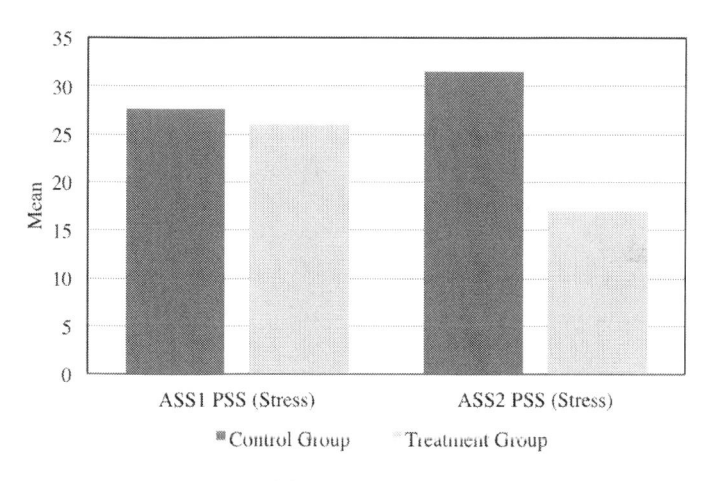

FIGURE 3.4 PSS: MEAN SCORES FOR TG AND CG AT ASSESSMENT 1 AND ASSESSMENT 2

Paired *t*-test results showed that mean differences of PSS scores between Assessment 1 and Assessment 2 were statistically different for the CG and were also significantly different for the TG (see Appendix 12, Table A12.2). Finally, a statistical *t*-test was computed to analyze the mean value variations of the CG and TG as between pre- and post-intervention using the *delta* variable created. Results showed that the mean variation of the PSS score was significantly higher in the TG when compared with the CG (see Appendix 12, Table A12.3). These results suggest that the participation in the MBSR program improved levels of stress among participants of the TG.

Correlations between the level of participation that included daily practice with CDs, daily informal practice, and attended sessions indicated that PSS was negatively correlated as between daily practice with CDs, daily informal practice, and number of sessions attended (see Appendix 12, Table A12.4).

Quality of life

Quality of life was assessed using the WHOQOL-BREF (Skevington *et al.*, 2004, Vaz Serra *et al.*, 2006). The WHOQOL-100 instrument (Canavarro *et al.*, 2009; WHOQOL Group, 1998) was used to assess the dimensions of the physical and spirituality.

WHOQOL-BREF

WHOQOL-BREF included these several dimensions: physical, psychological, social relations, and environment. Means and standard deviations results for both groups are presented in Appendix 13, Table A13.1.

A statistical *t*-test revealed that at Assessment 1 the differences between TG and CG scores in WHOQOL-BREF were not statistically significant. This was observed in the following dimensions: physical, psychological, social relations, and environment (see Appendix 13, Table A13.2). The same was observed at Assessment 2 in the following dimensions: physical, psychological, social relations, and environment (see Appendix 13, Table A13.3). The statistical results of paired *t*-tests looking at group differences between Assessment 1 and Assessment 2 for all WHOQOL-BREF analyses revealed that for the CG a significant difference (lower score in Assessment 2 than Assessment 1) was found in the psychological dimension. For the TG a significant increase in mean scores was found in the physical, psychological and environmental dimensions (see Appendix 13, Table A13.4).

Finally, a statistical *t*-test was computed to analyze the mean value variations of the CG and TG as between pre- and post-intervention using the *delta* variable created for WHOQOL-BREF. Results showed that the difference of the mean variation was statistically significant for these dimensions: physical, psychological, and environment. However, there were not statistically significant differences for the dimension of social relations. These results revealed that the participation of the TG in the MBSR program had a significant effect on WHOQOL-BREF physical, psychological, and environmental scores (see Appendix 13, Table A13.5).

Correlations between the level of participation that included daily practice with CDs, daily informal practice, and attended sessions showed significant positive correlations between daily practice with CDs and the subscales psychological and physical (see Appendix 13, Table A13.6).

WHOQOL-100

WHOQOL-100 included two dimensions: physical and spiritual. Means and standard deviations for both groups are presented in Appendix 14, Table A14.1.

A statistical *t*-test revealed that at Assessment 1 the difference between TG and CG scores in WHOQOL-100 were not statistically significant. This was observed in these dimensions: physical and spiritual (see Appendix 14, Table A14.2). At Assessment 2 differences were statistically significant for both dimensions: physical and spiritual (see Appendix 14, Table A14.3).

Paired *t*-tests assessed the statistical significance of differences as between Assessment 1 and Assessment 2 for the CG and TG in both dimensions of the WHOQOL-100. Results revealed that the CG did not present a significant difference between Assessment 1 and Assessment 2 in these dimensions: physical and spiritual. The TG showed statistically significant differences in both the physical and the spiritual dimensions (see Appendix 14, Table A14.4).

Finally, a statistical *t*-test was computed to analyze the mean value variations of the CG and TG as between pre- and post-intervention using the *delta* variable created for WHOQOL-100. Results showed that difference of the mean variation was statistically significant for both dimensions: physical and spiritual (see Appendix 14, Table A14.5). These results reveal that the participation of the TG in the MBSR program had a significant effect on WHOQOL-100 physical and spiritual scores.

Correlations between the level of participation that included daily practice with CDs, daily informal practice, and number of sessions attended were computed for the physical and spiritual dimensions. The dimension of physical showed no significant correlation with daily practice with CDs, daily informal practice, and number of sessions attended. The spiritual dimension also showed no significant correlation with daily practice with CDs, daily informal practice, and number of sessions attended (see Appendix 14, Table A14.6).

Physical health/symptoms

Physical health was assessed using the SHCI (Alves and Figueiras, 2008, Eriksen *et al.*, 1999) and the physical domain (Domain 1) of the WHOQOL-100 assessment instrument (Canavarro *et al.*, 2009; WHOQOL Group, 1998), which evaluated pain and discomfort, energy and fatigue, and sleep and rest. The results of the latter tests were presented in the section above.

SHCI

At Assessment 1 SHCI scores were lower for the CG and higher for the TG and differences were statistically significant. The CG scores showed an increase at Assessment 2, while the TG showed a decrease at Assessment 2. Differences were not statistically significant (see Figure 3.5 and Appendix 15, Table A15.1).

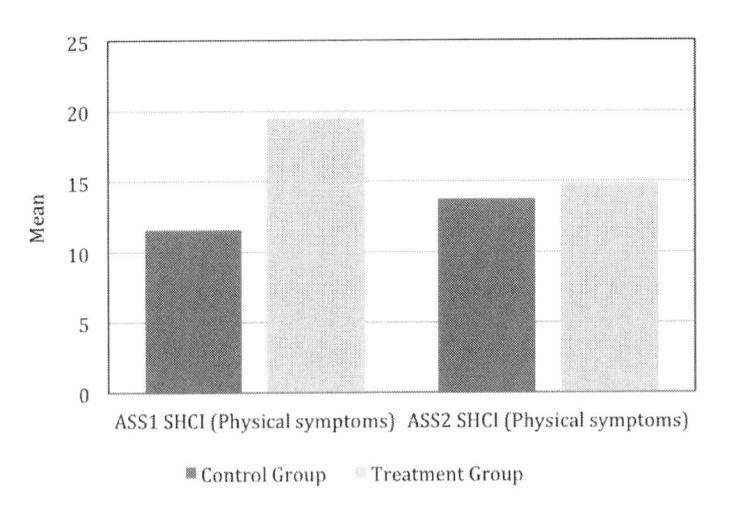

FIGURE 3.5 SHCI: MEAN SCORES FOR TG AND CG AT ASSESSMENT 1 AND ASSESSMENT 2

Paired *t*-test results showed that mean differences between Assessment 1 and Assessment 2 were significantly different for the CG and the TG (see Appendix 15, Table A15.2). Finally, a statistical *t*-test was computed to analyze the mean value variations of the CG and TG as between pre- and post-intervention using the *delta* variable created. Results showed that the mean variation of SHCI score was significantly lower in the TG when compared with the CG (see Appendix 15, Table A15.3). These results showed that the participation in the MBSR program significantly reduced the physical symptoms of participants. The increase of physical symptoms in the CG was also statistically significant.

Correlations between the level of participation showed significant negative correlations between daily practice with CDs and daily informal practice with SHCI scores (see Appendix 15, Table A15.4).

Death perspectives

Death perspectives were assessed using the DPS (Spilka *et al.*, 1977; Barros-Oliveira and Neto, 2004). This scale assessed death from eight different perspectives: death as pain and loneliness, death as afterlife or reward, indifference towards death, death as unknown, death as forsaking dependents plus guilt, death as courage, death as failure, and death as a natural end (Spilka *et al.*, 1977). Means and standard deviations are presented in Appendix 16, Table A16.1.

A statistical *t*-test revealed that at Assessment 1 the differences between TG and CG scores in DP scales were not statistically significant. This was observed in the dimensions of pain and loneliness, afterlife reward, indifferent, unknown, dependents and guilt, courage, failure, and natural end (see Appendix 16, Table A16.2).

The same was observed at Assessment 2 for the dimensions of pain and loneliness, afterlife reward, indifferent, unknown, dependents and guilt, courage, failure, and natural end (see Appendix 16, Table A16.3). Paired *t*-tests looking at group differences between Assessment 1 and Assessment 2 for all death perspectives scales showed no significant differences (see Appendix 16, Table A16.4).

Finally, a statistical *t*-test was computed to analyze the mean value variations of the CG and TG as between pre- and post-intervention, using the *delta* variable created for DPS. Results showed that difference in the mean variation was not statistically significant for the dimensions of pain and loneliness, afterlife reward, indifferent, unknown, dependents and guilt, courage, failure, and natural end. These results revealed that the participation of the TG in the MBSR program had no significant effect on DPS scores (see Appendix 16, Table A16.5).

Spirituality

Spirituality was assessed using the spirituality domain (Domain 6) of the WHOQOL-100 assessment instrument (Canavarro *et al.*, 2009; WHOQOL Group, 1998) and the SWBQ (Gomez and Fisher, 2003; Gouveia *et al.*, 2009). Statistical results for the domain of spirituality of the WHOQOL-100 were presented previously.

SWBQ

At Assessment 1 SWBQ scores were lower for the CG and higher for the TG but differences were not statistically different. The CG scores showed basically the same mean score at Assessment 2, while the TG showed an increase at Assessment 2, and differences between the two groups were statistically significant (see Appendix 17, Table A17.1).

Paired *t*-test results showed that mean differences of SWBQ scores as between Assessment 1 and Assessment 2 were statistically different for the CG and were also significantly different for the TG (see Appendix 17, Table A17.2). Finally, a statistical *t*-test was computed to analyze the mean value variations of the CG and TG as between pre- and post-intervention, using the *delta* variable created. Results showed that the mean variation of the SWBQ score was significantly higher in the TG when compared with the CG (see Appendix 17, Table A17.3). These results revealed that participation in the MBSR program improved the SWBQ scores of the TG as compared to the CG.

Correlations between the level of participation that included daily practice with CDs, daily informal practice, and attended sessions showed significant correlations with the SWBQ (see Appendix 17, Table A17.4).

Statistical analysis was also conducted to look at the different dimensions of the SWBQ, including personal, community, environment, and transcendental subscales and no significant differences were observed (see Appendix 17, Table A17.5).

Paired *t*-test results showed that mean differences of SWBQ scores between Assessment 1 and Assessment 2 were not statistically different for the CG in any of the dimensions of the SWBQ and were significantly different for the TG for the dimensions of environment and the transcendental (see Appendix 17, Table A17.6). Finally, a statistical *t*-test was computed to analyze the mean value variations of the CG and TG as between pre- and post-intervention, using the *delta* variable created. Results showed that the mean variation of all SWBQ dimensions was similar for the dimension of community as between the TG and CG and slightly higher for the dimensions of the personal, environmental, and transcendental for the TG but that differences were not statistically significant (see Appendix 17, Table A17.7).

Neuropsychological performance

Neuropsychological performance was assessed using two indexes of the Portuguese version of the WAIS III (Barreto *et al.*, 2008), including (a) the working memory index that includes the arithmetic and digit span subtests that assessed working memory (i.e., the system involved in temporal storage and manipulation of the information required for complex cognitive tasks such as language, comprehension, reasoning, and learning, a system that stores and processes information and is subdivided into three systems, including the central executive that resembles attention, the visuospatial sketch pad that stores and rehearses speech-based information, and the phonological loop that holds information in phonological form; Baddeley, 1992; Eysenck and Keane, 1995) and (b) the processing speed index that includes the digit symbol coding and incidental learning in a pairing of subtests to assess processing speed and memory (Strauss *et al.*, 2006). The Trail Making A and B Test (TMT, Army Individual Test Battery, 1944) was used to measure attention, executive functions, and motor speed.

Working memory index

The working memory index is composed of the direct digits, inverse digits, and arithmetic subtests. *T*-test statistics revealed that at Assessment 1 the direct digits subtest composite score was lower for the CG and higher for the TG, but differences were not statistically significant. At Assessment 2, the CG had a slight increase and the TG had a more prominent increase. The differences between CG and TG were statistically significant (see Appendix 18, Table A18.1).

At Assessment 1 the inverse digits score was lower for the CG than for the TG, but differences were not statistically significant. At Assessment 2, the CG showed a slight increase, but the TG had a higher increase and differences between the two groups were not statistically significant (see Appendix 18, Table A18.2).

At Assessment 1, arithmetic was lower for the CG than for the TG and differences were statistically different. At Assessment 2, there was a slight decrease in the CG scores and an increase in the TG, and differences between the two groups were statistically significant (see Appendix 18, Table A18.3).

Paired *t*-test results showed that mean differences for the working memory index as between Assessment 1 and Assessment 2 were not statistically significant for the CG and the TG except for the direct digit score among participants of the TG (see Appendix 18, Table A18.4).

Finally, a statistical *t*-test was computed to analyze the mean value variations of the CG and TG as between pre- and post-intervention, using the *delta* variable created. Results showed that the mean variation of the working memory index was significantly higher in the direct digits test for the TG when compared with the CG. The same was observed in the arithmetic test: TG when compared with the CG (see Appendix 18, Table A18.5). Results suggested that participation in the MBSR program improved the performance of the TG in some of the measures assessing working memory.

Correlations between the level of participation that included daily practice with CDs, daily informal practice, and attended sessions showed significant correlations with working memory index scores (see Appendix 18, Table A18.6).

Processing speed index

The processing speed index included two tests: the digit symbol coding and the symbol incident. At Assessment 1 digit symbol coding was lower for the CG than for the TG, but differences were not statistically significant. At Assessment 2, the CG showed an increase, but the TG had a higher increase, and differences between the two groups were not statistically different (see Appendix 19, Table A19.1).

At Assessment 1, digit symbol incident was lower for the CG than for the TG, and differences were not statistically significant. At Assessment 2, there was an increase in the CG scores and an increase in the TG scores, and differences between the two groups were statistically significant (see Appendix 19, Table A19.2).

Paired *t*-test results showed that mean differences for the processing speed index between Assessment 1 and Assessment 2 were statistically significant for the CG only for the digit symbol coding test but not for the digit symbol incident (see Appendix 19, Table A19.3).

Finally, a statistical *t*-test was computed to analyze the mean value variations of the CG and TG as between pre- and post-intervention, using the *delta* variable created. Results showed that the mean variation of the processing speed index was significantly higher in the symbol coding test for the TG when compared with the CG. In the symbol incident test no significant variation was observed for TG and CG. Results reflected that participation in the MBSR program improved the performance of the TG in some of the measures assessing processing speed (see Appendix 19, Table A19.4).

Correlations analysis as between levels of practice and processing speed index revealed significant positive correlations between the digit symbol incident with daily practice with CDs and daily informal practice (see Appendix 19, Table A19.5).

Memory

Memory was assessed using the free recall test. At Assessment 1 free recall was lower for the CG than for the TG, but differences were not statistically significant. At Assessment 2, the CG showed a slight increase, but the TG had a higher increase, and differences between the two groups were not statistically significant (see Appendix 20, Table A20.1).

Paired *t*-test results showed that mean differences for the memory free recall between Assessment 1 and Assessment 2 were not statistically significant for the CG but were significant for the TG (see Figure 3.6 and Appendix 20, Table A20.2).

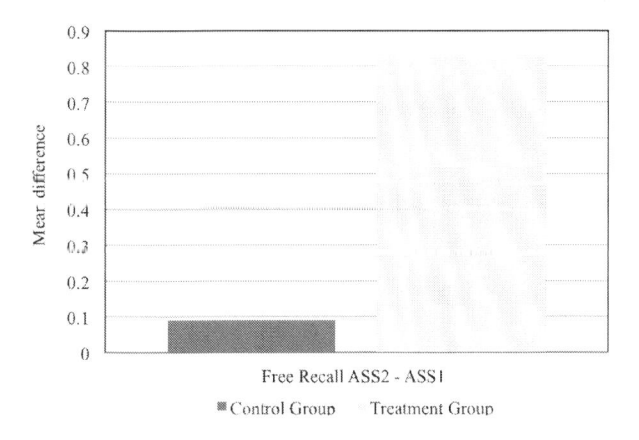

FIGURE 3.6 FREE RECALL: MEAN DIFFERENCE BETWEEN ASSESSMENT 1 AND ASSESSMENT 2 FOR TG AND CG

Finally, a statistical *t*-test was computed to analyze the mean value variations of the CG and TG as between pre- and post-intervention, using the *delta* variable created. Results showed that the mean variation of the free recall test was significantly higher in the TG when compared with the CG (see Appendix 20, Table A20.3). Results suggest that participation in the MBSR program improved the episodic memory performance of the TG.

Correlations between memory free recall and levels of practice revealed no significant correlations with respect to daily practice with CDs, daily informal practice, and number of sessions attended (see Appendix 20, Table A20.4).

Trail making

At Assessment 1 trail making was higher for the CG than for the TG, but differences were not statistically significant. At Assessment 2, the CG showed a slight decrease, but the TG had a higher decrease, and differences between the two groups were not statistically significant. A lower score in the Trail Making Test (TMT) equates with a better score, as it indicates that participants have spent less time completing the exercise. (see Appendix 20, Table A20.5). Paired *t*-test results showed that mean differences for the TMT between Assessment 1 and Assessment 2 were not statistically significant for the CG and for the TG (see Figure 3.7 and Appendix 20, Table A20.6).

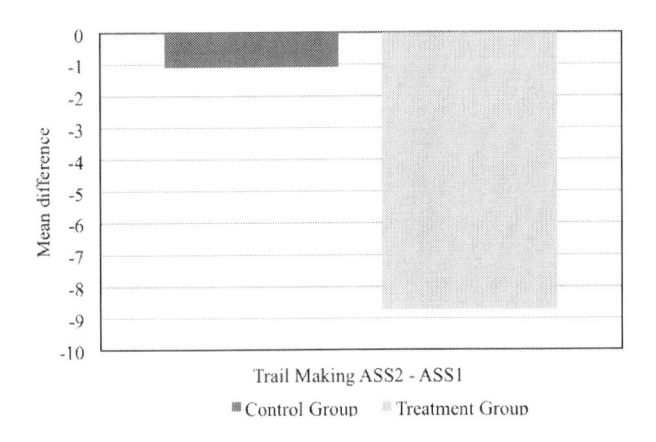

FIGURE 3.7 TRAIL MAKING: MEAN DIFFERENCE BETWEEN ASSESSMENT 1 AND ASSESSMENT 2 FOR CG AND TG

Finally, a statistical *t*-test was computed to analyze the mean value variations of the CG and TG as between pre- and post-intervention, using the *delta* variable created. Results showed that the mean variation of the trail making was not significantly higher for the TG when compared with the CG. Results suggested that the participation in the MBSR program did not improve the attention, executive functioning, and motor speed performance of the TG (see Appendix 20, Table A20.7). Correlations between memory free recall and levels of practice revealed no significant correlations with respect to daily practice with CDs, daily informal practice, and number of sessions attended (see Appendix 20, Table A20.8).

Summary of quantitative results

The statistical analysis conducted revealed that the participation in the MBSR program positively improved participants' mindfulness, including the capacities to observe the present-moment experience, to describe what is happening with oneself, and to act with awareness, nonjudgment, and nonreaction. Self-compassion was also improved, including measures of self-kindness, self-judgment, and common humanity. The capacity for decentering also improved after the MBSR among the TG's participants. TG participants also showed improvements in subjective well-being (i.e., satisfaction with life and affect) and psychological well-being, including scores on autonomy, environmental mastery, personal growth, relations with others, purpose in life, and self-acceptance. Psychological symptoms also improved as reflected in lower levels of tension, depression, hostility, fatigue, and confusion and higher levels of vigor in the TG after completing the MBSR program. Stress levels were also reduced. TG participants also showed increased quality of life in physical, psychological, and environmental dimensions. Physical symptoms decreased and quality of life in terms of the physical domain improved. Quality of life in the spiritual domain improved also, as did spiritual well-being. No impact was observed in terms of death perspectives. Neuropsychological measures revealed that the participation in the MBSR program improved episodic memory (i.e., free recall), speed processing, and working memory performance. No impact was observed in terms of attention, executive functioning, and motor speed.

In many of these measures the CG showed a decrease in scores at Assessment 2, including with respect to mindfulness, self-compassion, psychological well-being, psychological symptoms and stress, and physical well-being. It was hypothesized that the significant decreases observed could be related to the current economic crisis that Portugal was experiencing during this period, which was affecting the living conditions of this age group: Portuguese older adults experienced cuts in their pensions, and government also applied cuts in the National Health System and increased prices of doctors' appointments at National Health Centers and Hospitals, all of which could be affecting their economic capacity to use these services and, in turn, might impact their well-being, and their psychological and physical health. In neuropsychological tests the CG also showed improvement in some measures, which might be associated to the learning that might have occurred due to the exposure to the same tests at Assessment 1 and Assessment 2. It is important to note that these same stressors occurred for the TG, but that, for the TG, perhaps their practice of MBSR had buffered them against the deleterious effects of the economic crisis.

These results clearly reveal that the MBSR program has a significant effect on older adults' psychological well-being, physical health, neuropsychological performance, and spirituality. The results also suggest the potential of MBSR intervention to buffer against the stressors of life, in older age specifically, as well as in life globally (e.g., with respect to the economic crisis). Therefore, the MBSR program did for these participants provide a complementary and holistic intervention for older adults and foment participants' conscious aging.

Furthermore, results revealed an association between mindfulness, compassion/acceptance, and decentering, as the mean variations were significantly correlated among these three variables. Also, the observed changes in well-being, psychological and physical symptoms, quality of life, and spiritual well-being suggest that these three mechanisms may have mediated and enhanced these observed outcomes.

» Chapter 4 «

Qualitative Results

This chapter presents the qualitative findings of this study. These rely on heuristic inquiry, which, in this study, involved the use of several heuristic tools that included self-dialogue, tacit knowing, intuition, indwelling, and focusing. After following the analysis protocol outlined in Chapter 2 for each interview, I identified the individual depictions of each participant, using the code number attributed to each participant during the study in order to protect their identity. These individual depictions are presented in this section.

Individual depictions

The interviews of the seven participants were analyzed following the heuristic inquiry process and Colaizzi's (1978) strategy detailed in the description of the treatment of qualitative data (see Appendix 3). The analysis was guided by the main research question of the study: What are the effects and lived experiences of the MBSR program for older adults in terms of psychological well-being, subjective well-being, physical health, neuropsychological performance, and spirituality? The individual depictions provide information on participants' demographic, health, and religious background, his or her pattern of compliance throughout the MBSR program, information on new illnesses or significant events that occurred during the program, and a narrative constructed from the interview responses in relation to the lived experience and effects of the program in the life of that participant. At the end of each individual depiction, there is a presentation of that participant's replies to the last question of the interview: can you say three words that best describe your experience and the impact of the MBSR in your life? Results of these analyses included some main themes and the respective dimensions of those, which are presented for each participant in a table.

Participant ID Number 2

Participant ID Number 2 was a 69-year-old woman, married, Caucasian, and Catholic. She had a graduate degree and was currently retired. She suffered from excess cholesterol and took medication to control its levels. During the program she did not experience any new illness and did not start any new medication. She had previous contact with the concepts presented during the program mostly through reading, but did not have any previous experience in mindfulness meditation practices and had no regular practice of any other type of meditation. A month before she was recruited, she had lost her husband. At the moment of the initial interview she reported that she was still depressed and experiencing the impact of her loss in her life and was still dealing with this loss and how to adjust to her daily life without her husband's presence. She had the support of family and friends. She did not experience any major life event during her participation in the study. She was present for all sessions of the program and her home practice compliance was 90 percent for the formal practices with the CDs and 100 percent for the informal practices, including the exercises to be completed in the manual.

During the interview Participant ID Number 2 revealed that the course was very positive for her: "I have a very positive memory of the course...it was really good." She shared that she was going through a very difficult period in her life due to the loss of her husband:

> I was feeling very upset with his death, upset with the world and with life... I lost hope and will to live... I felt I as if I lost contact with reality... I was facing a reality I did not know and I did not want.

The participation in the program allowed her to learn to bring her attention to the present moment, to the here and now, allowing her to "reconnect with reality and with myself...and most importantly to accept his death." The systematic mindfulness training throughout the program allowed her to cultivate the bringing of attention and awareness to the present moment and, although bringing the mind to the present helped her reconnect with herself and reality, she did report that there were times that it was difficult and painful to face the loss and the reality of her life:

> It was really difficult for me to come back again and again to the here and now moment, and I was unwilling to do so... I felt more comfortable trapped and attached to memories of the past,

experiences and moments we lived together, and also wishes about the future with his presence, instead of having to face his absence.

The ability to be in the present moment allowed her to bring acceptance to the reality she was experiencing and helped her deal with her loss. She stated that the increased presence and capacity to observe what was happening in herself moment by moment helped her deal with the memories and pain:

> Although, the program helped me to recover, to feel more confident… to wake up in the morning and face the day, there are moments where I am still very sad… I feel sad and lonely, he comes to my mind, and memories arise…and I miss him, I miss him a lot. In these moments I observe these feelings, observe the memories, and I avoid getting into any kind of judgmental process or get attached to these memories… I observe and cultivate my presence, my acceptance… my equanimity. Oh my God this is hard sometimes, but brings me peace and a sense of presence, and I feel alive.

Instead of resisting or repressing these emotions, as she did in the beginning of the process, allowing herself to observe what was happening and bringing courage to face the pain, loss, thoughts, and memories were opportunities to cultivate acceptance and equanimity towards these events, which, in turn, allowed some healing to take place.

She clearly revealed an increased ability to accept her loss and pain: "I learned about the awareness of each moment, consciousness of life, and acceptance…mainly acceptance, which made me let go of the resistance I was feeling towards my husband's death," and realized that pain is not only a reality in her life, but rather a universal reality: "I am not the only one in pain…pain is a reality in everyone's lives…the course helped me realize this." She shared that this grieving process was a "learning process" and that, by bringing into awareness the emotions she was experiencing, even if they were difficult and painful, this "helps me to be healthier, emotionally and physically." Observing and embracing the pain helped her to "gain more distance and space to breathe."

She also showed an increased acceptance towards her emotions: "Sometimes I cry but I know that this is OK… I do not judge myself anymore. This is my present moment…the present moment I am living and I accept the tears." She also cultivated acceptance towards herself:

> I learned to accept myself with my virtues and my failures…there is no right or wrong…but a continuity of experience. If I fail I try

to accept the failures instead of criticizing and ruminating on these failures.

and acceptance of life: "I learned to embrace life completely with the good and bad moments, the moments of happiness and unhappiness" and aging: "One needs to accept. Everyone goes through these changes."

Increased presence and awareness was observed in evidence from several aspects of her life:

> I feel myself, I feel life, I feel the breath, I hear the birds, I taste the food I eat… I feel my body, I am aware of my body, I am aware of my thoughts and my emotions… I am not a victim of all these things, but an observer. I learned to look at life with a fresh new look.

This outlook reflected an increased awareness of emotions, thoughts, bodily sensations, and the external world. Throughout the interview she shared that the participation in the program had impacted her in terms of an increased sense of peace and aliveness: "That brings me a sense of peace… I feel alive…and I am learning to live again," of strength, "I found strength in myself…more strength to deal with the situations of daily life… It is amazing the strength that meditation brings to us," of confidence, "I feel present…emotionally confident and stable, less judgmental, peaceful, calm…all this is experienced in more happiness and sense of belonging," and of feeling healthier, "I feel stronger, I feel healthier, my body and mind feel healthier," more positive, "I feel calmer and more positive, more present… In the middle of chaos I find harmony," and more balanced emotionally:

> Generally I feel better, I feel less anxious about things. I used to feel anxious when difficulties came up. Now I feel less anxious trying to figure out how I will solve situations or face the future…being present allows me to worry less, to let go and face the moment with more clarity.

She also showed an increased discernment arising from the participation in the program, and the practices learned allowed her to approach the situations differently: "Instead of getting all nervous and lost, feeling incapable or useless, I try to observe the feelings that arise instead of getting involved in them…and I find a way to solve them… I try to… mindfully respond to the issue instead of reacting and allowing these emotions to cause me any kind of physical instability and emotional turmoil." She noted her increased motivation:

> I have always been careful with my diet, but since E. died I feel that I was less motivated to cook only for myself... The course allowed me to realize that I need to take care of myself... It is very important to take care of myself.

She reported a positive impact of the program on her physical well-being, including her health: "I feel stronger... I feel healthier...my body and mind feel healthier," her increased sense of physical relaxation "connecting with the flow of my breath... My body starts relaxing...my heart...my heart rhythm slows down... I feel that I come back 'home'," and being more active: "I started walking every day for an hour... I feel more energetic." Her general habits in terms of physical well-being were also affected as she started walking on a daily basis and her relationship with her diet also changed: "I am much more mindful about my diet habits, the way I eat and prepare the food... It was a very important step for me." She also reported improvements in her sleep: "I am also sleeping better, and even during the nights that I wake up with insomnia, I start meditating, and it helps me go back to sleep or to be calmer rather than worrying that I am not sleeping."

In terms of perceptions of aging and how she was experiencing this period of her life, Participant ID Number 2 reported that she did not feel the age she was and that she believes that "inside we do not age, it is just the outside that changes...the body." She felt that, due to her age she feels more experienced, less impulsive and more accepting of things that happen in her life. This period of her life is a learning process, like any other period of her life. Death and suffering were perceived as integral parts of life now, and, although these are difficult realities, she tries to accept them, and the program helped her in increasing this ability to be in the present moment and accepting what arises. She stated also her beliefs about the time after death: "But I feel that beyond that...beyond pain and physical death there will be complete peace and harmony."

Suffering was perceived after her participation as a learning process in life: "The course helped me realize this...suffering is a way of learning." Life was then seen in its impermanent nature: "Everything is impermanent, flowing, and changing...we are also changing at every moment."

Completing the program and establishing a daily practice of mindfulness allowed her to get in contact with herself; she realized that she had been disconnected with herself before starting the program and that completing the program had "allowed me to get in contact with myself again...it helped me to get away from everything that affected me negatively and get in touch with my inner self… You know, my true self, my essence…my soul." These statements suggested an awareness of a transpersonal self that is capable of observing what arises in the physical and emotional bodies and then remaining focused in a place that reflects peace and strength: "I let myself surf through the pain, through the emotions and it led me to my core…to my inner being…to a presence that is unshakable and unbreakable." Participating in the program reinforced her beliefs that she is more than the physical body and that her existence extends to other realms of existence: "What I truly am is present in this unshakable and peaceful place where my soul is present… Participating in the program allowed me to get in touch with this place again."

When questioned about the meaning of life and existence this participant shared that her belief relied on the concept that life has a purpose and that she walks a path to arrive at a defined destiny. This path has ups and down, easy moments and difficult moments in all facets of her life, but, post treatment, they were seen as part of life, so that thereafter she could grow and evolve as an individual. Life was seen as a school:

> I see that this life was a school for me, and it still is… I am learning and learning, and experiencing…and it is hard to face certain moments, but I got through them and I go on… This is the way life is!!!! I am very grateful for everything in life… Even the difficult moments.

In this school we call life, opportunities arise for growth and transformation, and completing the MBSR program "reminded me and reaffirmed my deep feeling of what life is… Life is an opportunity to grow and evolve." These beliefs guide her experience and give meaning to what she has gone through in her life: "This gives meaning to my life, because I know that all I experience has a reason… Even though I did not accept it many times, I know there is a reason…learning and growing." This gives meaning also to the painful experiences that she has had: "Even when I suffer emotionally or physically there is a reason…there is some kind of lesson behind it… I might not see it, but it is there."

During the program, in particular in the first three sessions, Participant ID Number 2 had some difficulties in sitting or lying still throughout the sessions and practices: sometimes there were tears, and I observed that, gradually, she learned to use deeper breaths to release the emotional tension that was present in these moments of agitation, possibly because during these moments she was facing the emotions that were present in her emotional and physical body. She did not share much during sessions and I saw this not only as based on her personality, as she revealed herself to be a reserved person, but also due to the emotional difficulties that she was experiencing.

After the program was completed, she maintained a regular formal practice of mindfulness meditation. The informal practices occurred naturally on a daily basis. She felt more conscious and aware throughout the day and less prone to do things on automatic pilot. She stated that she had become "more aware of things…of my inner world and outer world…my inner world are my thoughts and emotions…the outer world I am more aware of the noises, the movement of the cars, the trees, nature." This awareness affected positively her quality of life, as she felt generally better and more present.

This increased presence and awareness also impacted her social interactions, as she felt that her presence increased while listening and talking with others and that, therefore, these interactions improved: "Now I'm more accepting and compassionate… I feel this is also reflected in the way I interact with other people… I feel that I am more patient and understanding." The three words or phrases that she used to describe her experience and the impact of the MBSR in her life were: acceptance, awareness/presence, and impermanence.

The analysis of the interview guided by the main research questions of the study revealed the following themes (see Table 4.1).

TABLE 4.1 PARTICIPANT ID NUMBER 2: THEMES AND DIMENSIONS

Themes	Dimensions
Mindfulness	Observation, presence, awareness/consciousness, attention, decentering
Acceptance	Life, self, aging, loss, emotions, pain, suffering
Impermanence	Life
Psychological Well-Being	Confidence, peace/serenity, strength, aliveness, balanced, positivity, happiness, discernment, motivation, identity (see transpersonal self in spirituality theme)
Physical Well-Being	Health, relaxation, active, general habits, sleep
Perceptions of Aging	Ageless, wisdom, death
Spirituality	Transpersonal self, interconnectedness/universality, purpose in life, growth and transformation, suffering

cont.

TABLE 4.1 PARTICIPANT ID NUMBER 2:
THEMES AND DIMENSIONS *CONT.*

Themes	Dimensions
Social Interactions	Positive, compassion
Daily Life	Regular formal and informal practice, quality of life
Overall Experience	Positive

Participant ID Number 7

Participant ID Number 7 was a 67-year-old woman, Caucasian, living with a partner, with a graduate degree, and currently retired. She did not have any diagnosis of chronic illness and was not taking any regular medication when she enrolled in the study. Her religious background was considered spiritual. She had had a few experiences with meditation in her life but had never had a regular practice of meditation. She was familiar with some of the concepts presented during the program and had always been interested in participating in workshops, activities, and courses that cultivated her personal development. During the program she had to miss two sessions due to a backache crisis caused by a hernia, but she continued to do the practices while she was at home. Her home practice compliance was 76 percent for the formal practices with the CDs and 100 percent for the informal practices, including the exercises to be completed on the manual. During the program she did not experience any significant life event and did not start taking any medication apart from medication and treatments mostly based on herbal preparations and alternative protocols (e.g., acupuncture) to control and treat her backache crisis.

Apart from the moments when I asked the group about their experiences during the practices, she manifested her opinion or lived experience of the practices only a few times, but, when she did, she revealed a strong presence and ability to demonstrate the impact that the program was having in her daily life. There were moments of difficulties when she observed that her thoughts and emotions started growing and intensifying in stressful situations, but she clearly revealed a strong discernment and ability to bring awareness and acceptance to those moments. It was clear that the path that she had already completed in her personal development was also influencing this ability to incorporate the principles and practices being presented in the program.

At the interview, the participant revealed that the participation in the program was very positive, and that she had understood the processes being presented: "It was very positive to be present in this study, I really enjoyed it and I feel I followed the sessions and practices well." She said that she had some difficulties with the sitting meditation that lasted 45 minutes because this practice had more moments of silence during which she was able to observe and be aware of the agitation in her mind, and sometimes it was difficult to keep the observation on the breath or bodily sensations; however, she kept practicing it and accepted the difficulties as part of the learning process. She reported that, out of all the principles presented during the sessions, the one that had the greatest impact was the importance of bringing the mind to the present moment. She revealed an increased post-treatment ability to be attentive and aware of her daily actions, emotions, physical body, and how she was present with others: "I started to be more attentive of the things of my daily life…the things I do and what I feel emotionally and physically…to what I hear and how I hear other people." This ability to bring the mind to the present moment allowed her to find time to be with herself, to slow down, and to be more attentive: "The practices allowed me to find more time to be with myself…to stop and be with myself," and noted of this ability to observe what was happening in herself that "this being with myself is being in silence…having time to observe what is happening with me, how I feel and how I am." This being with herself was not only manifested in relation to the formal practices during which she actually found time to sit and be with herself in silence, but also in relation to the things she did in her daily life, as she reported that the formal practices helped her increase her ability to be more present in the moment-to-moment experience of her daily life. Instead of constantly being in her thoughts and preoccupations all the time, she reported an increased ability to experience her life. She stated her observations in that regard:

> I am more present when eating, walking…and I notice that when I practice formally it is easier to be present…present in these little things of daily life… I remember to pay attention, to be here and now…instead of being in my thoughts and mental worries all the time.

She reported an increased ability to observe the moments when she was involved in thoughts and emotions, and when she was performing tasks on automatic pilot. In these moments she reminded herself to bring her mind to what she was doing:

> I [am] more able [to] notice my thoughts and emotions…and when I am doing things in automatic pilot…sometimes there is no

awareness, I am completely lost in them...but other moments I am here, I notice them...which is a good thing, it is an improvement.

The participant also showed an improvement in her ability to realize the impermanence of things that occurred in her life, including how she felt and how she experienced her daily life: "By learning to be in the present moment I am able to see how things are constantly changing...outside and also in the way I feel in relation to things...it is amazing how things change," and that, instead of wanting to change things, she was able to cultivate an acceptance towards what was happening and let herself follow the flow of life: "I step back and observe what is happening ... I try not to grasp or hold anything...just let myself experience what is arising."

She also shared an increased ability to accept emotions:

> I learned to be more gentle with myself when these moments arise and accept these emotions and the preoccupations of my life... It is not easy but I try to observe and accept...sometimes I do not seem to be able, but I try [to] accept that as well... I notice a lot of individualism in people...and accept.

After her participation in the MBSR, she also cultivated acceptance towards pain: "I notice that when I had a physical problem, such as the backache crisis I had during the MBSR, I was able to accept what I was experiencing and the limitation that it was bringing in my daily life." This acceptance allowed her to relax emotionally, and, consequently, she reported an improvement in her physical well-being: "Accepting allowed me to become more serene emotionally, and in spite of not recovering from the physical pain, I ended up with less tension as I was emotionally calmer." She said that during the period she was at home with the backache crisis she had more time to practice and that she was able to recognize the thoughts and emotions of being tense and frustrated about the pain. She observed these moments, her thoughts and emotions, and connected with the breath. She stated that: "it was funny because it seemed that there stopped [being] any thoughts...and this allowed me to be more relaxed." In one session she shared that she had this back crisis every now and again, and although it always caused her some frustration and emotional upset, in some ways she had learned to accept that reality, but the practice had improved this ability to accept in deeper ways, as she was able to observe, breathe, and release to the present-moment experience.

The increased physical relaxation was associated with the observed changes in the emotional component of her life: "Physically I noticed that I was much better... I felt improvements in my physical well-being and health, physically relaxed...and I think it has to do with the fact that emotionally I felt better."

Apart from the increased sense of relaxation, she also manifested improvements in her sleep "Now I sleep much better... Before it was hard to fall asleep, but now it is much better." She associated these improvements in her sleep with the increased sense of relaxation and also the observed changes in her psychological well-being, including an increased sense of peace and serenity: "I felt an increased serenity," less mental agitation, "I noticed that by being in the present moment, my mind is calmer and more silenced," and discernment in her daily life:

> It is not always easy to put into practice the principles we know are better for us. With the program I noticed that I was able to put some distance in my experiences, I was able to observe my emotions and thoughts, bring acceptance and calm the mind...and act with more discernment.

When asked about her age, the participant reported that she did not feel her age and that the only thing that reminded her of her age was when she had some physical problem. She shared that she experienced some fears about how she will end up later in her life, due to the social reality of how families deal with their old parents (i.e., nursing home, loss of autonomy, etc.). I prompted her about where she was when these thoughts arose and quickly she closed her eyes and breathed deeply saying: "I am here, in the present moment...my body and mind are already releasing...there is no fear...accepting, releasing."

She also shared that at this age she never fears death and she has accepted it as a reality of life, as well as suffering: "Suffering is present in everyone's lives, since the beginning of life...we suffer...it is natural... not easy, but part of life." However, she reported some concerns in relation to the suffering she may experience before she dies. She said that before the program this was something that used to make her anxious and now, when these thoughts arise, she tries to bring awareness and acceptance to what she is experiencing. She said, "It helps, but sometimes it seems difficult to create distance because these thoughts and worries involv[ing] emotions... I observe and accept...but I realize that the work of integrating these principles in my life has only started." Furthermore, she feels that, as a result of her life experience, she has more clarity and discernment towards life in general than when she was younger:

"Although, with age certain limitations arise, it also brought me more experience and clarity towards life."

The participation in the program and the cultivated ability to be in the present-moment experience also affected her ability to be with others. She felt calmer when interacting with others, more accepting, and more compassionate: "I also notice [I am] more compassionate towards others... instead of feeling the victim of the world." Changes were also observed in terms of cognitive performance. She said:

> In relation to memory I noticed a lot of difference... I think it is because I am more present in the moment... Before the MBSR started I was always forgetting this and that... I was feeling my memory failing me... Now I am much better.

When questioned about how she perceived life and her existence, the participant reported that she felt there was a meaning and purpose in life, a purpose to learn. This learning occurs in all spheres of life, she notes, either through physical pain, emotional crisis, social interactions, and even spirituality: "Our experiences in life: body, for example when we have a disease, emotions, the people we interact with...and even the spiritual experiences such as reading a particular spiritual book...they are all ways of learning." According to her view, this learning in life has no beginning and no end; it is a continuous journey where we all have free will to choose what to do, but, in the end, no matter what choices we make, we all get to the aimed-for destiny. She stated: "My existence is this journey of learning...a journey to grow as an individual person." She also said: "My purpose is to learn to live the rhythm of nature, the rhythm of the Oneness...learn that everything is an energy that connects us all, in Oneness...that I am energy...my body, mind, spirit are all energy." She revealed a strong awareness and sense of universality and interconnectedness between everything that exists: "We live in an individual way, but we are spiritual beings and together we are One." This underlying view of life guided her journey in life and was an important aspect in the way she perceived her life experiences and how she experienced her life: "This is what I try to bring to my daily life, to guide me in my choices and in the way I see what happens to me on a daily basis." The participation in the program did not change her perception of life and her life's purpose but reinforced her views and beliefs.

Spiritually, she had always felt that something was missing in her life, which is the force that motivated her throughout her life to look for answers about her life meaning and existence. Sometimes, the emptiness that she experiences had made her feel anxious about finding the answers. During the program she felt that the anxiety in relation to this topic improved because she was more present and the movement of wanting to go to the future to find the answers slowed down.

The program allowed her to establish a daily routine of mindfulness meditation that she recognized had been a little bit lower than she had wanted, due to the social events that occurred during Christmas and New Year, but she showed determination to re-establish a strong daily practice. The informal practice continued as she realized that she was more present and aware of what she was doing while she was doing it, but she observed that her formal practice provides a strong support for improving her ability to be present and more discerning in her daily life. She also revealed that, in her perspective, this informal practice is about integrating all the concepts learned in her daily life: "integration in the now, moment by moment, because if these principles are not applied it stays in my mental plane… I have to consciously work to bring these learnings to my existential life."

Overall, she stated: "I feel more calm and serene… It is this ability to be more calm that affects my physical and psychological well-being, my spiritual experience…and also my memory…it affects my general well-being, my quality of life." The three words she used to summarize her experience and the effects of the program in her life were serenity, presence, attention.

The analysis of the interview revealed the following themes (see Table 4.2).

TABLE 4.2 PARTICIPANT ID NUMBER 7: THEMES AND DIMENSIONS

Themes	Dimensions
Mindfulness	Observation, presence, attention, awareness/consciousness, slowing down, Be, decentering, returning to the now, flow of life
Acceptance	Others, death, aging, suffering, emotions, pain
Impermanence	Life
Psychological Well-Being	Peace/serenity, discernment, silenced mind
Physical Well-Being	Relaxed, sleep

cont.

TABLE 4.2 PARTICIPANT ID NUMBER 7:
THEMES AND DIMENSIONS *CONT.*

Themes	Dimensions
Perceptions of Aging	Ageless, wisdom, fear
Spirituality	Transpersonal self, interconnectedness/universality, purpose in life, growth and transformation
Cognitive Performance	Memory improved
Social Interactions	Presence, compassion, calm
Daily Life	Formal and informal practice, quality of life
Overall Experience	Positive

Participant ID Number 8

Participant ID Number 8 was a 70-year-old woman, married, and Caucasian. She was Catholic with no previous experience in mindfulness meditation practices, did not suffer from any chronic illness and was taking medication only to improve her blood circulation. During the initial assessment she revealed herself to be a very spiritual person, mostly as associated with the Catholic Church. She was present in all sessions of the program and her home practice compliance was 90 percent for the formal practices and 100 percent for the informal practices, including the exercises to be completed in the manual. During the program she did not experience any significant life event, but she experienced a new illness after the program was completed (i.e., dizziness and low blood pressure) and started taking new medication (herbal and allopathic medicines) for that condition.

This participant reflected a very fragile and insecure presence. She was always posing questions about the themes, not because she was not following but because she was afraid of not truly understanding what was being said. Sometimes, she asked me to repeat more slowly what I was saying in order to allow her time to write notes of the themes being presented. She shared these questions she had about the interview process, and I mindfully and compassionately replied to her concerns. Many times, information about other participants' experience was very useful to her in these moments, as she felt with that information that she was not alone in her doubts and difficulties in applying the principles in her daily life. In many ways, it seemed to me that she was rather a perfectionist and that her insecurity made her doubt her own capacity and value in the progress she was reporting. She showed great spiritual awareness throughout the sessions, in terms of perception of interconnection and universality, as well as her compassion towards others in the group. Her husband was also a participant in the study and she always sat in a chair that was not close to him. I noticed that, when her husband missed a few sessions due to health issues, she was more participative and more confident, although she always showed concerns about not being truly capable of following the concepts; however, she was following them, and she was open and motivated in participating in all pair and group discussions, as well as in the program practices. At the end of sessions she always came to me with more personal questions, things that she did not feel comfortable sharing with the group—questions about how to apply the principles in certain aspects of her life, such as dealing with her husband's anxiety and insecurity. This insecurity was a characteristic of her personality, which, according to what she had shared in the initial interview, was something that had been present in her life since she was a little child, probably due to her educational and religious background, It seemed that her experience of getting married and leaving her parents' house had been a big step towards improving some aspects of that insecurity. For example, after getting married she had started volunteering at the Church, teaching and helping children.

At the interview the participant revealed that she deeply enjoyed being part of this study and meeting all the group members, and she was very grateful for my patience and compassionate presence throughout the sessions: "I really enjoyed having the privilege to be part of this study… I really liked all participants…and you were so loving, caring, and patient with all of us." The impact of the program was very positive in her life, and she stated that the main learning that she brought from the sessions was the importance of being in the present moment with an open and receptive attitude towards what is being experienced, without judging or criticizing, and the importance of cultivating acceptance: "For me the most important learning was the benefit of being in the present moment… being open and receptive to what I am experiencing…accepting what is." She shared a self-reflective observation: "I used [to be], and I still am, very critical of myself, and this helped me to be more accepting of who I am… and also of others." She did share that sometimes she had in the program process experienced difficulties and needed to clarify certain concepts being presented, as they were all quite new for her, but that they had all resonated very positively with her own perspective on things:

> The concepts made so much sense to me. I felt that I needed to clarify things in some moments, to make more sense in my head to the true meaning and its applicability in daily life, but it all made so much sense.

She manifested the awareness that being present in her daily life allowed her to experience things more deeply. She was aware of things that before she had not even recognized or valued; she had learned to observe her emotions, thoughts, and bodily feelings, which observations had allowed her to be more conscious and aware in her daily life. She said this about that change in her consciousness:

> Now I can observe my thoughts, emotions, and bodily sensations... before, I did not pay attention to it, it was there and I was numb to all these experiences. I learned to observe, to take two steps back and be conscious of my experience.

This developing awareness was not always positive for her, because the emotions, thoughts, and physical sensations that arose at those moments caused an uncomfortable sensation, but she tried to cultivate acceptance, focusing on her breath, and tried to let go and stop resisting the pain:

> By acknowledging what is present in my mind, body, and emotions I noticed that this was painful sometimes...as if they were intensified... but I tried to focus on the flow of my breath as you taught us, and stop pretending or resisting to the reality that is present.

She stated that the practices allowed her to make time to be with herself, and that, in the beginning she had felt a little bit uncomfortable about that, as if she was not confident enough to be with herself in an accepting and loving way: "It was hard in the beginning to meditate and [be] with myself, I felt uncomfortable because I tended to engage in criticism about my capacity to practice or doubts about doing it correctly." Gradually, and with the help of the support provided during sessions, she cultivated acceptance and the confidence to be with whatever was present, even the thoughts of criticism, and tried to foment an observer stance towards those thoughts and emotions: "I learned to observe these thoughts and emotions and tried to cultivate acceptance... I think I am much better now, but I also think that there is still a lot to be learned here...and practiced." The practices, formal and informal, helped her to slow down her daily rhythm:

> By bringing the attention to the present moment I slowed down the rhythm I used to do things and when I use the CDs I feel my mind slowing down, silencing...my heart beat slows down, my breath... I feel peaceful.

These comments are evidence that the practices also helped her feel more peaceful, which was one of the benefits of MBSR indicated in terms of psychological well-being for her: "Generally, I feel more calm, more peaceful...which is more pronounced after the practices, but also during the day." She also reported increased discernment arising from the growing ability to observe her thoughts and emotions in more stressful situations. She gave the example of when she started to feel unwell right after the program finished:

> You know I started to feel unwell after the program and I noticed the emotions arising because of this...such as fear, tension, anxiety... because I did not know what was wrong with me. I started to observe that my mind would make possible scenarios about what could be the cause.

The practices had helped her to gain some distance, to accept the pain, and to act with more discernment towards this experience: "When I practiced I was able to look with more discernment to what I was feeling emotionally and physically instead of feeding fear and anxiety."

Another main impact of the program, she stated, was the concept of acceptance that was cultivated not only towards her and others, but also towards pain, emotions, thoughts, and suffering: "Looking back into my life, now I am more able to accept my suffering...before, I accepted some situations, but I realized that is now something I see with less frustration." Being in the present moment also brought awareness of the impermanence of life "Things change...always...inside, outside...the way I am feeling, my body, my state of mind...and aging also brings these changes... I recognize more this impermanence and how I react or respond to it in my daily life."

The improved psychological well-being was associated with improvements for this participant in physical well-being, including a general sense of physical relaxation: "Emotionally I feel more relaxed and calm, which I feel also allows me to feel more relaxed physically... I do not feel so tense in my body," and improvements in sleep: "as my mind is more silenced, I am able to fall asleep more easily... I do not need to be watching TV for hours in order to fall asleep." The exercises developed towards mindful eating fostered an increased awareness of her eating habits: "I was always careful with my diet but now I observe more carefully what I eat, how I prepare, and what I choose to eat." She also reported changes in her physical exercise routines: "I also started to exercise on a regular basis...not only the yoga CD of the program, but also walking with my husband."

She shared that, because of her familial and religious education, she had always been very careful in the way she interacted with others in order not to hurt anyone but that, with the program, she had started to feel more present and more compassionate towards others in her interactions: "I feel that by being present and more accepting I am more compassionate in my interactions with others... I feel more connected with people because I am truly there, listening," and that that increased awareness and attention had allowed her to act with more discernment: "When I respond in my interactions, I feel that I am less impulsive when things are being stressful...especially with my grandkids who are really 'terrible' sometimes." As a result she felt that her relationships were more positive than before: "I take more out of my interactions now...because I am there with the other."

She did not feel the age she is and does not believe that people can be characterized or judged by their age: "Who we are internally is what matters and I feel young inside." She stated "I love having my age and the only thing that sometimes stresses me is the physical limitations that arise, but I learned to live with this and the program helped me cultivate acceptance towards it." She is grateful for her life and all the learning, because she is the person she is because of these experiences: "I am grateful for my life, the good and the bad, I learned and grew, with the help of God I am a different person, hopefully a better person... more discerning." She revealed that "it does not matter how I look, if with more or less wrinkles...my main wish [is] to fulfill my purpose in this life, to be of service to God and others," as she believes that we are all connected and that whatever happens to one person affects the other: "We are all sons of God, and whatever we do to ourselves we are doing to the other, as well...to our brother; why can't we see that?" Growing and learning throughout life, finding the true nature of her existence, and being open to serve others was seen as the main purposes in her life: "For me life is a journey of growth, of becoming a better person, of moving closer to God...of finding out who I truly am...and being here in this life present for others, helping them see their value." She shared this about her history: "I suffered a lot, people suffer all the time...we cannot change that reality, we can be there for others...but suffering is part of life." The program helped her reaffirm this acceptance towards suffering, observing that "learning to cultivate acceptance, helped me firm this belief." When questioned about "who she truly was," given her mention of that in the answer above, she said that "I am a daughter of God, I am a spiritual being...present in this life... I know that I am not only this body, I have a soul," apparently revealing an awareness of a transpersonal self that goes beyond the physical body. With the mindfulness practices she also experienced awareness of the interaction between body, mind, and emotions:

> I noticed with the practices that my body, my mind, and my emotions they are all connected...one is affecting the other and the other all the time... It is amazing...and I feel that by observing my body, mind and emotions it is as if my soul is observing my experience... there is no separation...all these are connected.

This realization allowed for seeing her experience with increased awareness and perceiving that the mind, body, emotions, and spirit are interrelated in her experiences. Her comments revealed that her spiritual life was very important to her and guided her in life, such as in the way she experienced suffering: "I know that I suffer for some reason...there is always a reason for everything in life" and in her service to others "helping others gives meaning to my life...it is a way to learn and grow, to see our true nature and the true nature of others...we are all God's sons."

When talking about her aging process, she shared that "I am not afraid of dying or death... I believe we go to some place peaceful...but what kind of pain will I have to go through when I am close to this reality?!" She used to feel bad for having fears about how she would experience the time of her death; now she tries to accept the fears by focusing on her breath and on the present moment. Although she realized that suffering and pain were realities of life, she also had this fear and concern regarding the pain and suffering she might go through at the moment of her death. She stated, "Death is part of the life...there is nothing we can do about it...just prepare ourselves mentally and emotionally to accept what comes."

She continued the practices after the program finished and the informal practices came to her as a natural result of her increased ability to be in the present moment:

> I am more present and conscious of all I do in my daily life. Obviously there are still many moments that I am not aware and [am] involved

in so many other thoughts about what I have to do…but I am more attentive towards everything I do.

She reported feeling better generally and that this improved the way she feels in her life every day. The three words or phrases that she used to describe and summarize her lived experience and the effects of the program were: presence, acceptance, ability to see. The analysis of the interview revealed the following themes (see Table 4.3).

TABLE 4.3 PARTICIPANT ID NUMBER 8: THEMES AND DIMENSIONS

Themes	Dimensions
Mindfulness	Observation, presence, attention, decentering, awareness/consciousness, slowing down, Be
Acceptance	Others, aging, suffering, emotions, thoughts, pain, self
Impermanence	Life
Psychological Well-Being	Peace/serenity, discernment, silenced mind
Physical Well-Being	Relaxed, sleep
Perceptions of Aging	Ageless, wisdom, death
Spirituality	Transpersonal self, interconnectedness/universality, purpose in life, growth and transformation, suffering
Social Interactions	Presence, discernment, positive, compassion
Daily Life	Formal and informal practice, quality of life
Overall Experience	Positive

Participant ID Number 13

Participant ID Number 13 was a 73-year-old male, Caucasian, married, with nine years of education, and currently retired. His religious background was Catholic. At the initial assessment, he had reported suffering from hypotension but that he did not take any medication for that condition or any other medications. During and after the MBSR program and prior to the final interview, he did not experience any new illness and did not start any new medication. He did not have any previous experience in mindfulness meditation, and all the concepts presented during the program were new to him. He was present in all sessions of the program and his home practice compliance was 86 percent for the formal practices with the CDs and 90 percent for the informal practices, including the exercises to be completed in the manual.

Throughout the sessions this participant was not very expressive when providing feedback. He was concise and direct, and, when asked to expand on his feelings or emotional reactions, he revealed great difficulty in expressing them, not because he was not aware of them, but because he did not know how to do it. During the interview, I observed the same difficulties for him, and, although I tried to prompt him in every possible way, his replies were overly concise. He was clear about how he had experienced the program and the effects of the program in his life. He was very kind, polite, and respectful of all participants. The way he spoke to me and others revealed a great awareness and compassion towards other people.

He shared that the participation in the program was very positive, in terms not only of the practices but also of the concepts being presented. He enjoyed the group and the context and environment created in each session. He said: "The learning was very positive." He felt that during and after the program he was undoubtedly more present and attentive to his experiences in his daily life: "I am more attentive to what I do, the way I do things, the way I experience my life, and with others…the way I relate with the present moment and with life changed." He became more aware of the moment-to-moment experiences and more capable of bringing his attention to the present moment. However, he recognized that there were still moments when he was not present and that he was performing things automatically, but that now he remembered to come back to the present moment and was able to observe the thoughts that were disconnecting him from the present-moment experience. He showed an increased ability to observe his thoughts, emotions, and bodily sensations resulting from the practices learned and practiced during the program: "The practices clearly showed me that I can observe what I am feeling and experiencing…now I observe my bodily sensations, my emotions, and my thought." He also shared this: "I am more present in the little things of life…such as brushing my teeth, eating, walking… and I notice that I slow down."

The changes observed in the way he related to the present moment and with life were associated not only with this increased ability to be in the moment with more awareness and consciousness, but also with the increased acceptance towards his experiences and awareness of the impermanence of life: "I can see more deeply the degree of impermanence of life: it is everywhere…the practices helped me to see things in terms of my thoughts, emotions, and bodily sensations." In terms of acceptance, he reported an increased acceptance towards his emotions:

> I notice myself accepting more things that I feel and that I used to criticize or judge, because I thought they were not correct…and, although I still feel they are not, I accept that it is natural to have these feelings.

Increased acceptance towards himself was also reported: "I noticed that I tended to criticize myself a lot…in relation to things that I was not doing, things that I was feeling or thinking…and now I can look at these moments with more acceptance." I believe this highly critical perspective he experienced, like a sef-directed punishment, was related to the fact that he had had a very strict Catholic education. He shared this about his upbringing: "My family was very Catholic and my father was very strict in his education and expectations towards us in relation to our Catholic values." When he was younger he had applied to study to be a priest, but his parents did not have enough money to make the enrollment at that time, and this was something that was very traumatic for his life. He said that:

> The life I have is not what I dreamt or wanted for me, and a lot of frustration, resentment, and anger followed me throughout the years of my life, because I always wanted to be a priest…the program helped me to cultivate more acceptance towards these feelings.

Although he still had moments when he felt sad and frustrated when he looked back, now he was able to cultivate acceptance, release these emotions, and look at the good things he had achieved in his life, which revealed an increased positivity. He said that "I do not feel so angry or frustrated. These feelings sometimes arise…but I try to observe, breathe, and accept…release…it helps…not always, but it helps many times." Even when he remembered the moments of his life when he had suffered, such as when he had lost close relatives or when difficulties in his life were so challenging that he lived in emotional and physical pain, he shared that he has now noticed that bringing awareness to his breath and cultivating acceptance has helped him remember these moments with increased acceptance and internal harmony.

When questioned about the effects of the program, this participant shared that the program had had positive consequences in terms of his psychological and physical well-being, and in his social interactions. In terms of psychological well-being, he reported that the practices explored during the program had had an effect in terms of emotional balance, sense of peace, and serenity. He said that "emotionally, I feel calmer... I feel more balanced, present, and more serene" and that these emotional changes had also impacted his physical well-being, "as my head is not everywhere and I feel calmer... I think this also affected my physical sense of relaxation and calmness."

He also said that the ability to experience with increased awareness his daily life allowed him to live more and feel more of his life, "It is very interesting how you see life with mindfulness... I see more and live more my life," and to act with more discernment in several situations, in particular challenging ones when he feels more stressed or confused about what to do. He stated that:

> I noticed that being more aware of my experiences and in the present moment helped me to know better what to do and how to do it...as if the answer was clearly present...this was especially true in moments of stress that I experienced during the program.

This discernment and awareness was expanded to his social interactions, as exemplified in his comment that "I feel that even when I am with others I have more clarity in terms of what I want to say or what I should say," and that, as a consequence, this improved the quality of his relationships. In terms of social interactions he also shared that being more present when he was with others allowed him to be more compassionate, "I feel more present in the interaction with others, I am more careful with what I say to others in order not to hurt them or not to talk impulsively," and to show more gratitude towards others "For me it is important to show gratitude...and because through mindfulness I feel more the present moment... I am more attentive and aware of the situations [for which] I want to share that gratitude."

In terms of his physical well-being, increased physical relaxation, and ability to move, he commented that "I feel more free to move...this was more obvious when we started the yoga practices," more awareness of how to move, "the practices helped me to move with more consciousness," and respect for his limitations that are reflected in the increased concern in taking care of his body:

> I am more aware of when I am overdoing or doing things that I cannot... I also started taking care of myself better, taking care of my body by walking and doing yoga, and being more mindful of my eating habits.

He also reported feeling healthier: "I feel healthier as a result of feeling physically more relaxed, freer, flexible, and in shape." When asked about how he felt about his age, he said he did not feel his age, "I do not even remember," and that the only moments this was more present was when physically he felt his age limitations that did not allow him to do the things he did when he was 30 or 40. He said that the program helped him to be more present, observe his limitations, and respect these limitations, "without a doubt that it is important to listen to our body… to pay attention to what we are doing and listen to the limits of our body in order to protect and take care of our body." He also stated that: "the program made me feel even younger" because he felt more relaxed, flexible, and enjoying more the little things in life.

It was apparent throughout the interview, and even in some of the sessions of the program, that his spiritual practices, such as going to the Mass at the Catholic Church and the way he tried to apply the Catholic principles in his life (e.g., showing gratitude, being honest, etc.) were very important for him and guided his way of being and acting in his day-to-day life: "What I learned in my spiritual or religious practices means a lot to me and I try to bring these principles to my daily life, since I was very young." He shared that, as he became more present and aware of his experiences, due to his ability to be in the present moment, he also noticed that when he was praying the words he was repeating were not coming out automatically, he noticed that the words were repeated with a deeper meaning as if he was feeling the words in his heart. The same happened when he was at Mass listening to the sermon: rather than being lost in his thoughts about his life he felt an increased presence and awareness of what was being said.

In terms of his perception of existence and his life he shared that:

> It is a learning journey, a continuous learning journey… It is incredible to look back…see where I came from, the path I walked, and where I am…sometimes it was hard, other times less hard, but life is life, this…and the connection I have with God helped me a lot in these difficult moments… We see suffering everywhere, it is part of life…we suffer when we are physically unwell, when we lose others, when we are sad or depressed…but these experiences are the way God gives us to learn and grow…we need to trust God…and we need to help others through their suffering.

This commentary revealed that his spiritual beliefs were very important in the way he perceived life and his existence and the way he saw suffering as a natural way to learn and grow in life. His spiritual beliefs gave meaning to the experiences in his physical, psychological, and social world. He stated that, during this learning process (of life), he learned and grew a lot and that participating in the program had reinforced this already established perspective on life. He added this:

> At a stage in my life where I thought I had not a lot of things to learn, I had this opportunity to do the program and to learn to live life in a different way, to see me in a different way: with openness, gratitude, and acceptance... I see myself more deeply... Before, I was not aware of the interconnection with the body and mind... [but] now I can see that it is all connected...in the same way that we are all connected in life, through God.

He also showed an awareness of this interconnection and universality when he stated that all the actions that one takes affect someone else and that, because of this relationship between people, we all need to be conscious and aware of our actions. This interconnection made him feel grateful because "we are dependent on each other...we serve each other."

He continued to practice after the program ended and continued to cultivate his presence and awareness in his daily life: "I bring my attention to everything I do...brushing my teeth, walking, talking with others... it is a very positive exercise," thereby revealing that, not only did he continue to find time in his daily life for the formal practices, but he applied the principles and exercises learned in his daily routine. Overall, he stated that he felt more present, emotionally and physically better, and that "because all is interconnected...this impacts the way I life my life: [I] live my day-to-day life with more quality. I feel better generally: with more attention, more present, alive...calmer...relaxed."

The three words he used to summarize his experience and the effects of the program in his life were freedom, well-being, attention. The analysis of the interview revealed the following themes (see Table 4.4).

TABLE 4.4 PARTICIPANT ID NUMBER 13. THEMES AND DIMENSIONS

Themes	Dimensions
Mindfulness	Observation, presence, awareness/consciousness, attention, slowing down, decentering
Acceptance	Life, self, aging, pain, suffering, emotions
Impermanence	Life

cont.

TABLE 4.4 PARTICIPANT ID NUMBER 13:
THEMES AND DIMENSIONS *CONT.*

Themes	Dimensions
Psychological Well-Being	Peace/serenity, aliveness, balanced, positivity, discernment
Physical Well-Being	Health, relaxation, active, general habits, respect for limitations
Perceptions of Aging	Ageless
Spirituality	Interconnectedness/universality, purpose in life, growth and transformation, suffering
Social Interactions	Positive, gratitude, discernment, compassion
Daily Life	Regular formal and informal practice, quality of life
Overall Experience	Positive

Participant ID Number 14

Participant ID Number 14 was a 65-year-old male, Caucasian, married. He completed high school and was currently retired. His religious background was Catholic. At the initial assessment he reported suffering from hypertension and that he took medication to control this condition. During and after the MBSR program he did not experience any new illness and did not start any new medication. He did not have any previous experience in mindfulness meditation, and all the concepts presented during the program were new to him. He was present in all sessions of the program and his home practice compliance was 90 percent for the formal practices with the CDs and 86 percent for the informal practices, including the exercises to be completed in the manual.

This participant was very participative during all sessions: he was always very open to sharing his experiences and asked questions to clarify doubts and difficulties he experienced in relation to the concepts and the practices presented. In particular, this participant revealed great difficulty in understanding and embracing the concept of acceptance. During three sessions he always presented his concerns in relation to the concept, as he was experiencing difficulties in going beyond his established concept of the word being used. He always saw the word *acceptance* as implying complete and blind acceptance, without questioning or taking any action to change anything. He asked me "How can I accept violence in the world, children dying in Africa, or the corruption in the world?" In the context of the MBSR, acceptance did not imply passivity towards the reality being experienced or acknowledged. With respect to mindfulness, acceptance is about embracing the present experience because things are as they are in a particular moment and by accepting it, we experience that the emotional reaction is lessened, we gain the ability to respond to the situation with more discernment, and clarity is enhanced. The acceptance and ability to embrace is what allows us to have more clarity about the reality being experienced. It does not mean that we cannot or should not do anything to change a reality we do not agree with but that, by accepting it, we are in a better position to act with more assertiveness. Although he mentally understood that concept, in his heart it was difficult to own the ability to accept the injustices he saw in the world. Gradually, as he progressed in the practices, he was more able to embody the meaning implied in this context.

During the interview, he stated that the program was a surprise to him. He had thought he was going to learn interesting concepts and practices, but it was a surprise to him the impact that all the learning principles and practices had had in his life. He stated that: "I was sure that it was going to be interesting, in particular because it was all very new to me, but it went beyond any expectation I had... It was an amazing and revealing experience." He referenced the fact that for him the main concepts that had impacted his way of experiencing life and seeing things was the notion of being in the present moment: "Learning to be in the present moment was so important to me... I learned to see things in a different way, to see myself and others in a different way...to see life in a completely new perspective," and the notion of acceptance: "The concept of acceptance was hard for me to embrace and understand, but slowly I realized what it meant...not the meaning of the word and of the words you used to explain the concept, but I understood it in my heart... I was able to experience what it meant to accept and not meaning passivity." He explained how being in the present moment had changed his experience of his life: "By being in the present moment I started to notice more... to see things more profoundly, because I was not always rushing to get somewhere or doing something...and always thinking about what I was going to do next." He learned to be in the present moment in his daily life with more attention and awareness of what was happening inside and outside: "Now I can observe how I feel in my mind and body... I feel what I am doing, sometimes even the environment around me... the sounds." By being in the moment and connecting with his present-moment experience he was able to slow down: "It is obvious to me that

I slowed down... I do not rush from one thing to another... I am more present...more attentive to what I do." He shared that there were still moments when he became aware that he was living in the same patterns of rushing, doing things automatically, and getting lost in thoughts about what he had to do afterward, but there were moments when he was present and able to observe what was arising. He stated that: "when my mind is wondering I am more aware of this movement... I am able to recognize when I am no longer in the present moment and I come back to the now." He was aware that this was not an easy process and that he still had much learning ahead of him, but he recognized the value of the changes he noticed in his life and in his ability to experience his life:

> It is amazing what I feel when I am focused in the present moment... it seems that nothing else is there, my concerns, my doubts, my fears... I am in the moment, really living my life. I know that there is still a lot to be learned, but I am grateful for the changes I am already experiencing in the way I experience my daily life.

He shared that the first moment he realized he truly understood the concept of acceptance was during a meditation practice when he was observing some thoughts and emotions he was having. He was not pleased with himself about the thoughts he was having because they were unwholesome and judgmental about some people close to him:

> I noticed that I accepted myself for having those thoughts... I accepted my imperfection and inability to control these thoughts... because in my heart I truly did not feel that way...at this moment I understood that acceptance was not sitting still and not wanting to change anything... I felt that I was accepting myself for not being perfect, and at the same time, I wanted to be a better person...to find ways of being that better person... I noticed that finding time to Be with myself during the practices [was] important...because I could be experiencing moments of being able to be with myself...with an awareness and capacity of observation that I never experienced before.

This revealed not only that the moments of practice had allowed him to find space and time to be with himself but also that it had helped him to cultivate an increased awareness about himself, his thoughts, his emotions, and accept his imperfections. He also stated that this increased acceptance was observed towards his life and the moments he suffered:

> I started to look at my life, the things I liked and the things I did not like...or even moments of deep suffering...with more acceptance...

> Clearly there are still moments when I feel frustrated and sad about the things I did not achieve or was unable to experience, or even things I experienced when I was young that were very painful, but... I notice that sometimes when these memories arise... I focus on my breath and there is acceptance...my body releases.

He mentioned that these painful experiences were related to the loss of his older sister when he was 12 years old. When he talked about this event, he cried, and he then shared that, in retrospect and observing his experiences during mindfulness practices, he could recognize the impermanent flow of life that had been discussed during the program. He said, "Impermanence is painful...not only because our life is constantly changing, but also because we see people we love suffer and passing away." Not only did he show an increased perception and awareness of the impermanence of life, but he demonstrated that attitude also towards death: "I can look back and feel more acceptance towards her [his sister's] death... I am able to recognize my pain because I was really young... I think I accept because I look at it and feel more at ease," and he noted that he now recognized that death is a reality of life: "Now I accept death and recognize that it is part of the life process."

He revealed that the participation in the program had affected his psychological well-being, as he felt an increased sense of peace and serenity, "I feel more peaceful...especially after practicing, but even during my day-to-day life...if I am more agitated I remember to breathe...to focus on the breath...and I feel calmer," as well as a sense of being more alive: "I live more...because I am more present in my day-to-day life," more balanced, and with increased discernment:

> I do not feel so agitated emotionally...even in moments of stress... I feel that I am more able to stay balanced...observe what is arising and then act with more awareness. There are moments that there is still difficulty and I react impulsively, but I recognize this after... As you told us several times...this is an ongoing learning process.

This increased discernment affected his social interactions, as he stated that: "because I am more present I also notice more what happens when I am with other people...when I talk or when they talk... I notice when I react emotionally or when I am about to react... This allows me to have a better perspective of things and act with more clarity." This increased awareness improved his social interaction, in particular with close relatives with whom he had difficult interactions: "I noticed that my interactions improved, in particular with my daughters with whom I tended to argue very often... I notice and they notice." He also realized that, because of his increased acceptance towards himself, he was also more compassionate and comprehensible towards others: "This was not immediate, but when I think about it... I notice that I am more comprehensible and accepting... towards others...if I make mistakes...others do, too... We are all human beings...we make mistakes."

His increased ability to be in the present moment and observe his moment-to-moment experience helped him cultivate an increasing capacity to recognize the good things in his life:

> I realized that I tended [before] to focus on the negative aspects of my life... I was always complaining about this or that... The exercises we made on focusing on the positive events of our lives helped me train myself to do this every day... Now I recognize that every day there are things that I can smile at...and be happy for... not everything is bad... Thank God!

He shared that the increased sense of calmness he was experiencing in his life was also affecting his physical well-being, as he realized that he was not accumulating as much tension in his body (e.g., shoulders) as he had before. He said, "I think that because I feel calmer emotionally, my body is not so tense...also the practice with the CD1 helps me relax, but I feel that even when I do not use that CD... I feel more relaxed...healthier." He associated this healthier feeling with the yoga practices explored during the program, the fact that he started doing yoga on a regular basis in a center near his house, and also the moments he had every day to be with himself during the meditation practices: "I am more active physically... I started doing yoga in a center near my house. I am more careful about my time and my needs. I always try to have time for myself every day...to be quiet and in silence." Moreover, he shared that "the practices allowed me to be more present with my body... I am more aware of what I need, so I tend to respect more what my body is saying...and because of that I feel healthier." He also revealed an increased awareness and respect for his bodily limitations, "I accept my limits... I try not to push myself to do things I know I am not well [enough] to do," improvements in the quality of his sleep as a result of feeling emotionally and physically more relaxed, and an increased acceptance towards physical pain:

> I remember in some practices my body would start hurting... I used the techniques presented...breathing in to the pain, breathing out and releasing...it helped me be with the physical pain with more

acceptance...well, sometimes I was not successful and I moved my posture to relieve the pain...but other times it worked!

When questioned about his experience of being his age, he stated, "I do not even remember my age... I feel young inside, in particular when I am with my grandchildren." He shared that he knew he was getting old and that his physical body was giving signs of his age, but generally he felt good, and he noticed that what had changed most in his life with age was the way he looked at life: "I know that physically I changed with age, but, when I look back, my perspective of life is so much different...more mature, more experienced...more balanced."

Spiritually, he revealed that the Catholic values he was taught at a young age were still very present and guided him in difficult moments of his life: "What my parents taught me about the basic values of life... the meaning of life...they always gave meaning to my life and helped me deal with difficult moments I experienced throughout life...loss, pain, disease." He did not attend Church on a regular basis, as he believed that more important than going to the Mass every week was to behave according to his beliefs in his daily life: "I do not feel the need to go to the Church every weekend... I know that more important than that is what I do every day...what I bring in my heart." He shared that: "it is in the everyday living that we can find the answer to our existence, to what we are doing here." According to his view "Life is a journey...a journey with a beginning and an end... The journey itself is the purpose...a purpose for learning and growing...for Being who we really are... The MBSR reinforced this idea I already had." Completing the program allowed him to reinforce the belief of the importance of his daily actions, as he was even more focused on the moment-to-moment experience of his daily life. He believed that human beings are united in some invisible plane, as we are all sons and daughters of God and, with the practices of the program, "We are all connected and interrelated... It is true that we forget...and being in the program allowed |us| to be more present with this reality...the reality that we are One." He stated that the raisin mindful eating exercise (an exercise presented during the first session of the MBSR program where participants mindfully eat three raisins), allowed him to pay more attention to the physical extension of this interconnection, as we all depend on each other for everything: "Some are plumbers, some are doctors, others are fishers... We all play a role and what one does has an effect on the other."

After the program was completed, he continued to maintain a regular practice of meditation: "I continue to meditate…not every day as I used to do during the program, but I keep a regular practice," and he continues to maintain and cultivate the ability to be in the present moment in his day-to-day tasks. Overall, he noticed that the program improved his general well-being and that, because of his increased ability to be in the present moment, the practice had improved the way he relates to life, which impacted his life positively "Generally, I feel better… I appreciate life better…my life improved." The three words or phrases used to summarize his experience and effects of the program were presence, acceptance, seeing life. The analysis of the interview revealed the following themes (see Table 4.5).

TABLE 4.5 PARTICIPANT ID NUMBER 14: THEMES AND DIMENSIONS

Themes	Dimensions
Mindfulness	Observation, decentering, presence, awareness/consciousness, attention, slowing down, Be
Acceptance	Life, self, aging, pain, emotions, suffering
Impermanence	Life
Psychological Well-Being	Peace/serenity, aliveness, balanced, positivity, discernment, identity (transpersonal self)
Physical Well-Being	Health, relaxation, active, general habits, respect for limitations, sleep
Perceptions of Aging	Ageless, wisdom, death
Spirituality	Transpersonal self, interconnectedness/universality, purpose in life, growth and transformation, suffering
Social Interactions	Positive, discernment, compassion
Daily Life	Regular formal and informal practice, quality of life
Overall Experience	Positive

Participant ID Number 16

Participant ID Number 16 was a 73-year-old female, Caucasian, single, with a graduate degree in religious studies, and currently retired. Her religious background was Catholic, but she had always been interested in different religions and read a lot about different religious perspectives (e.g., Western and Eastern). At the initial assessment she reported suffering from diabetes and hepatitis C and was taking medication for diabetes. During and after the MBSR program she did not experience any new illness and did not start any new medication. She had practiced meditation before but did not have a regular practice of meditation. Given her educational background and personal interest in religious philosophy, the concepts presented during the study were not unfamiliar to her. She was present in all sessions of the program and her home practice compliance was 87 percent for the formal practices with the CDs and 70 percent for the informal practices, including the exercises to be completed in the manual.

This participant was very participative throughout the sessions and, given her knowledge of the concepts presented as a result of her educational background and personal interest in religious philosophies and its practices for personal development, she shared with the other participants her own experiences in applying some of the concepts in her life. She clearly revealed an already established awareness and ability to be with herself, given that she had been involved in contemplative practices before in her life and considering the previous meditation practice she had. When she enrolled in the study she did not have a regular practice of meditation, and one of her objectives was to re-establish this routine in her life. I noticed that many times her questions were asking for deeper and more profound discussions on the issue of acceptance, life, and existence and its relation with mindfulness practices (formal and informal), but it was clear for both of us that, given the group context, these discussions were not expanded. At the interview she stated: "I really enjoyed participating in the program... But I feel I wanted more...a group that was more participative, stronger, and more profound... It was a very heterogeneous group," because some of the questions, concerns, and difficulties they presented throughout the sessions were perceived as "basic" for this participant, which is normal given the level of experience that other participants had had of mindfulness meditation. Even so, it was clear that she was enjoying the program and, throughout the sessions, she shared how gratifying it was to be there and to learn about mindfulness in the way that was being presented. She stated in one of the sessions: "For me it's amazing how the program was developed and how it presents the formal practices, and how it foments the informal application of the concepts... I see how deeply this is affecting my daily life...how I am going deeper into embracing the concepts and experiencing them in deeper layers of my existence." She expanded a little on "deeper layers of her existence," saying that it had to do with the meaning she attributed to life, existence, and reality and how she experienced this in her moment-to-moment experiences.

During the interview she revealed that one of the main impacts of the program was related to acceptance towards the other participants in the group. She stated that: "participating in the program was a challenge for me…to my capacity of being flexible and [having] adaptability towards the group…of tolerance and acceptance of their rhythm" given that she recognized that she tended to be demanding of others and tended not to respect their natural rhythm. She added that: "it was a learning process of respect for others, for their rhythm, and for the differences between us all…because we are all different, but part of the same nature, of Oneness." She felt afterward more open towards others, open to accept the differences between individuals. Furthermore, this acceptance expanded to accepting her tendency to be demanding and inflexible with others: "I was able to do a profound work of accepting myself for being this way… demanding and inflexible towards others." As a consequence, she observed that, throughout the program, she was more tolerant and respectful of others, some of her social interactions improved and were more positive, and she noticed that the increased ability to observe what was arising in each passing moment allowed her to have more discerning and assertive responses when interacting with others. She added this explanation:

> I can better observe myself when I am interacting with others… I cultivate acceptance and when I notice my inflexibility and intolerance arising… I breathe… I try to bring my awareness to the moment and observe from a broader perspective… This allows me to act and respond mindfully to what is present.

The mindfulness practice was experienced as an essential moment in her daily life, as it was the moment when "she met with herself" by finding time to be in stillness and silence. She added that:

> With meditation I make that invitation to be with myself in that moment, moment-by-moment, in silence…with the formal practice this being with myself is extended and prolonged throughout the rest of the day…and the more I practice the easier it is to come back to that moment of being with myself, in stillness.

She started practicing regularly, almost every day, and, as a result, she noticed an increased and deeper capacity to observe and be aware of her moment-to-moment experience throughout the day: "I observe myself more and more deeply—my emotions, my bodily sensations, my limits when I am doing certain things…now that I am more attentive I take care of myself much better." She also shared these observations:

> I am aware of things more quickly...everything seems to arise in a more gentle way, my awareness, my capacity for being in the present moment, my ability to observe my experiences and myself...and to pay attention to what is arising within myself and outside in the world... It arises more naturally...even my ability to observe my thoughts comes out more naturally...the ability to shift my attention from one object to the other is more gentle and effortless... Before, when I learned to practice and during the period I practiced regularly...it was not so easy.

She recognized that there were still moments in which she was performing things on automatic pilot, but she was quicker to recognize this disconnection with herself and the present moment, and she gently brought the attention to what she was doing. This increased ability of meta-wareness and decentering allowed her to experience the reality of the impermanence of life in deeper ways:

> Sometimes I sit in the park... I intentionally bring my attention to the breath...bring my awareness to the present moment...then I gently shift my attention to observe the things around me...and I notice the constant movement of everything around me: sounds, people, clouds...everything is changing constantly... I can see myself changing at the same time things are changing.

She reported that the improvements of her ability to experience the present moment fomented her capacity to change and adapt to new rhythms and that she moved beyond her comfort zone, such as when meeting certain people that she avoided because it would cause pressure and facing challenging circumstances. She also changed the rhythm of her daily routine in order to foment her flexibility, and began to work on that within the group. She stated, "I gradually changed some of my routines, such as what I eat for breakfast, where I sit to read, when I meditate... I am trying to foment my flexibility."

She suggested that the meditation practice was very important for her spiritual development and that, as a result of this developmental process, she had observed in herself an increased acceptance towards life, pain, and suffering, as well as increased awareness of interconnection among all the manifestations of life. She said this in that regard:

> I have always been interested in the spiritual aspect of my life...and for me meditation is a tool in this spiritual developmental process because I can observe myself and the world better...know me better.

> With the regular practice I notice more deeply the interconnection between all manifestations of life…it helps me to be present in this journey of life…helps me to enjoy each moment…to appreciate the beauty of life with all its difficulties and moments of happiness… It helps to accept all this…the difficulties, the pain, my emotions… life! Accept the constant impermanence of life…the changes inside and outside…even the changes in my body…acceptance of myself.

She also manifested that this increased awareness and connection with herself and the world fomented her well-being, as she felt more calm, serene, flexible, and patient: "with the regular practice I became more serene, calmer…more flexible and patient with myself and others." She noticed that she was more balanced emotionally: "I feel less irritated." She was aware that the emotional and physical bodies were constantly interrelating with one another and noticed that with the regular practices this awareness improved. In this line, she suggested that, as a result of her feeling more balanced emotionally and calmer, she also noticed that, physically, she felt healthier, more relaxed, and active: "We know that our emotions are constantly affecting the body, and the other way around… With the practices I noticed that I felt better emotionally, more balanced… calmer…and maybe as a consequence I felt healthier and more relaxed in my body." She added that: "Physically, I also feel calmer…as if my body is more relaxed, more at ease" and "I feel more dynamic…not only cognitively but physically. The yoga and the meditation helped me have more energy, and because of that I feel more active…healthier."

This participant was a writer and she was currently finishing her second book. She revealed that, when the program started, she had been stuck in her writing process and that, as she gradually adapted a regular practice and noticed all the described changes in her life and well-being, she also recognized that she felt more creative and dynamic in her work: "I feel more creative and dynamic… I returned to my book writing and it was flowing very well."

When asked about her experience of being her age, she laughed, replying that she does not feel the age she is. She stated: "I feel very well with my age… I feel good with my life…in the end of the day, our age is how we experience life inside…our head…in our spirit… I feel young." She added that:

> Life is a learning journey…and in this journey I learned about Being—TO BE—to be happy in my intrinsic nature, my nature as a sentient being… The more important things, apart from my age, is

> the learning, the wisdom and the discernment age brings... Today I feel that I am living life in a different way...with more clarity, more balance...less impulsivity... I accept things better, accept suffering...life...death...aging... I accept myself...because all that is in our material plane of existence...in reality I am much more than that... I am a spiritual being...evolving and learning in this life.

She revealed that she was very happy with her life and with what she had achieved. She showed tears of happiness while sharing how happy, as she said that:

> It was a long journey...a very hard and long journey to get where I am today...to live the purpose of my life: learning, knowing me, being, and realizing myself...a journey with a lot of tears, pain, suffering...always going up, up, up...with a lot of strength and resilience.

She revealed gratitude for those who had helped her in this process, to overcome certain obstacles in her life, to all that crossed her path, but, most of all, she said: "I am grateful to life...to the life force that guided me in this journey." It was this belief that her life's purpose was to grow and evolve as a sentient being and the belief that this life force was guiding her in this journey that gave meaning to her experiences in her life. She said that "Walking the path of life... I found me, got to know me...saw beyond my physical, emotional, and mental bodies... and had a glimpse of the true nature of my existence...connected with everything." The program did not change all this perception of life and existence, but reinforced these views, as she had realized that: "I feel more deeply connected with my present moment, with myself, as a result of the practices... I see more...and I am able to experience my body, mind, emotions, and spirit interacting in each passing moment."

Overall, she stated: "I feel more tolerant and open, more alive, more present...more aware of myself, others, and the connection between everything." The three words used to summarize her experience and the effects of the program were flexibility, present, and connection. The analysis of the interview revealed the following themes (see Table 4.6).

TABLE 4.6 PARTICIPANT ID NUMBER 16: THEMES AND DIMENSIONS

Themes	Dimensions
Mindfulness	Observation, decentering, presence, awareness/consciousness, attention, Be
Acceptance	Life, self, aging, pain, suffering, others
Impermanence	Life
Psychological Well-Being	Peace/serenity, aliveness, balanced, flexibility to change, patient, identity (transpersonal self)
Physical Well-Being	Health, relaxation, active
Perceptions of Aging	Ageless, wisdom, death
Spirituality	Transpersonal self, interconnectedness/universality, purpose in life, growth and transformation, suffering
Social Interactions	Positive, discernment, adaptability, tolerance, openness, acceptance, respect
Daily Life	Regular formal and informal practice, quality of life
Overall Experience	Positive

Participant ID Number 18

Participant ID Number 18 was a 67-year-old female, Caucasian, single, with nine years of education, and currently retired. Her religious background was Catholic. At the initial assessment she reported suffering from hypertension and that she was taking medication to control this condition. During and after the MBSR program, she did not experience any new illness and did not start any new medication. A few weeks before being recruited to the study, Participant ID Number 18 had lost her father, whom she she had cared for over several years, and she had been present during his passing. She did not have any previous experience in mindfulness meditation, and all the concepts presented during the program were new to her. She was present in all sessions of the program and her home practice compliance was 100 percent for the formal practices and 100 percent for the informal practices, including the exercises to be completed in the manual.

This participant was very quiet during all sessions. She shared her experience when asked to, in pairs and to the entire group, but never asked questions or raised any concerns. Before and after the sessions, she always engaged in conversations with me and other participants. Overall, she did not show any major difficulties in terms of practice, and throughout the eight weeks she revealed that she was enjoying the program.

At the initial interview she shared that she felt depressed and still going through her grieving process, due to her father's death, but she also said that in some ways she had been already prepared for his death, because her father had been unwell for some time and she knew that he would not last very long.

She shared that: "the experience was very positive" and that, although the themes and principles were very new to her, she had noticed that: "I was able to absorb and apply them to my daily life very naturally." She said that the main effects of the program in her life were the increased ability to experience the present moment: "I notice that I learned to live life in a different way… I am more present…now. I notice that, but, before, I was always worried about getting to…the future." She also shared that, with the practices: "I observe myself more and more deeply—my emotions, my bodily sensations, my limits when I am doing certain things… Now that I am more attentive, I take care of myself much better," and she noted that, in moments when she is in the future, she quickly becomes aware of it, because, in these moments:

> I feel more nervous…agitated…and that manifests not only emotionally, but physically. I feel tenser… I notice my thoughts arising more quickly… In the moments when I feel disconnected, I stop…even if it's just for a few seconds… I observe the breath, return to the present moment…and I feel everything slowing down inside me and my body relaxing… This returning to the breath is almost automatic… I do not need to think too much about it… I stop, breathe, and here I am…in the present.

She realized that, having participated in the program, she now does things:

> More calmly…with more awareness and consciousness… Of course I still do many things in automatic pilot, but I recognize these moments…and quickly come back to the moment…bringing my awareness to what I am doing…and I feel myself slowing down and returning to what I am doing.

Moreover, she shared that she was more aware of her emotional and physical bodies: "I feel more conscious emotionally…more aware of my body… I am more attentive to the way I feel emotionally, the interaction between the emotions I am having and my well-being…my physical body." She added "I can also observe my thoughts... This is more difficult, but I see how they impact my well-being and the way I experience my daily life." This awareness was also observed by her in terms of the way she interacted with others:

> I also feel more present when I am with others...especially with my daughter, I notice that, before, I was always projecting my own stress and emotional conflicts towards her...because she lives with me and is the closest person I have... Now I am more patient and I actually do the exercise of being more careful in terms of my emotions and how I react when I am with her. This awareness and bringing my attention to the breath allow me to act more calmly and with more clarity...less impulsively...or emotionally.

She also observed that this increased presence and attention influenced her presence at Mass and when she was praying:

> I noticed a lot of difference when I pray... I remember that, before the program started, I decided to stop praying at home because I recognized that after a few minutes I was repeating the words automatically and thinking about all sorts of things...but not praying... This was not good! Now I am present... I notice the thoughts arising and sometimes I even get lost in them, but I am there...present with the words and with my intention.

It was clear to her that this increased attention, awareness, and capacity to be in the moment-to-moment experience was having positive effects in her life not only in terms of the quality of her social interactions, in particular with her daughter, but also in terms of her psychological and physical well-being. She stated that: "emotionally I feel calmer... more serene... I no longer feel that imminent stress and anxiety. I feel less irritated," and that "the retuning to the Now... I feel it is living... I am living more." Physically, she stated, she felt "more relaxed...lighter, released!" and, as a consequence, she felt healthier "I feel healthier... I think because emotionally and physically I am more relaxed." She became more aware and respectful of her body: "Now I observe my body, I notice what it is saying to me...and things that I used to do before, without even realizing that I was pushing myself too much... now I recognize these moments... I stop and respect if I need to rest or do things more slowly." She also reported that her sleep improved:

> I noticed a great impact in my sleep...before I always had great difficulties falling asleep... I went to bed and I used to stay awake

for hours thinking about my day…the day after…things I had to sort out or things that were worrying me… Now I notice that when I go to bed my mind is calmer and I can easily fall asleep.

She also shared that the participation in the program had a great impact in terms of how she accepted and faced her father's death. She elaborated on that observation:

> As you know, my father passed away a few weeks before the program started…and it was very important for me, the concept of acceptance…and of looking at the positive side of our experience in life… It helped me overcome this difficult moment of my life with more calm and serenity. This acceptance helped not only in terms of accepting his death, because deep down I knew this was something that was going to happen very soon…but also it helped me accept how I was feeling and emotionally responding to the situation. For example, there were moments when I felt sad and cried when I thought about my father…when images came up in my mind of moments I was taking care of him in my house… They were painful… I accepted them and all the emotions that arose rather than repressing and thinking that I was not being strong enough… I felt myself surrendering to these emotions…accepting and being with these emotions…with the pain…the emptiness…and breathing in and out…accepting… I was able to experience these emotions releasing…feeling peace… I remembered the discussions we had about impermanence…and I could see that life is impermanent in every way…not only in terms of life and death…but every moment there is always something changing… I could see my emotions changing…in that precise moment… And death…it is painful and hard to experience the loss of a loved one… It is scary even…but it is part of life.

She shared some difficulties of her life, such as having to raise her daughter on her own because her partner did not assume his parental responsibilities and had different priorities in his life. She shared this about accepting those circumstances:

> I thought I had accepted this before, but during the program these thoughts came up…and I saw that I was actually accepting this… in a deeper and more profound way…accepting my suffering and the way my life turned out during that period in my life.

She revealed great happiness and satisfaction with her life in the midst of all the difficulties and obstacles she had had to overcome and face in her life, and she loved being her age. As she stated it:

> I do not feel my age... I am happy. I am very happy with my age... I feel very happy with my life, with my journey and learning throughout these years... The program allowed me to recognize even more profoundly this gratitude I have towards life and accept all the difficulties I have experienced. There were a lot of difficult moments, but they are part of life... I always fought and walked with strength...because I knew that I was never alone... God was guiding me and giving me the strength I needed... Looking back and looking to my life right now... I am happy and fulfilled. I love to live, to serve and help others.

She also said that the concept of acceptance helped her face her physical limitations and pain associated with age with more acceptance. After the end of the program, she had a pain in her knee that was limiting her movements and slowing down her normal pace. She said that: "this situation with my knee, I have been cultivating acceptance towards what is happening and I am calmly waiting for it to recover and come back to my normal pace in life."

Helping others was a very important part of her life. She had spent several years taking care of her frail and dependent father, volunteering at Church, and now, a few months after his death, she was already looking for other places to provide the same kind of support to frail older adults. She explained that intention:

> Helping others is very important for me... I always felt that we need to be here for each other...to show our compassion and love towards other human beings because we are all living the same journey...suffering...we are all part of God's creation... Helping is in my nature; it gives me strength and courage in my own life.

For her, life was a journey of learning and growth: "For me, life is a learning process, a journey that we need to complete to grow and evolve as spiritual beings." Participating in the program confirmed and reinforced these beliefs. She shared her thoughts in that regard:

> I have always tried to focus on the good things of life and on the value of our journey as individual and spiritual beings...on the fact that life is a learning process and even if difficult moments arise...it

does not matter... It will always be a beautiful journey...because we are doing what we were meant to do...learn and experience life... experience how we are all deeply connected with each other...due to our spiritual nature... We're are interrelated to nature, to others, to animals... Every action we have interferes and affects everything around us.

Again, spiritually, she noticed that the program had affected her life:

Spiritually, I noticed changes... I feel more connected with everything around me. I notice things more, I look at myself and see myself in ways I was never aware before... I recognize much more easily the interconnection between my thoughts, emotions, and physical body... I feel the connection between these expressions of my being... I always felt connected with others, but now this is present more deeply... We are One manifestation of God's creation.

Overall, she stated that the participation in the program had impacted her ability to be in the present moment with more calm and tranquility, that she observes herself better, including her emotions, bodily sensations, and thoughts, and the ability to accept life:

I feel that these principles are so simple and true...concepts that arise from our own capacity of living in harmony... It is amazing how unaware I was about all these things, and now that I am aware I recognize the importance they have in my life.

The three words or phrases that she used to summarize her experience and the effects of the program in her life were: presence, perception of life and everything in her daily life, and tranquility/serenity. The analysis of the interview revealed the following themes (see Table 4.7).

TABLE 4.7 PARTICIPANT ID NUMBER 18: THEMES AND DIMENSIONS

Themes	Dimensions
Mindfulness	Observation, decentering, presence, awareness/consciousness, attention, slowing down
Acceptance	Life, emotions, pain, suffering, loss
Impermanence	Life
Psychological Well-Being	Peace/serenity, aliveness, balanced, positivity, discernment

cont.

TABLE 4.7 PARTICIPANT ID NUMBER 18:
THEMES AND DIMENSIONS *CONT.*

Themes	Dimensions
Physical Well-Being	Health, relaxation, sleep, respect for limitations
Perceptions of Aging	Ageless, death
Spirituality	Transpersonal self, interconnectedness/universality, purpose in life, growth and transformation, suffering
Social Interactions	Presence, attention, positive, discernment
Daily Life	Regular formal and informal practice, quality of life
Overall Experience	Positive

Global results

The stages of immersion, incubation, and illumination, which were explained in Chapter 2, allowed me to identify the main themes that emerged from the seven interviews, which resulted in a creative synthesis of the phenomenon being investigated, as is presented in Table 4.19 and as a poem.

Be
Experience the flow of life
Embrace all that arises
Openly
Receptively

Accept life, yourself, others . . .
The clouds
The sun
Life
Death
The beginning . . . and the end
There is no end . . .

Experience yourself
Changing, growing
Connected, embodied
Here

Mind and emotions
Body and heart
You know who you are
Your essence . . .
Spirit, Energy, Light

Follow the path
Find your meaning, your purpose
Find yourself

Be still
Breathe
Connect
Listen. . .
Shhhh. . .
What is it saying???
I AM!

(Martins, 2012; unpublished)

Each theme identified is explained in the next section, and examples of significant statements from participants' interviews are presented, each followed by that participant's code number. From the seven interviews, I identified three core themes: mindfulness, acceptance, and impermanence. These core themes had an effect on secondary categories that constituted the secondary themes: psychological well-being, physical well-being, perceptions of aging, spirituality, social interactions, and daily life. Each core theme and secondary theme included several dimensions.

The three core themes were determined based on the participants' answers during the interviews. When interviewees were asked to share their experience of the MBSR program (which was the first question of the interview protocol), they all mentioned that, with the program, they were more present in their daily lives, more mindful of the things they experienced moment-to-moment and of how they were more accepting of things, and aware of the impermanence of their daily experience. These major learning principles that were cultivated during the program affected their lives in several domains, and these constituted the secondary themes. These domains were indicated in the interviews when participants were asked about the effects of the program in their daily lives. They all reported effects in terms of psychological and physical health, social interactions, aging, and spirituality. The spiritual effects were more present in participants' replies when they were questioned about the impact of the program in terms of their views and experience of life. The impact of the program in terms of perceptions of aging was more present when questioned about the effects of the program on how they were experiencing this stage of life.

Core themes

Three core themes were identified: mindfulness, acceptance, and impermanence. These themes are explored below, including the description of their respective dimensions. It is important to note that the same statement can refer to different themes and different dimensions; they are not exclusively descriptive of any one theme.

MINDFULNESS

All participants revealed that the participation in the MBSR program and the regular practice of mindfulness had promoted their ability to be mindful of their present-moment experience. They reported increased capacities of observation, presence, and attention, as well as an increased awareness and consciousness of their present-moment experiences. This increased mindfulness was recognized in relation to their emotions, thoughts, bodily sensations, and interaction between mind and body, among others. Furthermore, they shared an increased ability to slow down in their daily lives and to be in the present moment with themselves rather than only being engaged in doing. This ability to be in the present moment allowed them to see themselves and life more deeply and appreciate their life more. Examples of significant statements from participants' interviews for this theme and respective dimensions are presented in Table 4.8.

TABLE 4.8 MINDFULNESS AND RESPECTIVE DIMENSIONS:
EXAMPLES OF SIGNIFICANT STATEMENTS

Core Theme	Dimension	Significant Statements
Mindfulness	Observation	"I observe these feelings, observe these memories." (ID Number 2) "I observe myself more and more deeply—my emotions, my bodily sensations, my limits when I am doing certain things… now that I am more attentive I take care of myself much better." (ID Number 18) "My attention is more often in the present moment." (ID Number 16)
	Decentering	"I am more able to observe what is happening in my present-moment experience rather than emotionally reacting to what is occurring… I stop and observe, I act with more awareness and discernment." (ID Number 7) "Sometimes the automatic pilot starts and my mind goes around and around the emotions I am feeling… As soon as I realize that, I stop and breathe… I focus on the present moment and try to observe what is arising…observing and letting it go." (ID Number 14)
	Attention	"I see life with more attention…everything that I experience… I see with more attention." (ID Number 13) "I started to be more attentive to the things I experience in my daily life: the things I do, my interactions with others, my emotions, my body, my mind." (ID Number 7)
	Presence	"The MBSR helped me to get in touch with the present moment… I learned to bring mindfulness to the present moment." (ID Number 2) "I am more present in the things I do while I do it… I am more present in the day-to-day living." (ID Number 13)

cont.

TABLE 4.8 MINDFULNESS AND RESPECTIVE DIMENSIONS: EXAMPLES OF SIGNIFICANT STATEMENTS *CONT.*

Core Theme	Dimension	Significant Statements
	Awareness/ Consciousness	"When my mind is wandering, I am more aware of this movement... I am able to recognize when I am no longer in the present moment and I come back to the now." (ID Number 14) "We see more and more deeply... I am more aware of my emotions, thoughts, feelings, bodily sensations... I move more consciously and act more consciously." (ID Number 8)
	Slowing Down	"I feel much more present in the little things I do in life: while washing my teeth, eating, walking...and I observe that I slow down." (ID Number 3) "It is obvious to me that I slowed down... I do not rush from one thing to another... I am more present... more attentive to what I do...and, as a consequence, I feel that I slowed down a lot." (ID Number 14)
	Be	"The mindfulness practices allowed me to find time to be with myself...with my inner self." (ID Number 7) "In the moments when I feel disconnected I stop...even if it just for a few seconds... I observe the breath, return to the present moment...and I feel everything slowing down inside me and my body relaxing." (ID Number 18)

ACCEPTANCE

All participants shared that the participation in the MBSR program fomented their ability to be more accepting of their present-moment experiences. This acceptance was observed towards life, self, aging, emotions, pain, and suffering. Suffering was seen as being an integral part of life and a way through which, as individual beings, we experience life and learn. At the initial assessment two participants revealed that a close relative had died during the prior month. Only these two participants revealed that the MBSR program had helped them deal with their loss, because they had shared that they were grieving during the program. Given the relevance of their statement at the final interview, I decided to include this secondary theme in the global results. Examples of significant statements from participants' interviews for this theme and respective dimensions are outlined in Table 4.9.

TABLE 4.9 ACCEPTANCE AND RESPECTIVE DIMENSIONS: EXAMPLES OF SIGNIFICANT STATEMENTS

Core Theme	Dimension	Significant Statements
Acceptance	Life	"I became more accepting and flexible before life." (ID Number 16) "My life was very difficult…but now I look back and accept life for what it was and what it taught me." (ID Number 13)
	Self	"I accept myself… I observe when thoughts of condemnation arise… I accept them and it helps to accept myself." (ID Number 14) "I learned to accept myself with my virtues and with my failures… There is no right or wrong [event]… but a continuity of experiences." (ID Number 2)
	Aging	"But even when these changes happen I hope to face them with acceptance and lightly." (ID Number 2) "I do not feel my age…but when things happen physically and I feel more limited I notice that." (ID Number 13)
	Loss	"The MBSR course helped me to get in touch with the present moment…to reconnect with the reality… and with myself…mmmm… and most importantly to accept his death." (ID Number 2) "Finally, participating in the program also had a significant impact in the way I accepted my father's death… As you know, he passed away a few weeks before the MBSR started." (ID Number 18)
	Emotions	"I am more able to accept the way I feel emotionally." (ID Number 18) "The practices help me to accept my emotions when I become worried about things." (ID Number 7)

cont.

TABLE 4.9 ACCEPTANCE AND RESPECTIVE DIMENSIONS: EXAMPLES OF SIGNIFICANT STATEMENTS *CONT.*

Core Theme	Dimension	Significant Statements
	Pain	"I notice that when I have some physical pain, I am more able to observe and accept what I am feeling, which helps to release tension." (ID Number 8) "You know that I had a back pain crisis during the program... I noticed that I was more accepting of what was happening...of the pain and the limitations it was bringing." (ID Number 7)
	Suffering	"We suffer but it is part of life." (ID Number 18) "I suffered a lot during my infancy and adolescence... I always looked back with a lot of pain... Now I am starting to look at things with acceptance and I feel that the pain subsides...releases." (ID Number 14)
	Others	"The program helped me to be more accepting and respectful of others." (ID Number 8) "I also noticed that when I was with others I felt mentally calmer, less stressed...reacting less towards what was being said. This helped me to be more accepting... I notice people are very individualistic... and I accept." (ID Number 7)

IMPERMANENCE

Some participants revealed an increased ability to recognize the impermanence of life. Things are always changing in life, and these include not only things that happen outside of oneself but also one's emotions, feelings, thoughts, and so forth. Accepting the present-moment experience allowed the participants to be more present with whatever was happening in their lives or themselves in each passing moment. Examples of significant statements from participants' interviews for this theme and its respective dimension are presented in Table 4.10.

TABLE 4.10 IMPERMANENCE AND RESPECTIVE DIMENSION: EXAMPLES OF SIGNIFICANT STATEMENTS

Core Theme	Dimension	Significant Statements
Impermanence	Life	"Life is always changing… Things never stay the same… Now I recognize more this impermanence… and accept it." (ID Number 14) "Everything is impermanent, flowing, and changing… We are also changing at every moment." (ID Number 2) "Things change…always…inside, outside… the way I am feeling, my body, my state of mind…and aging also brings these changes… I recognize more this impermanence and how I react or respond to it in my daily life." (ID Number 8)

These principles—mindfulness, acceptance, and impermanence—when cultivated formally through mindfulness practices and informally in one's daily life (i.e., when performing one's daily actions such as eating, walking, and responding to stressful events of life) had a powerful impact in several domains of the participants' existence, including: psychological well-being, physical well-being, social interaction, perceptions of aging, spirituality, and daily life.

Secondary themes

Seven secondary themes were identified that represent the domains of participants' lives that were influenced by the MBSR program and mindfulness practices. These themes include psychological well-being, physical well-being, perceptions of aging, spirituality, social interactions, cognitive performance, and daily life. Each of these themes has several dimensions, which are detailed below.

Psychological well-being

The impact of the MBSR program on participants' psychological well-being was evident. All participants reported an increased sense of peace and serenity. Some shared that they felt more alive, balanced, positive, happy, and emotionally strong. Others reported an increased discernment due to their newfound or newly strengthened ability to observe their thoughts, emotions, feelings, and the totality of their experience in the present moment. Some participants revealed that the regular practice of mindfulness allowed them to find time and space to be with themselves and get in touch with their inner self (i.e., transpersonal self), which they recognized as being an important moment in their days. Table 4.11 provides examples of significant statements from participants' interviews for this theme and its respective dimensions.

TABLE 4.11 PSYCHOLOGICAL WELL-BEING AND RESPECTIVE DIMENSIONS: EXAMPLES OF SIGNIFICANT STATEMENTS

Secondary Theme	Dimension	Significant Statements
Psychological Well-Being	Peace/ Serenity	"With the regular practice of mindfulness meditation and yoga I became more serene." (ID Number 16) "When I return to the breath emotionally I feel that I gradually become more calm and peaceful." (ID Number 18)
	Aliveness	"I am learning to live again." (ID Number 2) "I live more…because I am more present in my day-to-day life." (ID Number 14) "The returning to the Now… I feel it is living… I am living more." (ID Number 18)
	Balanced	"I feel better…feel more balanced emotionally…less anxious and stressed." (ID Number 13) "I feel less irritated." (ID Number 16)
	Positivity	"The practices allowed me to keep bringing the mind to the present moment and valuing the positive side of every experience." (ID Number 18) "The practices helped me to be less frustrated and angry about my past… I accept what was and try to look to the positive side of it." (ID Number 13)

Physical well-being

The MBSR program affected participants' health, as they generally felt better physically and, as a result of being more relaxed emotionally, their physical body also released, and the general sense of well-being improved. They reported an increased ability to relax as a result of the mindfulness practices. Several participants revealed an increased awareness and respect for their physical limitations (i.e., health and/or age-related), and others also shared that their sleep improved. It was also reported that the practices changed their general habits (e.g., started doing regular exercise) and improved their activity levels, as they felt more active and flexible as a result of being more relaxed. Table 4.12 provides examples of significant statements from participants' interviews for this theme and its respective dimensions.

TABLE 4.12 PHYSICAL WELL-BEING AND RESPECTIVE DIMENSIONS: EXAMPLES OF SIGNIFICANT STATEMENTS

Secondary Theme	Dimension	Significant Statements
Physical Well-Being	Health	"Because I feel more relaxed I feel healthier." (ID Number 8) "The practices allowed me to be more present with my body… I am more aware of what I need, so I tend to respect more what my body is saying…and because of that I feel healthier." (ID Number 14)
	Relaxation	"Physically, I also feel calmer…as if my body is more relaxed, more at ease." (ID Number 13) "If my body is tense… I feel that it relaxes after the practices." (ID Number 16)
	Active	"I feel more dynamic…not only cognitively but physically. The yoga and the meditation helped me have more energy, and because of that I feel more active…healthier." (ID Number 16) "I started walking every day for an hour… I feel more energetic." (ID Number 2)
	General Habits	"I am more conscious of my diet… I also started to exercise on a regular basis…not only the yoga CD of the program, but also walking with my husband." (ID Number 8) "I am more active physically… I started doing yoga in a center near my house. I am more careful about my time and my needs. I always try to have time for myself everyday…to be quiet and in silence." (ID Number 14)

cont.

TABLE 4.12 PHYSICAL WELL-BEING AND RESPECTIVE DIMENSIONS: EXAMPLES OF SIGNIFICANT STATEMENTS *CONT.*

Secondary Theme	Dimension	Significant Statements
	Respect for Limitations	"I observe me more…my emotions, bodily sensations, my limits when I am doing certain things… Sometimes I start to feel tired and probably in a normal situation I would continue to do it… Now I am more aware and I take care of myself in a better way." (ID Number 18) "I accept my limits… I try not to push myself to do things I know I am not well [enough] to do." (ID Number 14)
	Sleep	"I am also sleeping better, and even during the nights that I wake up with insomnia, I start meditating, and it helps me go back to sleep or to be calmer rather than worrying that I am not sleeping." (ID Number 2) "Now I sleep much better… Before it was hard to go fall asleep, but now it is much better." (ID Number 7)

Perceptions of aging

Most participants revealed that their participation in the MBSR program confirmed their perspectives of how they were experiencing life during this period of their lives. They all revealed that they do not feel their age (i.e., feel ageless) and that the only thing that reminds them of their age is when they look in the mirror or when they feel that their body is limiting themselves in some way. Some also revealed that they believe and experience that aging brings more wisdom as a result of their life experience. Furthermore, some showed that they see death as part of the life process, not something to be feared or rejected, but something to be accepted as part of the natural cycle of life. Table 4.13 provides examples of significant statements from participants' interviews for this theme and its respective dimensions.

TABLE 4.13 PERCEPTIONS OF AGING AND RESPECTIVE
DIMENSIONS: EXAMPLES OF SIGNIFICANT STATEMENTS

Secondary Theme	Dimension	Significant Statements
Perceptions of Aging	Ageless	"I do not even feel the age I have." (ID Number 7) "I do not feel the age I have." (ID Number 18) "I do not even remember... I do not feel the age I have." (ID Number 13)
	Wisdom	"The more important things apart from my age is the learning, the wisdom and the discernment age brings... Today I feel that I am living life in a different way...with more clarity, more balance...less impulsivity... I accept things better, accept suffering...life...death...aging." (ID Number 16) "Now I am less impulsive... I ponder more about things, and if I cannot get what I want or if things do not go as I plan... I feel less frustrated." (ID Number 2)
	Death	"Now I accept death and recognize that it is part of the life process." (ID Number 14) "Death is part of the life... There is nothing we can do about it...just prepare ourselves mentally and emotionally to accept what comes." (ID Number 8)

Spirituality

Some participants shared that the participation in the MBSR program confirmed their beliefs that life is a learning process, a journey of growth and transformation, which is seen as the purpose in life that can be manifested in different ways in the material world, including physical, psychological, social, and transcendental (e.g., church) experiences. The participation in the program and the regular practice allowed some participants to cultivate time to be with their inner self and to foment their awareness that they are more than just their mental body, that they are an integral and whole being with a body, mind, emotions, and spirit, all of which interact in each passing moment (i.e., the discovery of the transpersonal self). For some participants the MBSR program also allowed them to cultivate their perception of interconnections among everything in life, while for others it was a confirmation of an already present interconnectedness and universality awareness. Examples of significant statements for this theme and its respective dimensions are presented in Table 4.14.

TABLE 4.14 SPIRITUALITY AND RESPECTIVE DIMENSIONS: EXAMPLES OF SIGNIFICANT STATEMENTS

Secondary Theme	Dimension	Significant Statements
Spirituality	Transpersonal Self	"Well, the participation in the program allowed me to get in contact with myself again… It helped me to get away from everything that affected me negatively and get in touch with my inner self… You know, my true self, my essence…my soul." (ID Number 2) "My life is a learning journey…to learn how to live according to the rhythm of nature, the rhythm of the Whole… to see that I am more than my thoughts…to connect with my inner self. The practices allow me to go deeper in this sense…to see myself better and more deeply." (ID Number 7)
	Interconnectedness/ Universality	"We are all connected and interrelated… It is true that we forget…and being in the program allowed us to be more present with this reality…the reality that we are One." (ID Number 14) "The MBSR also reinforced my perspective that reality is interconnected…everything in the world is… We do not live isolated from the rest… We are interrelated to nature, to others, to animals… Every action we have interferes and affects everything around us." (ID Number 18)
	Purpose of Life	"We all have a purpose in life… The practices and being in the present moment with myself…allow me to be aware of this purpose in my daily life." (ID Number 8) "Well…life is a journey…a journey with a beginning and an end… The journey itself is the purpose…a purpose for learning and growing…for Being who we really are… The MBSR reinforced this idea I already had…" (ID Number 14)

Growth and Transformation	"I see that this life was a school for me, and it still is… I am learning and learning, and experiencing…and it is hard to face certain moments, but I got through them and I go on… This is the way life is!!!! I am very grateful for everything in life… Even the difficult moments." (ID Number 2) "I feel very happy with my life, with my journey and learning throughout these years… The program allowed me to recognize even more profoundly this gratitude I have towards life and accept all the difficulties I have experienced." (ID Number 18)
Suffering	"When we stop and look with our inner eye we realize that suffering is indeed what helps us learn in this journey… I am learning to accept life as it comes, even the suffering I experience in the present and what I have experienced in the past." (ID Number 13) "What can we do??!!! Nothing can change the reality of suffering… It is part of life. Being aware of it and present with it is a wonderful way of experiencing it…no rejection… accepting what arises…breathing in and breathing out." (ID Number 8)

The interviews also revealed that, when participants were asked about how they perceived their existence in this period of their lives, they all referred to their spiritual beliefs in relation to how they see themselves, their journey, and the meaning of their existence, which seemed to be reflected in all domains (i.e., physical, psychological, social interactions, etc.) of their lives, as they would refer to God or some other spiritual belief to make sense of their experiences and suffering in their daily life in their relations with others; their own physical, psychological, or other state; the cycles of growth and transformation; and their purpose in life, as these participant comments illustrate:

> Because I was raised within the Catholic beliefs it was always important for me to help others, to be thankful and grateful for everything they do. Today, I still do it because I know we are all sons of God. The mindfulness practice allowed me to be even more

attentive and present in my interactions with others, to say thank you, and to be grateful for whatever they offer. (ID Number 13)

When I am unwell, I always thank God that what I am experiencing is not as bad as other people around me, some even younger. I am thankful for what I have... Connecting with God allowed me to be strong throughout my journey in life. (ID Number 18)

Some participants indicated that serving and providing support to others was a very important function in this period of their lives. They volunteer to help frail older adults, teach children in Church, or provide help for the homeless:

> I used to be there for my father before he passed. I would do everything I could to be with him and relieve him from his pain. Now, that he passed, I decided to continue with this support to other older adults that are in bed and need company and support. It is important to me to continue doing that... I feel fulfilled and I am helping. (ID Number 18)

> I volunteer at the church where I follow children's working in several tasks in the green garden, in creative arts, or simply in religious classes. I love interacting with them... They have so much to teach me... I feel really happy to go. (ID Number 8)

Most participants were also responsible for caring for their grandchildren after school time, and other participants revealed the great importance that gardening and taking care of the green garden had in their daily routines:

> For me, being in the green garden every day is like a mindfulness practice... Now I realize that, because when I am there, my mind silences and during and after the MBSR program, I noticed it even more—the impact that this activity has in my daily life, to slow down my thoughts. (ID Number 2)

Social interactions

Some participants stated that the participation in the MBSR program improved their ability to relate with others, thereby making their interactions more positive. This was a result of their improved ability to be present and to exercise discernment during interactions. Some also reported an increased gratitude and compassion towards others. Examples of significant statements from participants' interviews are presented in Table 4.15 to illustrate this theme and its respective dimensions.

TABLE 4.15 SOCIAL INTERACTIONS AND RESPECTIVE DIMENSIONS: EXAMPLES OF SIGNIFICANT STATEMENTS

Secondary Theme	Dimension	Significant Statements
Social Interactions	Discernment	"Because I am more aware of how I feel and think when I am with others…and of what they say… I tend to be more careful in the way I say things or do things." (ID Number 14) "Being present helped me to be more aware of how to interact with others… My family notices that difference, as well." (ID Number 8)
	Presence	"I noticed that when I was with others I was more present, mentally calmer and less stressed." (ID Number 7) "I feel more present when I am with others. I am more attentive to what others say and present in my interactions with others." (ID Number 18)
	Positive	"As I am calmer and less stressed the way I interact with other people improved, as well." (ID Number 2) "I also notice that because I am calmer my interactions with others flows in a more positive way." (ID Number 18)
	Compassion	"I feel more present in the interaction with others, I am more careful with what I say to others in order not to hurt them or not to talk impulsively." (ID Number 13) "It was a learning to respect and accept others, their rhythm…the difference between everyone… I am more tolerant towards [others]." (ID Number 16)

Cognitive performance

Two participants reported improved cognitive performance during and after the MBSR program. One participant observed improved memory, while the other shared that her creativity had improved. The other participants reported that they had not had any memory complaints before the MBSR program started, so they did not notice any difference in this respect. Of the two participants who reported cognitive performance changes, one reported memory complaints at the initial assessment and the other was cognitively active before and during the program, as she was writing a book. Although only two participants revealed that the MBSR program had effects on their cognitive performance, this secondary theme and its respective dimensions were included in the results. Among all participants only these two participants had significant concerns about their memory performance at their initial assessment (i.e., one because she noticed she was forgetting a few things and the other because she was cognitively active in writing a book). In Table 4.16 examples of significant statements selected from these two participants' interviews are presented to support this theme and its respective dimensions.

TABLE 4.16 COGNITIVE PERFORMANCE AND RESPECTIVE DIMENSIONS: EXAMPLES OF SIGNIFICANT STATEMENTS

Secondary Theme	Dimension	Significant Statements
Social Interactions	Memory Performance	"In relation to memory I noticed a lot of difference ... I think it is because I am more present in the moment... Before the MBSR started I was always forgetting this and that... I was feeling my memory failing me... Now I am much better." (ID Number 7)
	Creativity	"I feel more creative and dynamic... I returned to my book writing and it was flowing very well." (ID Number 16)

Daily life

Their participation in the MBSR program allowed all participants to establish a regular practice of mindfulness, both formal and informal, which generally improved their quality of life. Examples of significant statements from participants' interviews for this theme and its respective dimensions are presented in Table 4.17.

QUALITATIVE RESULTS

TABLE 4.17 DAILY LIFE AND RESPECTIVE DIMENSIONS: EXAMPLES OF SIGNIFICANT STATEMENTS

Secondary Theme	Dimension	Significant Statements
Daily Life	Regular Practice (formal and informal)	"I continue to do my practices... the formal and informal practices... not as regularly as during the MBSR, but it is an integral part of my daily routine." (ID Number 13) "I continue to use the CDs and also paying attention to the everything I do in my daily routine... sometimes the mind wonders... but I keep reminding myself to bring it back to the present moment."(ID Number 7)
	Quality of Life	"Generally; I feel better... I appreciate life better... My life improved" (ID Number 14) "The quality of my life improved because I am less stressed, less anxious...physically I feel better and I am enjoying life with a smile." (ID Number 8)

Overall experience

All participants revealed that the overall experience of the MBSR program was very positive and gratifying not only because of the learning process and perceived effects in their lives and well-being but also because of the group interaction and exchanges during the sessions of the program (Table 4.18).

TABLE 4.18 OVERALL EXPERIENCE: EXAMPLES OF SIGNIFICANT STATEMENTS

Secondary Theme	Dimension	Significant Statements
Overall Experience	Positive	"I really enjoyed having this opportunity... It was very gratifying to be present and to learn so much." (ID Number 8) "For me it was very positive. I liked a lot the practices that were presented, your presence and way of being and interacting with the group. The group was very good, as well... It was a very positive learning process." (ID Number 13)

Table 4.19 presents a summary of core themes, secondary themes, and respective dimensions. Frequencies of core themes, secondary themes, and dimensions among the seven participants interviewed for this study are given in brackets.

Summary of results

Results of qualitative analysis revealed that the MBSR program improved participants' mindfulness skills. They revealed an increased capacity of observation, attention, and awareness, as well as consciousness of their moment-to-moment experience. The participants reported that these practices allowed them to slow down in their daily lives and to find time to be with themselves. This increased ability to be in the present moment was accompanied by an internal attitude of acceptance of whatever arises, hence the reported increased acceptance of what they experience in their lives. The increased mindfulness was also associated with the recognition and acceptance of the impermanence of life. These major principles learned or reinforced during the MBSR program and adopted in their daily lives had a positive effect in terms of psychological well-being, physical health, perceptions of aging, spirituality, social interaction, cognitive performance, and daily lives. These changes were evident not only among participants who had had no previous experience with or knowledge of meditation and related concepts, but also among those who had some previous contact with these practices and an inherent philosophy in their regard, therefore revealing that learning is continuous.

TABLE 4.19 CORE THEMES, SECONDARY THEMES, DIMENSIONS, AND RESPECTIVE FREQUENCIES

Core Themes	Learned principles from MBSR program adopted in daily life			
	Mindfulness (7)	Acceptance (7)		Impermanence (7)
Dimensions	Attention (7) Observation (7) Presence (7) Awareness and Consciousness (7) Slowing Down (5) Be (4) Decentering (7)	Life (5) Self (5) Aging (6) Loss (2) Others (3)	Emotions (6) Pain (7) Suffering (7)	Life (7)
Secondary Themes	Effects of these Principles			
	Physical Well-Being (7)	Perceptions of Aging (7)		Spirituality (7)
Dimensions	Health (6) Relaxation (7) Active (4) General Habits (4) Respect for Limitations (3) Sleep (5)	Ageless (7) Wisdom (4) Death (5)		Transpersonal Self (6) Interconnectedness/Universality (7) Purpose of life (7) Growth and Transformation (7) Suffering (6)
	Psychological Well-Being (7)			
Dimensions	Peace/Serenity (7) Aliveness (5) Balanced (5)	Discernment (6) Positivity (4) Identity (see Transpersonal Self; 3)		
Secondary Themes (cont.)	Social Interactions (7)	Cognitive Performance (2)		Daily Life (7)
Dimensions	Discernment (5) Presence (3) Positive (6) Compassion (5)	Memory (1) Creativity (1)		Regular Practice (formal and informal; 7) Quality of Life (7)
Overall Experience	Positive (7)			

» Chapter 5 «

Mixed-Methods Results

This study employed convergent parallel mixed-method design as quantitative and qualitative data were gathered concurrently, and both data sets were equally prioritized during analysis. Quantitative and qualitative strands were kept independent during the analysis and then mixed during the overall interpretation. Combining both quantitative and qualitative data allowed for a broader and more complete understanding of the phenomena and increased the overall strength of the study (Creswell, 2009). Table 5.1 shows the quantitative and qualitative results for the dimensions assessed in terms of *yes* and *no* responses to whether the data shows participants had generally experienced the designated changes.

TABLE 5.1 QUANTITATIVE AND QUALITATIVE RESULTS FOR THE DIFFERENT DIMENSIONS

Dimensions	Qualitative	Quantitative
Mindfulness	YES	YES
Self-Compassion Acceptance	YES	YES
Decentering	YES	YES
Psychological Well-Being	YES	YES
Physical Well-Being	YES	YES
Spirituality	YES	YES
Death Perspectives	YES (Acceptance)	NO
Aging	YES	YES
Social Interactions	YES	YES
Quality of Life	YES	YES
Cognitive Performance	YES	YES
Daily Practice	YES	(NA)

This study provides robust evidence of the effectiveness of MBSR for older adults. Results strongly reflect that this program can function as a holistic intervention for this age group, as participants showed significant improvements in terms of their inherent mindfulness capacities and ability to accept and be compassionate with themselves. Mindfulness also impacted their ability to observe their thoughts, feelings, and bodily sensations as temporary, with an internal attitude of acceptance and nonjudgment. The changes in their ability to be in the present moment, observing their moment-to-moment experience with an accepting and compassionate internal attitude, had profound effects on their well-being (i.e., subjective and objective) and physical health. The perceptions of their aging process were also affected, as they showed an increased capacity to accept the changes associated with aging and also supported an already present experience of being ageless. They also reported that age brings wisdom as a reflection of their life experience. Also, death was perceived and accepted as part of the natural process of life, including the death of close relatives.

Significant effects of the program were observed in terms of participants' spiritual well-being and spirituality. Throughout the MBSR program, participants found support and confirmation for their established beliefs that life's major purpose involves growth and transformation as sentient beings. They also fomented ways of finding time and space to be with their inner self, contemplate their whole existence (i.e., physical, mental, emotional, and spiritual bodies), and cultivated the ability to perceive and experience the interconnectedness among everything in life.

The changes observed in their internal attitude towards their moment-to-moment experience also impacted their social interactions, as they became more accepting, respectful, present, and compassionate with others, thereby improving the quality of their interactions with others. Their quality of life also improved. Moreover, the fomented ability to maintain their attention in the present-moment experience also enhanced their cognitive performance, which might also be reflecting the improved well-being, physical health, and quality of life.

Figure 5.1 summarizes the integration of both quantitative and qualitative results. The oval shape of the diagram and the inside square having rounded corners were intentionally selected to imply a continuous, dynamic, and cyclic movement of the learning process within and between each principle, domain, and their respective dimensions, which is reinforced by the circling arrows included in the figure. The circling arrows selected are meant to mirror the same dynamic movement that is observed in everything in the Universe (e.g., galaxies and atoms). Results revealed that the participation in the MBSR program fomented in older adults some basic learning principles inherent in the program. These included: mindfulness, observation, impermanence, presence, act with awareness, acceptance, compassion, nonjudgment, decentering, and awareness of impermanence of the present-moment experience. These principles were transmitted and learned throughout the sessions of the MBSR program. As the principles learned in the program came from the outside world, rather than their inner world, they are presented in the outer limit of the diagram. However, it is important to state that these capacities are not extraneous to human being's inherent nature; they are capacities that we all have inherent in our existence: the capacity to observe, pay attention, be present, be aware, and so forth. Throughout the program participants had the opportunity to develop, cultivate, and foment these capacities, as well as to learn how to deal with any difficulties that arose during this learning process.

The different principles that were developed and cultivated during the program affected participants' lives in terms of well-being, physical well-being, social interactions, daily life experience, death perspectives, and cognitive performance. These are not independent domains; they interact with each other; thus, they are presented within the same square in the diagram. At the very core of the diagram there is the domain of spirituality; according to the interviews, I perceived that participants' spiritual values and beliefs guided their journey in life. It is at the heart of their existence, because it is what they refer to when they refer to their understanding of who they are and the meaning of their lives and existence. This domain affects and is affected by other domains (i.e., physical, psychological, social, etc.). Spirituality affects the other domains because it helps participants deal with experiences in the outer world and daily lives. At the same time, spirituality is affected by their physical, psychological, social, and cognitive aspects, and by daily life because these experiences are the means through which they experience life and their existence and learn their true nature. Lastly, all the domains and principles learned are being dynamically affected in a bidirectional way, that is, the diagram implies a movement from the outside-in, but the movement also occurs from the inside-out, as the continuous experience of the principles in the different dimensions of individuals' lives dynamically affects the understanding and experience of the principles learned.

Overall, this study provides strong and robust evidence of the effectiveness of this intervention in older adults. It reveals that the MBSR program had a significant impact on their well-being, physical health, neuropsychological performance, spirituality and spiritual well-being, perceptions of aging and death, quality of life, and social interactions, thereby functioning as a complementary and holistic intervention for this age group.

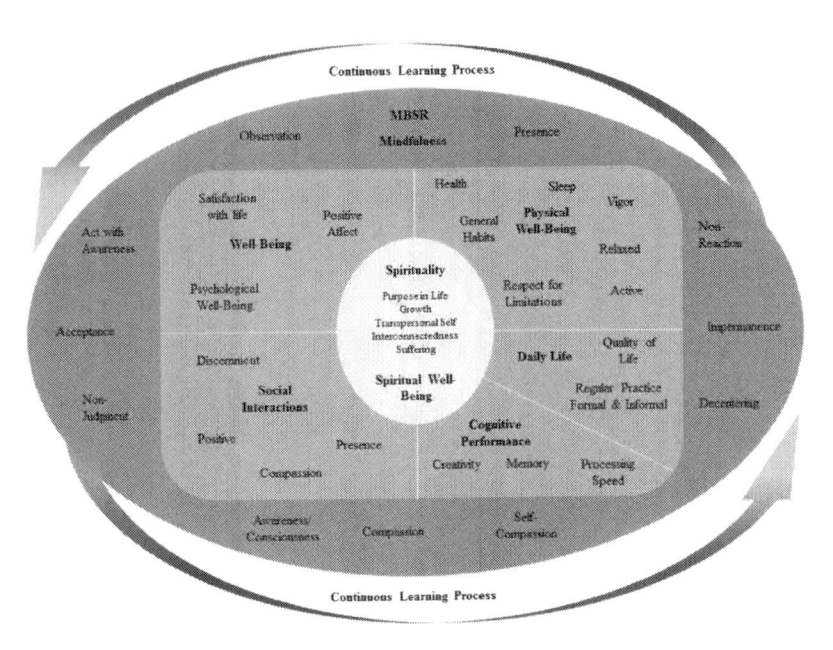

FIGURE 5.1 MIXED RESULTS: MBSR FOR OLDER ADULTS

» Chapter 6 «

Integral Results

I was supremely happy, for I had seen. Nothing could ever be the same. I have drunk at the clear and pure waters and my thirst was appeased… I have seen the Light. I have touched compassion which heals all sorrow and suffering; it is not for myself, but for the world… Love in all its glory has intoxicated my heart; my heart can never be closed. I have drunk at the fountain of Joy and eternal Beauty.

Jiddu Krishnamurti[1]

The main themes that arose from the analysis of my journal notes, related to the integral aspects of participants' experiences, involved *change: openness versus resistance to change, wisdom, spiritual development,* and *adaptation*. The themes will be explored in more detail separately.

Change: openness versus resistance to change

I observed that participants' experiences throughout the program were always changing. I noticed continuous changes in the way they expressed their experiences of mindful activities, emotional and mental states, difficulties, obstacles, excuses to justify not completing the exercises and practices at home. Change was present in the way they sat in the chairs throughout sessions and mindfulness practices and in the way they interacted with each other and with me. There was change within and without, and, several times, this change was not realized and perceived by participants. When participants realized and perceived this change, it allowed them to be aware of the possibility of transformation and growth that they still experience at this point in their lives. When this possibility

---

1 J Krishnamurti Online (2014) Daily Quote Archive, available at www.jkrishnamurti.org/krishnamurti-teachings/daily-quote-archive.php, accessed on 14 May 2014.

was accepted and their internal attitude was open and receptive to it, change was intensified, and it became even more obvious and noticeable. Several times, participants expressed their inability to learn or change deep-rooted patterns of behavior and emotional responses, seeing that as due to their age: "These meditation practices and the possibilities of transformation it offers are great for people your [my own] age. What are we going to do now with all this, when so little time is left for us to apply [them]?!" (participants' words). When they moved beyond these crystallized concepts that their age was an impediment to living their lives in a new way and were open to realizing the possibility of change and growth, the changes that I observed in participants from session to session became more apparent and present in them: their emotional and physical presence, actions, and words. They were more optimistic and, therefore, receptive to learning more about mindfulness, practicing more the meditations presented, and learning with each other as they shared their experiences. Also, they became more aware of these changes and the benefits they were experiencing with the practices from session to session.

A few participants stayed resistant to recognizing these small changes and their own ability to change and to live life with a fresh internal attitude. These participants at those times found constant excuses to justify their noncompliance with the exercises, their inability to change, and the perceived lack of beauty in life, as if life was as it was and there was nothing they could do to change at this point in their lives. They were attached to their fixed concepts and ideas about themselves and their possibility to change rather than directly experiencing their moment to moment right here where they would observe changes occurring in themselves and others. These participants did not meet the criteria for being interviewed for the study, as they had lower rates of compliance and/or exhibited health issues during the eight-week period of the program.

I realized that change can only take place when we open ourselves to it, to experience its manifestation in its full potentiality, and to the full potential that inhabits our own essence, in order to grow and evolve. When we open ourselves to life and to the possibilities that each moment brings for self-growth and transformation, we allow ourselves to die and to be reborn each moment, as concepts and perceptions of ourselves and life dissolve and the flux of life guides us in this journey. Kornfield (2008) expressed it this way:

> The reality of experience is an ever-changing river. Direct perception drops beneath the names of things to show us their ephemeral, mysterious nature. When we bring our attention to the direct perception of experience, we become alive and free. (p.88)

Some of the participants that were more resistant to change showed some changes, although these occurred in a more subtle way (e.g., how quickly they sat in the meditation position, how they reacted less emotionally to some of the discussions being presented, how they sat or lay down throughout the meditation practices). It was not clear to me whether they realized these changes or any difference that these might be having in their daily life. It was not clear whether these changes were affecting their way of thinking, feeling, and acting, or if these could have a long-lasting effect in their daily lives. What I could notice was that something was happening within them, and I compassionately allowed each participant to enjoy the journey of their process without projecting any expectation or demanding any compliance or change. Each of them was responsible for their own choices at each point in their learning process throughout the program, and my role was to be mindfully present with an internal attitude of openness and compassion as the practices and themes were presented.

Wisdom

One of the mindful activities that were performed in the first session of the program was the mindful eating of raisins. When participants shared their experiences, they revealed awareness of interconnectedness (i.e., interconnectedness in relation to the entire process associated with the production and the necessary elements of nature involved). This awareness was very present in a way that I had never observed before in other MBSR participants of other age groups. I interpreted this awareness as a sign of wisdom: a wisdom that arises as a result of the natural flow of life experience allowing individuals to perceive the interconnection of all existence. There is something that life on its own brings to each individual's development—experience—and with experience comes wisdom. Wisdom is something that cannot be learned mentally or conceptually but only with time and experience in life, through the natural development of individuals throughout their life span. Tornstam (1997) stated that aging is a process of "natural progression towards maturation and wisdom" (p.143) and that, in this period of life, individuals move towards a more spiritual and transpersonal perspective of life. Similarly, several authors (Erikson, 1997; Jung, 1939b, 1971; Reed, 1991; Schachter-Shalomi, 1995) suggested that aging is characterized by a process of individuation and transcendence, spiritual development, and unity with all people and the Divine. In the Upanishads, it was presented that wisdom was not related to what is knowable in the sensory world, but was defined as an intuitive understanding of the nature of life and death (Birren and Svensson, 2005). Similarly, according to Buddha's teaching, wisdom was related to "knowledge" that arises from personal observation and experience (Birren and Svensson, 2005). Birren and Svensson (2005) revised other Eastern perspectives on wisdom (e.g., Confucius, Tao-te-Ching), showing that Eastern perspectives do not focus the concept of wisdom on the physical world, but on an "enlightened understanding of the relationships between the natural world and the Divine" (p.9). In this same line, another observation that I interpreted as a sign of wisdom was participants' very present perception of the interconnection of life as a sign of this spiritual development that goes beyond their personal self and is connected with everything in life: people, animals, nature, and beyond.

Spiritual development

One participant shared that the raisins that were eaten during this exercise served their purpose and that she hoped to fulfill hers in her lifetime. I perceived this to be for her a step in the search for meaning and purpose in life that occurs in all individuals throughout their lives (Frankl, 2004a, 2004b). In old age, many of us experience loss of a social role with retirement, fear of isolation and of losing autonomy, which is experienced by some as a loss of meaning in life (MacKinlay, 2001; Missine, 2004). In old age, rather, the search for meaning in life is found in experiences with the world and others, including relating with our families, the quest to address our spiritual needs, and the role of helping others (Missine, 2004). I observed that this search for meaning and purpose in late life in this group was very much present when participants shared how much they were learning to integrate the mindfulness presence and attention in their daily lives, in particular in activities that give meaning to their days, such as taking care of their grandchildren and volunteering in Church and other organizations that offer support to individuals with health issues (e.g., terminal illness, chronic diseases, and physical disablity). The way they talked about the voluntary activities they were involved in revealed how important and significant being able to give and help others is in lending purpose and significance to their lives. For example, one participant said:

> I am learning to be present with my grandchild, to be more careful about how I condition him when I try to warn him of some things he does. I am being more mindful of the way I talk and act around him because I know it will affect his way of behaving. Being able to do this means a lot to me. I love taking care of him and I learn a lot with him. I wake up with a purpose.

Another participant shared that:

> Every week when I go to the farm, where I plant things and take care of the vineyards, I become even more aware of the interconnectedness between things. It has always been a very important thing in my life, but being mindful while I do it, made these moments even more a special for me. I love going there, taking care of the plants and the vegetable garden. It is my greatest hobby.

I observed that each participant was finding different ways to fulfill his or her purpose in life either through church, nature, volunteer work, or family support. There is an intrinsic need to have a meaning in life that guides and motivates us to wake up every morning and move along this journey, to continue to grow and evolve as individuals.

Some of the participants also revealed a very mature and balanced attitude towards the suffering in their lives, both present and past. One participant said that:

> I know that I am not young anymore, and my body aches and fails me sometimes, but I am so grateful to still be here learning and growing, enjoying and sharing my experiences with others, and experiencing life with happiness and gratitude.

Another participant shared this comment about aging while enjoying life:

> I am having difficulties with my knee for two weeks already. I can hardly bend it. It is only this kind of situation that remind me of my age. I do not like, but I accept it because I know that there are people of my age and younger that suffer much more than I do. I know that I have to be more careful and take it easier in my daily tasks, but I do everything I need. I am not going to allow these situations to make me feel sad or depressed. Every day is a good day to smile, to live, to enjoy life.

They accepted and were grateful for what life brings them and would not let these situations, in particular if they were related to physical limitations, to diminish their will to live and their joy towards life. Missine (2004) found that, in old age, individuals also find meaning in their lives by the attitude they bring towards their suffering. What I observed was exactly that: the way these participants faced their suffering allowed them to find meaning and purpose in their daily living. Life was still a journey to be enjoyed and experienced with an open heart.

Adaptation

This theme is related to the adaptation of the MBSR program to older adult groups. Throughout the program I observed that many aspects of the sessions needed to be adapted to this age population. The duration of the sessions per se were not problematic; the most difficult part was the duration of the practices, because it meant that they needed to lie down or sit still for about 45 minutes. I believe that it would be important to adjust the practices to 30 minutes in order to prevent any fatigue and physical discomfort. The yoga practices were well accepted, but, because every posture was new to them, I had to spend a lot a time explaining the postures and how to move the body from posture to posture to avoid any physical pain or strain. It meant that a predicated 45-minute practice took about 60 minutes to complete. Also, some of the postures I felt were too demanding on all of them. I believe that it would be more beneficial to include fewer postures in each yoga practice to exclude the ones that are more challenging, and to allow extra time to explain each posture, and to verify that each participant is doing it correctly. The intensive silent session was supposed to last six to seven hours, but, as based on their responses during the previous two-hour sessions, I shortened this session to five hours. When I scheduled the practices for this session, I was intentionally interspersing sitting, standing, walking, and lying-down meditation practices to prevent any overdoing and physical fatigue. Participants' response to this session was very positive, with no complaints. They were very pleased with the fact that they were not always sitting or standing, which was something that had tired them during the two-hour session. Some of the two-hour sessions had included only sitting. I concluded that this intensive silent session should be shortened to four to five hours with these age groups. These changes imply that the CDs provided with the practices should also be adapted according to the changes suggested.

» CHAPTER 7 «

Discussion

This chapter begins with a discussion of the research questions and respective findings of this study: (a) What are the effects of the experience of the MBSR on psychological well-being, neuropsychological performance, physical health, and spirituality in older adults? and (b) What is the essence of the lived experience of older adults during the MBSR program? Also discussed are the research subquestions, which included: What is the experience of aging and being old? How do older adults experience being part of the MBSR program? What is the perception of life and existence among older adults? How do mindfulness practices impact older adults' views and experiences of life? What is well-being in old age? What is the experienced impact of the MBSR program in individuals' sense of well-being (physical and psychological)? What are the cognitive changes experienced among healthy older adults? How do mindfulness practices impact elders' cognitive performance? and How do older adults commit to mindfulness practices in their daily life? These are interpreted and conceptualized according to the literature review presented in Chapter 2. The limitations and delimitations of this study are also presented, as well as the practical applications and implications of this research and suggestions for future research. Finally, a brief summary and concluding remarks are presented at the end of this chapter.

Interpretations and conceptualization of findings

Several studies have been developed to assess the effectiveness of the MBSR program in clinical (Carlson and Garland, 2005; Carlson *et al.*, 2009; Didonna, 2009; Kabat-Zinn, 1990; Kristeller and Hallett, 1999; Miller *et al.*, 1995) and nonclinical groups (Bédard *et al.*, 2003; Brown and Ryan, 2003; Chambers *et al.*, 2008; Davidson *et al.*, 2003; Didonna, 2009; Murphy, 1995), revealing very positive results in terms of its effectiveness in promoting psychological and physical well-being.

However, studies conducted with healthy older adults are few, and most studies with this age group included institutionalized (e.g., see Ernst *et al.*, 2008; McBee, 2008) and clinical older adults (e.g., see Prewitt, 2000; Morone *et al.*, 2008; Smith, 2004, 2006). Furthermore, as was reviewed in Chapter 2, most of these studies showed methodological limitations and poor control (e.g., see Smith, 2004, 2006), and no study looked at the impact of the participation in the MBSR program for older adults in terms of spirituality, cognitive performance, and the effectiveness of this intervention in affecting all dimensions of participants' lives, including psychological well-being, physical health, social interactions, neuropsychological performance, spirituality, perspectives on existence, life purpose, aging, death, and loss.

This unique and complex study provides an in-depth analysis of the effects and lived experiences of the MBSR program for older adults and revealed distinctive and robust evidence that the MBSR program had significant effects on this sample of older adults in terms of acquired mindfulness abilities and other associated dimensions, such as self-compassion, attention, observation, presence, and decentering; objective and subjective well-being; physical health; social interactions; spirituality and spiritual well-being; and neuropsychological performance. There was also evidence that participation in the program affected their perception of their lives, aging, death, and loss. These are explored individually in the following sections.

Mindfulness and self-compassion

The MBSR program is based on a systematic and rigorous practice of mindfulness techniques, mindful yoga exercises, and group discussions associated with mindfulness practice, emotional development, and stress reduction (Kabat-Zinn, 1990). The results of this study strongly support previous empirical findings on the effectiveness of the MBSR program in improving mindfulness skills in older adults who completed the program. Quantitative measures revealed that the TG showed a significant increase in mindfulness, as measured by the MAAS and the FFMQ, as compared with the CG's results. In the FFMQ, the TG showed significant mean variations from Assessment 1 to Assessment 2 in all the different subscales that included observation, description, act with awareness, nonjudgment, and nonreaction. They also reported increased self-compassion, as measured by the SCS, including self-kindness, self-judgment, and common humanity and increased decentering, as assessed by the EQ.

DISCUSSION

In terms of the qualitative analysis, the TG revealed increased attention to the present-moment experience, observation directed toward what is happening in each passing moment within and without, and increased presence and awareness of their thoughts, emotions, feelings, and bodily sensations. They also reported increased capacity to slow down, cultivate states of being rather than doing, and to accomplish decentering. These were accompanied by an increased acceptance of life, self, aging, loss, others, emotions, pain, and suffering and by an awareness and acceptance of the impermanence of life.

Overall, participants revealed an increased ability to be in the present moment, with attention and awareness to what was happening in their moment-to-moment experience. They showed an increased capacity to observe their experiences in the present moment (i.e., as in metacognitive awareness): their thoughts, emotions, and physical sensations, and to cultivate a more discerning and objective perspective of what they experience rather than engaging in automatic emotional reactions and mental processes. This increased capacity to observe the present-moment experience with greater clarity has been called *reperceiving* (Shapiro *et al.*, 2006). Participants revealed an increased ability to observe their thoughts and feelings as temporary, impermanent, and transient manifestations, objective events in the mind—as opposed to as true reflections of the self—with an internal attitude of acceptance and nonjudgment (Fresco *et al.*, 2007).

Mindfulness, self-compassion, and reperceiving have been suggested to be related to positive changes in psychological functioning (Fresco *et al.*, 2007) and to a mediating mechanism of the observed impact in terms of well-being (Orzech *et al.*, 2009). Orzech *et al.* showed that increased ability to be mindful and accepting of the present-moment experience and the increased capacity to reperceive were associated with observed improvements in well-being, quality of life, and physical and psychological symptoms. Self-compassion was also related with improvements in spiritual well-being. These results support the suggestions that mindfulness training involves these mechanisms in the learning process: mindful attention, acceptance, and decentering (Orzech *et al.*, 2009).

Another quality that increased with mindfulness training was the participants' self-compassion, that is, the ability to be kind and understanding towards themselves in difficult times rather than engaging in self-criticism and self-judgment (Orzech *et al.*, 2009). They also showed an increased awareness and accepting attitude towards painful feelings, thoughts, and physical sensations rather than overly identifying themselves with them. This was evident not only in relation to themselves and others, but also in relation to life, suffering, the aging process, and loss.

These results are in agreement with other research studies looking at the impact of the MBSR in mindfulness scores as measured by MAAS and FFMQ (e.g., see Carmody and Baer, 2008; Carmody *et al.*, 2009; Nyklicek and Kuijpers, 2008; Shapiro, Brown and Biegel, 2007), decentering as measured by the EQ (Carmody *et al.*, 2009), and self-compassion as assessed by the SCS (Birnie, Speca and Carlson, 2010) in the general population.

Carmody *et al.* (2009) were testing a psychological model that explains the mechanisms involved in the observed positive changes of the MBSR program, and developed a study with 320 adults, between the ages of 17 and 77. Results revealed that participation in the MBSR program had had a significant effect on mindfulness (as assessed by the FFMQ) and decentering (as assessed by the EQ). Similarly, Carmody and Baer (2008) investigated the relationship between home practice of mindfulness meditation exercises and levels of mindfulness and medical and psychological well-being in 174 adults, aged 19–68. Results of this study revealed that participation in the MBSR program had a significant pre-post effect in all FFMQ subscales: observation, description, act with awareness, nonjudgment, and nonreaction.

A randomized study looking at the effects of MBSR on psychological well-being and quality of life of 60 adults, with a mean age of 44 years, revealed that participation in the MBSR program positively affected mindfulness scores in the treatment group as compared with those of the control group (Nyklicek and Kuijpers, 2008). Another study (Birnie *et al.*, 2010) looking at the impact of the MBSR program on self-compassion and empathy in a sample of 51 adults aged 24–77, showed that participants showed not only significant increases in MAAS scores after the intervention but also significant increases in self-compassion as assessed by the SCS. Also, Shapiro *et al.* (2007), in a prospective, nonrandomized, cohort-controlled design, evaluated the effects of the MBSR program in 83 mental health therapists-in-training. The sample was divided into three groups that attended three different courses as part of their training: (a) MBSR program, (b) Psychological Theory, and (c) Research Methods. Results showed that there was an increase in self-compassion and mindfulness (assessed using the SCS and MAAS, respectively) in the MBSR program participants.

Among older-adult groups, Prewitt (2000), looking at the effects of the MBSR program in ten older adults with fibromyalgia in a qualitative study, also found increased mindfulness and increased awareness and self-acceptance among the participants who completed the program. Another study (Morone *et al.*, 2008) also showed that participation in an eight-week MBSR program increased the levels of acceptance of older adults towards their limits and pain. Turner (2010) conducted a randomized study looking at the effects of mindfulness meditation on successful aging. Twenty-two participants, aged 46 to 70, were randomly assigned to a treatment group or a control group. The treatment group completed an eight-week MBSR program and the control group completed a nutritional educational program. Participants were assessed in terms of mindfulness, emotional regulations, and perceptions of aging. The treatment group showed increases in mindfulness between pre- and post-intervention assessment, but differences were not statistically significant.

The results of this research study also support suggestions (e.g., see Shapiro *et al.*, 2006; Shapiro and Schwartz, 1999) that mindfulness involves several psychological processes: participants meditate with an intention to bring their attention to whatever is arising in the present-moment experience, with an internal attitude of acceptance and openness towards what arises moment by moment. It is the interaction of these three axioms that fosters individuals' transformation and observed changes, including the increased capacities of decentering (Fresco *et al.*, 2007), reperceiving (Shapiro *et al.*, 2006), and metacognitive awareness (Bishop, 2002; Bishop *et al.*, 2004; Teasdale *et al.*, 2002) of their present-moment experience. This presence, attention, and acceptance allows individuals to connect with their body and mind, affecting their emotional and behavioral self-regulation as their awareness fosters a more discerning and conscious response to their experience rather than their engaging in automatic, habitual, and impulsive patterns of reaction, a change that ultimately affects their internal balance and health. This increased ability to be with what is in the present-moment experience also influenced participants' ability to cultivate a state of being in the present moment rather than doing, to slow down, and to truly experience what is happening in their lives in each passing moment, with openness and acceptance.

Well-being and psychological symptoms

This study looked at the effects of the MBSR program for older adults in terms of well-being and psychological symptoms. Well-being was assessed quantitatively in terms of PWB and SWB. PWB is associated with self-acceptance, environmental mastery, positive relationships, personal growth, life purpose, and autonomy. These dimensions reflect the eudaimonic view of well-being (Ryan and Deci, 2001) and were assessed using the PWBS (Ryff and Keynes, 1995). SWB reflects the hedonic view of well-being (i.e., pleasure and happiness) and was assessed using measures to evaluate satisfaction with life, using the SWLS (Diener et al., 1985), and positive mood and negative mood, using the PANAS (Watson et al., 1988). Psychological symptoms were assessed using scales to measure perceived stress, mood, and quality of life.

Results revealed that older adults in the TG showed increased SWB after completing the MBSR program: there was a significant increase in satisfaction with life and positive affect, and a decrease in negative affect. In terms of PWB, results also showed significant improvement in older adults who completed the program. This improvement was observed in the dimensions of autonomy, environmental mastery, personal growth, relations with others, purpose in life, and self-acceptance. These results suggested that participation in the MBSR program had improved both eudaimonic and hedonic well-being in older adults.

In terms of psychological symptoms, older adults who completed the MBSR program showed a decrease in psychological symptoms that included depression, tension, hostility, fatigue, and confusion, while there was an increase in vigor indicated. The levels of perceived stress also decreased. Quality of life improved in the dimensions of the physical, the psychological, and the environment.

The qualitative analysis also supported results reflected in the quantitative findings. Participants showed increased sense of peace and serenity; they felt more alive, balanced, positive, happy, and emotionally strong. They also revealed an increased quality of life and improvements in their relations with others, as they were more accepting, present, and discerning in their interactions. This increased discernment was also present in their daily lives, as they showed an improved capacity to observe their thoughts, emotions, and feelings—and the totality of their experience—without being caught in emotional reactions and automatic patterns of response. They reported an increased ability to mindfully regulate their emotions, and manage and respond in an adaptive way to the inner and outer world.

DISCUSSION

The results of this study are in agreement with previous research. Several studies (Bédard *et al.*, 2003; Birnie *et al.*, 2010; Carlson and Garland, 2005, Carlson *et al.*, 2009; Carmody and Baer, 2008; Carmody *et al.*, 2008; Kabat-Zinn, 1990) evaluating the effectiveness of the MBSR program in clinical and nonclinical populations repeatedly revealed that participation in the program improved psychological symptoms, well-being, and quality of life. Similarly, studies conducted with clinical (Smith, 2004, 2006) and institutionalized (Ernst *et al.*, 2008) older adults also revealed that, after completing the MBSR program, participants showed improvements in psychological symptoms.

Turner (2010) revealed a decrease in PANAS NA (Newhill *et al.*, 2010) and in emotional dysregulation (i.e., low threshold or high sensitivity to emotional stimuli, high amplitude of emotional response, and slow return to emotional baseline). Other studies (e.g., see Lantz *et al.*, 1997; Lindberg, 2005; Moye and Hanlon, 1996) using meditation and relaxation interventions in clinical and nonclinical older adults also reported increases in well-being and quality of life, and decreases in psychological symptoms.

Mindfulness practice has been associated with the development of several psychological and cognitive processes (e.g., acceptance, metacognitive awareness, decentering, etc.) that modulate the psychological changes and increased well-being observed after participation in mindfulness training. It was suggested that the increased ability to observe and relate to the present-moment experience—including thoughts, bodily sensations, feelings, and emotions—with acceptance, openness, receptivity, and nonjudgment fosters a healthier and more adaptive ability to deal with daily life experience and emotional forces (Hayes and Feldman, 2004; Kabat-Zinn, 1990). The capacity for mindful emotional regulation enables individuals to recognize their emotions, create space and time to mindfully observe what they are experiencing in the present moment, and positively deal with what is arising rather than suppressing or repressing the emotions and engaging in automatic and habitual maladaptive patterns of response (Brown *et al.*, 2007; Chambers *et al.*, 2009). This capacity to observe emotions with acceptance, nonjudgment, and openness allows individuals to deal with these emotions with discernment, thereby allowing healing to take place by replacing unwholesome emotions with a wholesome presence (Welwood, 1985).

In Buddhist philosophy it is suggested that, with mindfulness meditation, a person finds that unwholesome emotions and attitudes are transformed by cultivating a calming observing mind and wholesome states, such as compassion and equanimity. It fosters the recognition of the beauty and simplicity of life that lies in living in the here and now, flexibility and adaptation to the changes occurring in life as a consequence of its impermanent nature, and cultivation of harmony and balance between the inner self and outer world (Thera, 1965).

Literature has shown that, in old age, psychological problems such as emotional distress, depression, and anxiety can occur (McBee, 2006; Smith, 2006), and that psychological symptoms and subjective well-being have an effect in terms of disability, disease outcomes, morbidity, and functioning status (Gruenewald and Kemeny, 2007; Pressman and Cohen 2005). This study revealed that the MBSR program alleviated psychological symptoms, improved subjective well-being and psychological well-being, and fomented elders' positive emotions, outcomes that have been shown to affect health, optimal functioning, and quality of life (Davis *et al.*, 2007). Overall, the MBSR program positively impacted older adults' well-being and reduced psychological symptoms, and it may also be seen to have been associated with improvements in physical health of participants who completed the program.

Physical health

With age, many physical changes occur that may limit individuals' bodily systems and, consequently, their health. The challenges that these changes pose in older adults' lives affects their psychological well-being (e.g., autonomy and environmental mastery) and psychological symptoms (e.g., stress), and, in some cases, increases fear of death (Jewell, 2004; MacKinlay, 2001). Physical health can also be affected by psychological symptoms in older adults (Gruenewald and Kemeny, 2007; Pressman and Cohen 2005). The MBSR program has been shown to improve health symptoms in clinical (e.g., see Carlson and Garland, 2005; Carlson *et al.*, 2009; Kabat-Zinn, 1982; Kabat-Zinn *et al.*, 1985) and nonclinical (e.g., see Davidson *et al.*, 2003) populations. Studies with older adults revealed that the MBSR is effective in reducing physical symptoms and improving health in noninstitutionalized older adults suffering from chronic pain (Morone *et al.*, 2008; Smith, 2004) and institutionalized older adults (Ernst *et al.*, 2008, McBee, Westreich, and Likourezos, 2004).

The results of this study coincide with the reviewed literature. Participants who completed the MBSR program revealed decreased physical symptoms as measured by the SHCI (Eriksen *et al.*, 1999).

Participants also showed increased quality of life in the physical domain of the WHOQOL-100 (Canavarro *et al.*, 2009; WHOQOL Group, 1998) that evaluated pain and discomfort, energy and fatigue, and sleep and rest. The qualitative analysis demonstrated that the MBSR program improved their general physical well-being as a consequence of their improved feeling of relaxation that resulted from the mindfulness practices. They also reported feeling more active and flexible as a result of being more relaxed. There was an increased awareness of and respect for their age-related physical limitations, as well as improved quality of sleep. These physical improvements could also be associated with the positive changes observed in terms of psychological symptoms and well-being.

Some participants revealed that the mindfulness practices had changed their general habits in their daily lives, as they started doing regular exercise. There is evidence that physical exercise has multiple positive effects in older adults. Yaffe *et al.* (2001) conducted a prospective study evaluating the effects of physical activity and cognitive function in older adults. They recruited a sample of 5925 predominantly white community-dwelling women aged 65 or above. Participants were assessed cognitively at baseline and again six to eight years later. Physical activity was measured using self-reported records of physical activity (e.g., walking and climbing stairs) and energy expended. Results revealed that women with greater physical activity at baseline were less likely to experience cognitive decline at the six to eight years follow-up. Chodzko-Zajko *et al.* (2009) overviewed several studies looking at the impact of physical exercise in older adults. They showed that physical exercise improved cognitive processing; influenced the aging process; and improved psychological health and well-being, and overall quality of life. Accordingly, the reported changes in general habits of participants of the TG may further foment their cognition, well-being, and health.

Another important aspect is the transpersonal qualities inherent in physical exercise. Although in the Western world most of the physical exercise performed does not reflect a valuing of the quality of embodied awareness, it is possible that cultivating mindfulness in their daily lives and/ or practicing physical mindful practices such as yoga could increasingly foster this awareness and, consequently, impact the way older adults experience and understand reality and express deeper meanings of their experience. The body is the most fundamental source of knowledge, the source of all perception and action, the heart of our ability to express the meaning of our experiences that goes beyond any word, and what allows us to connect the inner and the outer worlds (Merleau-Ponty, 1962).

Overall, the MBSR program had a positive effect on the physical well-being of the participants of the TG. It is important that future research studies evaluate which practices of the MBSR program more directly affected older adults' physical health—the mindfulness meditation or the mindful yoga practices—as studies have shown that yoga practice in older adults improves health and health-related quality of life (Oken et al., 2006). This randomized study recruited 135 individuals, who were divided into three groups—yoga group, aerobic exercise group, and waiting-list group—that participated in the study during a six-month period. The yoga group participated in a weekly Iyengar yoga class and was invited to complete yoga exercises at home. The aerobic exercise group also participated in a weekly class and was also invited to do daily home practices. The waiting-list group did not participate in any class but received monthly phone calls to assess changes in health. All participants were assessed before and after the intervention in terms of cognitive performance using tests of attention and alertness, episodic memory, and working memory; mood, quality of life; fatigue; and physical measures. Results revealed no group effect on cognitive functions, but showed that the yoga intervention group had significant improvements in terms of quality of life, vitality, and physical measures, and decreases in terms of fatigue and bodily pain, as compared with both the aerobic exercise group and the wait-list group.

Social interactions

Compared with results for the CG, participants of the TG revealed improvements in terms of relations with others as assessed by the PWBS. Qualitative data also reflected that participants who completed the MBSR program recognized that their interactions with others had improved. They verified that they became more present when they were with others, which allowed them to be more discerning in their relationships. They also reported increased gratitude and compassion towards others. These results are very positive, not only in terms of the observed improvement in participants' relationships with others, but also because this may have impacted other dimensions of their lives, such as health, quality of life, and well-being. Rook *et al.* (2007) reviewed several studies on the beneficial and detrimental effects of social relationships in later life, and they demonstrated that social functioning is related with several positive health outcomes, such as reduced risk of cardiovascular disease, cancer, infectious illness, and functional decline and lower risk with respect to mortality, as well as less risk of the onset and development of—and higher probablity of their recovery from—disability in later life. These social functioning patterns refer to the amount of interaction within and the structure of older adults' social network, such as group membership and familial ties (Berg et al., 2007). Moreover, the quality of relations in older adults also has an impact on their health and psychological well-being (Gruenewald and Kemeny, 2007; Rook et al., 2007). Empirical evidence showed that negative social relationships have been associated with adverse psychological and physical health effects, while positive social relationships were associated with favorable psychological and health outcomes (Rook et al., 2007).

In the same line, Finch et al. (1989) evaluated the impact of positive and negative social ties on psychological distress and well-being among older adults. They recruited 246 noninstitutionalized community residents between the ages of 60 and 80. Participants were assessed in terms of their social network, in which positive social ties were quantified in terms of the number of individuals named as providers of instrumental social support (e.g., financial assistance or help with shopping) and emotional social support (e.g., people that they confided in or with whom they could discuss personal worries). Negative social ties were measured in terms of the number of individuals that criticized, exploited, disappointed by breaking promises, or frequently caused feelings of anger for these older adults. Participants were also assessed in terms of psychological well-being (i.e., quality of life) and psychological distress. Results showed that negative social ties were significantly related with and strong predictors of distress and decreased psychological well-being, while positive social ties fostered older adults' psychological well-being.

Similarly, Seeman (2000) reviewed published studies on social relationships and health/health behaviors in older adults. The selected studies in the meta-analysis had been published between 1970 and 1998 and were identified through MEDLINE (an online database that contains journal citations and abstracts for biomedical and life science literature from around the world) using keywords such as social relationships, social support, and health. This study also reviewed health-related journals, including the *American Journal of Epidemiology, Annals of Epidemiology, American Journal of Public Health, Journal of Health and Social Behavior, Social Science and Medicine,* and the *Journals of Gerontology.* I gave preference to original research and studies with strong methodologies that included representative samples, longitudinal data, or multivariate analysis that controlled for possible confounders. Data were organized in major categories in order to extract a synthesis of the data found in the literature collected. The data clearly showed that the quality of social relationships in older adults played an important role in health promotion. Negative social relations (i.e., critical and/or demanding relationships) had more negative effects in older adults' health, such as depression and angina, which, in turn, were associated with physiological profiles reflecting elevated stress hormones, increased cardiovascular activity, and decreased immune system response. Positive social relations were associated with better health, which may reflect lower levels of stress and, consequently, better immune function. Given the importance of the quality of social interaction among older adults, further research is necessary to evaluate the impact of MBSR program on the quality of relationships of older adults.

Neuropsychological performance

As was reviewed in Chapter 1, the neurological changes that occur as individuals age have effects in terms of specific cognitive skills such as fluid intelligence, memory, speed processing, learning, and executive functioning. Mindfulness meditation practice has been associated with increased thickness in brain regions associated with attention, interoception, empathy, and sensory processing (Lazar *et al.*, 2005) and may have a neuro-protective effect in terms of grey matter decline in areas involved in mindfulness practice, such as attention and emotional regulation (Pagnogni and Cekic, 2007, Goleman, 2003). Moreover, empirical evidence showed that mindfulness meditation and the MBSR program involve the training in attention and inhibitory skills of automatic cognitive processes; in particular, it was shown that mindfulness practitioners improve attentional skills (Treadway and Lazar, 2009) and working memory processing (Chambers *et al.*, 2008).

One of the research questions of this study was: What are the effects of the MBSR program in older adults in terms of neuropsychological performance? It was suggested that, as older adults frequently exhibit deficits in processing skills due to the reduced working memory performance, deficits in inhibitory skills (McDowd, 1997) and suppression mechanisms (Palladino and DeBeni, 1999); and decline in processing speed, attention (Craik, 1999), and distraction control (Darowski *et al.*, 2008), they could benefit from mindfulness practice in terms of cognitive performance, in particular, with respect to attention, processing speed, and working memory. Quantitative results demonstrated that older adults who completed the MBSR program improved in some of the measures used to assess the working memory, speed processing, and episodic memory. Qualitative results showed that the two participants who had reported some difficulties in terms of memory at pre-assessment observed improvements of cognitive performance at post-assessment: one in terms of creativity and the other in terms of memory.

Overall, this study supports the hypothesis that the MBSR program was beneficial for older adults' cognitive performance. These observed improvements in cognition could be associated with improvements in health and well-being, reduced psychological symptoms, physical activity during the program, and the regular exercise participants started including in their daily routines. Empirical evidence suggests that cognitive performance in older adults is affected by health (Lopez et al., 2003), well-being and psychological symptoms such as depression (Lichtenberg et al., 1995), and physical activity (Chodzko-Zajko et al., 2009; Yaffe et al., 2001). A follow-up assessment taken a few months after the completion of the study could reveal whether these observed changes were maintained and that outcome's association with the rate of mindfulness practice at home between the end of the study and the follow-up assessment.

In terms of creativity, there is a study looking at the effects of mindfulness training in a business context that showed an association between mindfulness practice and creativity (Langer, Heffernan, and Kiester, 1988). It is possible that the increased creativity described was related with the improved attention, patience, and calmness experienced by the participant as a result of the mindfulness practices, which allowed an increased clarity and intuitive awareness of what she wanted to transmit to the reader. Furthermore, the increased ability to be in the present moment observing what is arising in the mental, emotional, and physical bodies could allow the participant to be more aware of insights arising, thereby facilitating the creative expression.

Spirituality, perceptions of existence and aging, death, and loss

The results of this study showed that participation in the MBSR program affected spirituality and spiritual well-being in older adults. Participants revealed increased spiritual well-being, particularly regarding how they relate to themselves in terms of meaning, purpose, and values in life; to the environment (i.e., nurture, enjoyment, and care for the physical world); and to their relationships with a higher reality (i.e., Cosmic force, God, or transcendental reality). Furthermore, they also revealed that the MBSR program fomented and/or confirmed an already present sense of interconnectedness and universality with others and nature, and helped them find time and space to connect with their inner self.

The MBSR program also promoted their sense of transpersonal self; that is, they see themselves not as separate entities in the world (i.e., separate from others and from nature), but as part of a larger and interconnected reality. They also cultivated an awareness of themselves as whole beings with body, mind, emotions, and spirit that interact in each moment of their experience, both within and without. These results are similar to those of previous studies looking at the effects of MBSR on spirituality that revealed that mindfulness practices were associated with an increased sense of awareness of interconnection among themselves, other individuals, and nature (MacKenzie *et al.*, 2007).

Spirituality was revealed to be an integral part of participants' lives, either through Church, belief in God, or other spiritual beliefs. Their spiritual beliefs supported and gave meaning to their lives and to their psychological, physical, and social experiences; the cycles of their life of development and transformation; and their purpose in life.

These results support the Buddhist principles and Buddhist psychology suggestions that meditation cultivates a "receptive consciousness" (Brazier, 2003) that fosters an awareness of the larger reality that contains the personal experience, the whole and the wholeness of being (Selby, 2003), the interconnection with the world, and the impermanence of self and reality (Brazier, 2003). It also supports Buddhist principles that suggested that mindfulness practices fosters a process of disidentification with the self and awareness of the interconnection with all reality (Ekman *et al.*, 2005).

Furthermore, the study's outcome confirms that, in old age, individuals are moving towards individuation and a more spiritual and transpersonal perspective on life (Erikson, 1997; Jung, 1939b, 1971; Reed, 1991; Schachter-Shalomi, 1995). It is a period of development of personal wholeness, unity with the Self, inner environment, integration, and being and of unity with the Self, the cosmos, and God (Brewi and Brennan, 1999). It is a period in which elders move towards maturation and wisdom (i.e., gerotranscendence) and shift their metaperspective towards a more spiritual understanding of themselves, life, and reality (Tornstam, 1997).

In this study, participants' learning journey during the MBSR program also confirmed an already established belief among participants that life is a learning process, a journey of growth and transformation as sentient beings. This learning journey was perceived as the ultimate purpose in life, which is developed and experienced in the physical, psychological, social, and spiritual dimensions of their lives. They saw suffering, learning, and death as an integral part of life, and the participation in the MBSR program allowed them to cultivate an increased sense of acceptance towards suffering, self, others, life, death, and the impermanence of life. This mindset reflects that old age is an opportunity to learn and to grow, to be aware of the beauty of this period of life, to connect with the inner self and the meaning of life, death, and mortality (Schachter-Shalomi, 1995).

The increased acceptance of death and the perception that death is part of the natural cycle of life reported by participants of this study could be attributed to the increased presence in the "here and now," awareness of their life in the present moment, improved acceptance towards life experiences of the past and present, acceptance of the impermanence of life, and the natural movement towards their inner world that characterizes this stage of life (Brewi and Brennan, 1999).

In terms of perception of aging, older adults from the TG demonstrated that they do not see themselves as being old and that the only factor reminding them of their age is their body, when it shows signs of physical aging and limitations that make them slow down in their daily lives. This may have a positive impact on their functioning and health, as it has been suggested that older adults with positive perceptions of aging have fewer declines in physical functioning and health (Gruenewald and Kemeny, 2007). This suggests not only that older adults in this study showed an ageless perception of themselves but also that they did not identify themselves with a materialist view of their existence (i.e., body), possibly due to their developing connection with their inner self and the Cosmos/God. The changes in the physical body in late life are opportunities for individuals to self-transcend and move to the inner world of their existence. Participants perceived aging as a sign of wisdom arising from their life experience, which conceptualization meets the Buddhist perspective of wisdom as being based on a personal observation and experience rather than on an intellectual achievement. Rumi (as cited in Barks, 1995) wrote:

> There are two kinds of intelligence: one acquired,
> as a child in school memorizes facts and concepts
> from books and from what the teacher says,
> collecting information from the traditional sciences
> as well as from the new sciences.

> With such intelligence you rise in the world.
> You get ranked ahead or behind others
> in regard to your competence in retaining
> information. You stroll with this intelligence
> in and out of fields of knowledge, getting always more
> marks on your preserving tablets.
>
> There is another kind of tablet, one
> already completed and preserved inside you.
> A spring overflowing its springbox. A freshness
> in the center of the chest. This other intelligence
> does not turn yellow or stagnate. It's fluid,
> and it doesn't move from outside to inside
> through conduits of plumbing-learning.
> This second knowing is a fountainhead
> from within you, moving out. (p.178)

Individuals have an intrinsic need to find meaning in life (Frankl, 2004a, 2004b) and, in old age, the loss of meaning that comes with the challenges experienced in this period of life—including retirement and loss of social role, dependency, and isolation—may cause individuals to experience a "crisis of meanings" (Missine, 2004). In this period of life, individuals find meaning in their experiences with the world and with others (experiential values) and by the attitude they bring towards their experience of suffering (attitudinal values), just as they find meaning in their family, attention to their spiritual needs, helping others, and suffering (Missine, 2004). The results of this study support these suggestions, as participants perceived that life's main purpose lies in growth and transformation in the school of life. Suffering is perceived as part of life's journey undertaken to grow and develop. They found meaning in helping their family by taking care of their grandchildren or by helping others in need (e.g., church, volunteer work, etc.), and mindfulness practice fostered their presence, their awareness, and the quality of these experiences.

MacKinlay (2001) suggested that the goal of human beings is to achieve spiritual wholeness, which is attained when individuals' identify and find ways to respond to their ultimate meaning in life; find hope and intimacy with God and/or others; and transcend limitations and loss. Participants of this study revealed a common ultimate meaning in life: to grow and develop throughout life, and that old age was just another period of their lives in which to grow and transform. This learning occurred in all dimensions of their lives, including the way they experience the physical, psychological, social, and spiritual. Through mindfulness, participants fomented their ability to mindfully accept life, their experiences, their suffering, and their limitations; and to be in their interactions with others with more presence and openness. For MacKinlay (2001), the ability to find the individual and final meaning in life was seen as wisdom, which was defined as an increasing ability to tolerate uncertainty and a deepening search for a meaning in life. Tornstam (1997) suggested that aging is "a natural progression towards wisdom" (p.143) that reflects a movement towards individuation, self-transcendence, spiritual development, and unity with all people and with the Divine (Erikson, 1997; Jung, 1939b, 1971; Reed, 1991; Schachter-Shalomi, 1995).

Results of this study also revealed that the MBSR program supported the grieving process of two elders that had recently lost a close relative, supporting them in ways that helped them to accept their loss and improve their psychological well-being. Bereavement has been shown to have nonclinical and clinical consequences in older adults. Nonclinical consequences include loneliness, personal functioning, personal control, social functioning, coping, and social participation. The clinical impact of bereavement in older adults includes depression, anxiety, traumatic grief, suicide, mortality (Hansson and Stroebe, 2007), guilt, frustration, and identity crisis (Kumar, 2010). Accordingly, the MBSR program seems to have a positive impact in older adults' bereavement process by providing support in terms of cultivating their attention in the present moment, accepting the present-moment experiences independently of their quality, and recognizing and accepting the impermanence of reality, which, according to Buddhism, is the cause of individuals' suffering (Brazier, 2003, Neale, 2006). These principles impacted participants' perspective on death, thereby aiding in their experience of losing others.

Evidence showed that the spiritual development that characterizes old age allows individuals to consciously and successfully adapt to the challenges of this period of life. Older adults retain a sense of self that is ageless, an identity that maintains continuity and integrity that transcends physical and psychological challenges that occur during this period of life. These challenges are perceived as part of the life's journey and internally accepted. Participation in the MBSR program not only fomented this acceptance of life and their awareness of the impermanence of life, but also fostered their connection with themselves and their inner nature and their awareness of their purpose and the meaning of life, death, and mortality. It fomented older adults' conscious aging (Moody, 2000; Robba, 2006), in which elders bring awareness, mindfulness, and acceptance to the aging process, learn from the process that arises from the experience of aging, and relate to the world in terms of individuation, self-knowledge, connection with the universal aspect of life, and service.

Overall, the MBSR fostered and fomented the development of personal and universal dimensions of elders' lives. Nevertheless, more studies need to be developed to replicate these findings and more deeply explore the impact of these changes in elders' lives during and after the completion of the MBSR program.

Formal and informal practices

In the MBSR program, the component of formal and informal practice is very important. In all eight sessions participants are guided on one or two formal practices of mindfulness (e.g., sitting meditation, body-scan meditation, or mindful yoga), and all participants are given CDs with the practices used to conduct daily formal mindfulness meditations at home, which last approximately 45 minutes. They are also invited to conduct several informal practices during their daily lives, such as mindful eating; observation and description of how they experience pleasant and unpleasant events, including their emotions, thoughts, and bodily sensations during the events; and level of awareness of these occurrences while the event is taking place.

In spite of the importance of formal and informal practice of mindfulness throughout the eight weeks of the MBSR program, few studies have looked at the effects of home practice and informal practice with respect to the observed positive changes in mindfulness and other dimensions (e.g., psychological well-being, stress, etc.) in individuals who completed the program. For example, Speca *et al.* (2000) conducted a study with cancer patients that completed the MBSR program. Results of this study revealed that home practice meditation was significantly related to improvements in mood. Similar results were reported by Carmody and Baer (2008) in a study looking at the relationships between mindfulness practice and levels of mindfulness, medical and psychological symptoms, and well-being that showed that mindfulness practice was significantly related to changes in mindfulness, psychological well-being, stress, and psychological symptoms.

Other studies (e.g., see Astin, 1997; Davidson *et al.*, 2003) reflected no such association. Astin (1997) looked at the effects of practice time and improvement in psychological symptoms in a sample of college students that completed the MBSR program. The study showed no significant correlations between practice time and symptoms improvement.

This study revealed that formal practice with CDs was related to improvements in mindfulness, reduction in perceived stress, psychological and physical symptoms, quality of life in the physical and psychological dimensions, and processing speed in older adults. Informal practices were related with mindfulness, reduction in perceived stress, decrease in psychological and physical symptoms, increased quality of life (in the physical and psychological dimension of the WHOQOL-BREF), decentering, dimension isolation of the compassion scale, and speed processing in older adults. The number of sessions attended by participants was related with mindfulness improvements, reduction in perceived stress, and decentering. The impact of the regular practice in participants' quality of life was also revealed by the qualitative analysis of this study. Overall, these results support the importance of regular mindfulness practice for fostering improvements of mindfulness, compassion, and decentering, and significant reductions in psychological symptoms, physical symptoms, quality of life, and processing speed.

In this study, participants who completed the MBSR adopted a regular formal and informal practice of mindfulness meditation during and after the program. During the program, the informal practices relied mainly on completing certain exercises that were presented in the manual given them at the beginning of the program, which included exercises such as mindful eating, observation and awareness of emotional reaction patterns, observation of mindful responses during the week, observation and awareness of eating patterns, and so forth. After the program, participants revealed that the informal practices were generalized to daily life tasks completed throughout the day, such as eating, brushing the teeth, interaction with others, walking, cooking, contemplation of nature, and others. They no longer perceived these as practices but as something that was occurring naturally in their lives and was a way of slowing down and experiencing life more fully. This evidence suggests that formal practices of mindfulness foster mindful living, which outcome is similar to the results found by Carmody and Baer (2008). Carmody and Baer revealed that the amount of time spent in formal practice of mindfulness predicted increases in the self-reported tendency to be mindful in daily life.

Furthermore, results of the present study support the suggestions that mindfulness is not only a formal practice through which we direct and cultivate mindful awareness when we sit on a meditation cushion or practice mindful yoga on our yoga mats, but mindfulness is also a way of being with oneself and life in each passing moment (Shauna and Carlson, 2009), a way of being that allows us to deeply experience each moment and know what is happening in and with us moment by moment. Shauna and Carlson (2009) stated:

> This knowing...it is a felt sense, a knowing with your whole being. This deep knowing is mindfulness. As you breathe in, knowing with your whole body 'breathing in.' As you breathe out, knowing with your whole body 'breathing out.' (p.4)

This way of being entails acceptance of whatever is arising in each passing moment, involves an open and receptive attention, and fosters a discerning attention that allows us to be aware and conscious of the quality of the present experience and our internal reaction and response to it. It allows us to cultivate a nondual awareness, so that, by accepting what is, we do not reject the experiences that cause us suffering; neither do we crave those experiences that bring us pleasure. We rest in the present moment free from our conditionings and mental patterns of aversion and craving. We experience the moment with all our heart: open, present, and receptive, embracing the totality of our experience. In this understanding, mindfulness is both a process (mindful practice) and an outcome (mindful awareness; Shapiro and Carlson, 2009).

The distinction between these two aspects of mindfulness was also reflected in my personal experience during the study and continue to be as as a mindfulness instructor and in my daily life, as I cultivate a kind, compassionate and mindful presence in my many moments of life. It is clear that both are inseparable and interrelated when we embark in this journey of experiencing mindfulness in ourselves and our daily lives. Mindfulness affects our well-being, as well as the way life is experienced and perceived. There is deeper knowledge and insight into the nature of oneself, others, and existence. There is no separation and no division: there is Oneness and interconnection. There is no past, no present: there is is-ness.

Another issue that I believe is very important in the field of mindfulness has to do with the personal practice of the teacher/instructor and psychotherapists using mindfulness approaches in their professional settings. Mindfulness cannot be taught conceptually and intellectually. In order to truly pass on the essence of mindfulness and guide individuals in this learning and transformational journey, teachers and professionals using mindfulness as a therapeutic tool need to be constantly investing in their own transformation process through mindfulness (and other personal inquiry approaches). The personal formal and informal practice of mindfulness fosters professionals' embodied awareness during interactions with clients. This allows an increased presence in the moment and discernment in terms of the adequate response, as well as a constant investment in strengthening positive states of mind such as lovingkindness, compassion, acceptance, receptivity, patience, openness, nonjudgment, and beginner's mind, which are all positive attitudinal elements for MBSR teachers to embody during instruction (Woods, 2009). In MBSR's teaching settings there is no separation between teacher/instructor and clients, as both are being influenced by each other in various ways. The teacher/instructor's awareness of his internal forces (i.e., unconscious material, ego, emotions, feelings, thoughts) arising in each passing moment allows him to be more aware of what is present within himself throughout the sessions, as well as what is arising from the environment and his internal reactions to what is taking place moment by moment. Also, it allows him to participate in the interaction with the group with awareness, detailed observation, contemplation, creativity, and openness. This awareness fosters a more discerning presence and dialogue with clients, and foments an internal attitude of co-operation with clients in which both are learning, growing, healing, and moving towards wholeness in each passing moment. Laing (1967) provided this reminder: "Psychotherapy must remain an obstinate attempt of two people to recover the wholeness of being human through the relationship between them" (p.45). The MBSR is not group psychotherapy, but it has therapeutic effects, and a therapeutic dynamic is being developed in each session, moment by moment.

The importance of mindfulness teachers' personal practice is valued in many mindfulness program trainings such as the training in MBSR and MBCT programs (Woods, 2009). It is important to evaluate in what way teachers' personal practice and developmental process in mindfulness might impact the teaching environment and the observed changes in participants who complete the program.

Older adults' experience of the MBSR program

Overall, the experience of the MBSR program in older adults had very positive impacts in terms of physical and psychological well-being, cognitive performance, spirituality and spiritual well-being, death perspectives, and loss. They all reported that the experience was very positive and gratifying in terms of the learned principles and developed practices; observed impact in their daily life in terms of mindfulness skills (i.e., observation, attention, presence, awareness, slowing down, and capacity of cultivating states of being in the present moment), and acceptance of life, self, the aging process, loss, and others; and their having experienced improvements in well-being, cognition, physical health, and social interactions. Participation in the program promoted their spiritual well-being, sense of interconnection, awareness of their transpersonal self, and perception of life's purpose as relying on growth and transformation. When participants were asked about the impact of the MBSR program in terms of their well-being, they focused their answers on psychological and physical health, social interactions, and spirituality, and some also manifested the impact of the practices in terms of cognition. The effects in spirituality were more present in participants' replies when they were questioned about their perception of life and existence and the impact of the program on their views and experience of life. This suggests that, for older adults, well-being relies on all these dimensions of their lives.

This study aimed to investigate the impact of the MBSR program in all dimensions of older adults' lives, that is, the psychological, physical, social, cognitive, and spiritual because all these different realms are part of individuals' whole existence, and they interact with one another in defining one's experience of life in each passing moment. This study revealed that participation in the MBSR program affected individuals' experience as a whole: physically, psychologically, socially, cognitively, and spiritually, thereby suggesting that the MBSR program can function as a holistic intervention for elders as a means for cultivating physical health, emotional balance, positive social interactions, and spiritual development during a period of life in which individuals experience many challenges associated with the aging process.

Adaptation of MBSR for healthy older adults

The MBSR program as elaborated by Kabat-Zinn (1990) consists of an eight to ten-week program with a weekly two-hour session and an intensive silent meditation day between the sixth and the seventh week. Participants are given four audio CDs containing guided formal practices (i.e., yoga and mindfulness meditation) and a manual with exercises to be completed throughout the program.

Several other mindfulness-based interventions have been developed to be adapted to specific clinical populations or age groups. Some of these programs include MBCT, particularly applied in cases of depression and suicidal ideations (Barnhofer and Crane, 2009; Segal *et al.*, 2002); acceptance and commitment therapy (ACT) for dealing with general anxiety disorder (Hoppes, 2006); dialectical behavior therapy (DBT), which has been effective in reducing multi-impulsive and suicidal behaviors in patients suffering from borderline personality disorder (Linehan, 1993; Rizvi, Welch, and Dimidjian, 2009); and the Inner Kids ABC program (Greenland, 2010) for children and for frail elders with significant physical and cognitive impairment (McBee, 2008). These interventions differ somewhat in terms of the approach and procedures used to teach mindfulness, but they share the same goal of teaching participants to become aware of thoughts and emotions and to change their relation to them so that thoughts and feelings are recognized as mental events rather than either aspects of the self or reflections of reality (Baer, 2003).

The results from the present study suggested that the MBSR should accept some adaptations for healthy older adults in order to address special needs of this age group. Although, the sample of this study did not suffer from major physical or cognitive impairments, they showed some difficulties that are associated with their age. These difficulties were observed during the practices, as they needed to be sitting or lying down for 45 minutes and some showed some fatigue. Some of the yoga postures included in the yoga practice sequences were a little demanding, due to some physical limitations associated with normal aging. Because the participants were slower-moving and needed more time to find their way into the posture, the sequence took 60 minutes, instead of 45 minutes. It is suggested that the MBSR for this age group should adjust the time of the practices to 30 minutes instead of 45 minutes and that some of the most challenging yoga postures should be excluded in order to decrease the time of the sequence, allow more extra time to explain each posture, and facilitate participants' practice. The intensive silent session was supposed to last six to seven hours, but, based on participants' feedback and my own observation during the weekly two-hour sessions, this session was shortened to five hours. The intensive should intersperse sitting, standing, walking, and lying-down meditation practices in order to avoid any overdoing and physical tiredness. These changes imply that the CDs provided with the practices should also be adapted according to the changes suggested.

Delimitations and limitations

Delimitations

Participants who were selected for the study were representative of the general population because they were selected from a pool of noninstitutionalized older adults. The target places of recruitment (i.e., Third Age Universities, yoga centers, etc.) possibly delimited the study, as these venues attract older adults who are more actively engaged in social and recreational activities.

The inclusion and exclusion criteria highly delimited the selection, as participants were included in the study only if they were 65 years old or above, with no regular practice of meditation, no cognitive impairment (as assessed using MOCA), no terminal illness or clinical diagnosis of depression or anxiety, no mobility difficulties, and a willingness to participate in an eight-week MBSR program with a 90-minute session per week and a full day (six to seven hours) session between the sixth and seventh week of the program. Participants were not accepted in the study if they lived in nursing homes. Another delimitation of the study was the selection of participants with no recent diagnosis of chronic illness. Those who had been recently diagnosed might not yet have experienced the stabilizing effects of medication or might still be unstable in relation to treatment approach.

Using spoken interviews rather than written responses from participants was also a delimitation. Some participants might feel inhibited or less comfortable in sharing their experiences verbally and written responses would allow responses to be reworked more carefully.

Limitations

One limitation of this study was the size of the sample, in particular in relation to the quantitative measures. However, given the selected battery of psychological and neuropsychological tests, as well as the mixed-method approach used in the study, this research gathered significant data to obtain solid and strong results reflecting the effects and life experiences of older adults during the MBSR program.

Another limitation was the fact that the sample included participants with the same ethnicity, almost all with the same religious background, and all from the same social class. Furthermore, the control group was an empty group (i.e., did not participate in the MBSR program and did not do anything) which may raise questions concerning the nature of the effects observed in the treatment group. It could be questioned whether the observed effects are attributed to the specifics of the MBSR program or the general factors (e.g., increased attention, interaction with individuals from the same age group, etc.) associated with the fact that the treatment group participated in an activity.

The method used in the study did not allow the generalization of the findings to the larger population. The findings offered an in-depth description of the lived experience of participants and cannot be applied to other groups or individuals.

Another limitation was participants' ability to share certain experiences or dimensions of experience, due to the complexity of the experiences being described. Also the language might have been a limitation, as verbal description tends to limit the complexity of nonverbal aspects of the experience, even though I prompted participants to use metaphors or images in order to convey the meaning of their experiences. Moreover, because participants were Portuguese, the Portuguese language might somehow have emphasized certain aspects of the experience or limited other aspects of the experience. Finally, because the analysis of the interview was translated to English (by myself) some of the meaning might have been lost in the translation process, although all attempts were made to use the English words that most fully reflected the intended meaning.

Factors such as medication and illnesses might have influenced the observed changes in psychological well-being, physical health, and neuropsychological performance in some of the elders who participated in the study. Finally, this research used the same neuropsychological tests for Assessment 1 and Assessment 2 (i.e., pre-intervention and post-intervention, respectively) which might have caused some learning effect as participants were exposed twice to the same tests.

Applications and implications of the study

As was discussed in this section, this study provides solid and robust evidence that the MBSR program provided a holistic support to foment the well-being, physical health, and spirituality of older adults, as well as stimulated and improved their cognitive performance and social interactions. This study also presents evidence that the principles and practices learned throughout the MBSR program also provided support for dealing with loss in older adults and the aging process. Accordingly, this study has significant applications to the field of gerontology, geriatric services for mental and physical health, and psychologists working with older adults. It revealed important findings for day centers, nursing homes, and Third Age Universities, which may be interested in including the MBSR program in their activities for older adults.

For researchers in the field of mindfulness, conscious aging, and aging, it may also provide inspiration for future research exploring the impact of the MBSR program and/or an adapted version of the MBSR for older adults in this age group and other associated interventions that foster conscious aging.

This study provided significant support to the advancement of Transpersonal Psychology as applied to older adults by revealing new data in terms of: (a) understanding of how the MBSR can be used as a holistic intervention for older adults; (b) the effects and lived experiences of the MBSR program for older adults in terms of spiritual development and spiritual well-being; (c) an in-depth analysis of how the MBSR program fomented new meanings and understanding about themselves, their existence, the purpose of their lives, the aging process, loss, and death; (d) understanding the transpersonal development in older adults; and (e) the interaction between physical health, well-being, spiritual transformation, social interactions, and cognitive performance in promoting older adults' well-being.

This study provided a broad and in-depth analysis of the effects of the MBSR program for older adults. However, future research will be important to replicate and generalize the findings. First, it would be important to collect a larger sample that included more racial, socio-economic, and religious diversity to observe whether the results are replicated in such a sample. Second, in order to evaluate the extent to which the MBSR program helps older adults to deal with and go through the experience of grieving and bereavement, a study focused on a sample of individuals who have recently lost a close relative would provide more in-depth analysis of how the program fosters the observed acceptance and positive emotional attitude towards loss. Third, a follow-up assessment would provide information of the prolonged effects of the MBSR program for older adults who have completed the program and how these practices affect participants in terms of conscious aging. Moreover, looking at long-term effects of the program in participants' lives would allow the understanding of how the participation in the program and maintaining a regular practice affect their aging process. Fifth, a question remains: what is it about the MBSR program that is behind the observed effects in older adults as compared with outcomes of regular sessions of mindfulness practice or regular practices of yoga? It would be important to develop a study with three intervention groups and a control group comparing the effects of the MBSR program with weekly mindfulness sessions and weekly yoga sessions in order to understand the difference between these interventions in older adults. Sixth, given the suggested changes to the MBSR program for older adults, a future study should look at how older adults experienced the program within this proposed adapted format of the MBSR, as compared with the one used in this study. Seventh, further research should be developed to look at the effects of the MBSR program on older adults' social interactions. Finally, it is important to note that each MBSR teacher/instructor will have had a unique personal history and individual transformation throughout his life and is going through a different learning process while he facilitates the program: How are individuals' experience of the MBSR program affected by these particular and individual characteristics of the teacher/instructor that is facilitating the program? How might this factor impact the changes observed in participants? A study designed to look at individual differences of MBSR teachers and the observed effects on his and participants' transformation could provide some insight into these questions.

Summary and conclusions

This study used a mixed-method and integral inquiry approach to look at the effects and lived experiences of older adults in the MBSR program. This method allowed me to honor both quantitative and qualitative methods of research. The quantitative data provided insights into effects of the MBSR program in terms of well-being, physical health, cognitive performance, and spirituality, while the qualitative methods allowed an in-depth exploration of participants' experiences during the program and the meaning of these experiences.

Twenty-four older adults between the ages of 65 and 73 participated in the study. The sample was randomly divided into two groups: the treatment group and the control group. The treatment group participated in the MBSR program while the control group did not participate in the MBSR program. All participants completed Assessment 1 and Assessment 2 (pre- and post-intervention, respectively) which consisted of a questionnaire on demographic and health status, and a psychological battery of tests used to assess their well-being, physical health, spiritual well-being, neuropsychological performance, and death perspectives. At Assessment 2, seven participants also completed a qualitative interview to explore their lived experiences of the MBSR program. The quantitative data were statistically analyzed using the SPSS program and the qualitative data were analyzed using the heuristic inquiry approach, which involved an in-depth immersion in the research question in order to derive a global creative synthesis of the interviews. Results were combined and merged concurrently to arrive at an overall analysis of the findings.

This research provided in-depth and comprehensive analysis of the effects of the MBSR program for older adults. It revealed significant and robust evidence showing that the MBSR program fomented older adults' physical health, subjective and psychological well-being, cognitive performance, social interactions, spirituality and spiritual well-being; affected participants' perspectives of aging, meaning of life, and death; and provided a positive support for bereavement process. This study suggested that the MBSR program functioned as an alternative holistic intervention program for elders that focused on improving individuals' integral well-being and transpersonal development and on fostering balance and harmony of the body, mind, and spirit.

What time is it?
Now
Where are you?
Here
Who are you?
The moment.

(Welch and Salva, 2006)

» Appendix 1 «

Description of Quantitative Measures

In order to assess the effects of the MBSR program on psychological and physical well-being, neuropsychological performance, and spirituality, several standardized instruments were used. I selected only scales (as listed on page 68 onwards) that had been translated and/or validated to the Portuguese population. *Validity* of an instrument has been defined as "the extent to which it measures what it was intended to measure" (Mertens, 2005, p.352). According to the Standards for Educational and Psychological Testing, validity is "a unitary concept that measures the degree to which all the accumulated evidence supports the intended interpretation of test scores for the proposed purpose" (as cited in Mertens, 2005, p.352). Usually, instruments are validated according to construct and content validity. *Construct validity* refers to the "evidence and rationales that support the trustworthiness of the score meaning" (Mertens, 2005, p.352), and *content validity* is related to evidence that shows that the "test covers the appropriate content" (Mertens, 2005, p.352). The instruments selected are described below.

Mindfulness Attention Awareness Scale

The Mindfulness Awareness Attention Scale (MAAS) was used in this study to assess the trait mindfulness of participants of the study. The MAAS was developed by Brown and Ryan (2003) to measure the general tendency to be attentive and aware of present-moment experience in daily life. The MAAS consists of a 15-item self-report test with various statements related to mindfulness. It has a single factor structure and provides a single total score. Each statement is rated on a six-point Likert scale of one (*almost always*) to six (*almost never*). The MAAS has been validated in college, working adults, and cancer populations. The authors reported internal consistency (Cronbach's alpha coefficient) of .82. The MAAS was significantly correlated with openness to experience, emotional intelligence, and well-being; negatively correlated with rumination and social anxiety; and unrelated to self-monitoring. MAAS scores were significantly higher in mindfulness practitioners than in a matched control group. A group of cancer patients who completed the MBSR program showed increases in MAAS scores that were associated with decreases in mood disturbance and symptoms of stress (Carlson and Brown, 2005). The MAAS appears to be sensitive to different degrees of mindfulness that can result from training. Other studies showed that participation in the MBSR program are associated with increases in mindfulness as measured by MAAS (Carmody *et al.*, 2008; Nyklicek and Kuijpers, 2008; Shapiro *et al.*, 2007).

The validation of the MAAS to the Portuguese population with a sample of 530 individuals revealed good internal consistency (alpha coefficient .88; Gregório and Pinto-Gouveia, 2011).

Five Facet Mindfulness Questionnaire

Baer *et al.* (2006) developed the Five Facet Mindfulness Questionnaire (FFMQ) that was derived from a factor analytic study of five independently developed mindfulness questionnaires, including the MAAS, the Freiburg Mindfulness Inventory (FMI), the Kentuchy Inventory of Mindfulness Skills (KIMS), the Cognitive and Affective Mindfulness Scale (CAMS), and the Mindfulness Questionnaire (MQ). The analysis resulted in a 39-item questionnaire regarding five factors that are associated with a general tendency to be mindful in daily life: observing, describing, acting with awareness, being nonjudging of inner experience, and nonreactivity of inner experience. Items are rated on a five-point Likert scale ranging from one (*never or very rarely true*) to five (*very often or always*). Results revealed good internal consistency (Cronbach's alpha coefficient range of from .84 to .87), significant relationships with a variety of constructs related to mindfulness (e.g., self-compassion, emotional regulation, etc.), and psychological well-being, with the exception of the observation facet. The FFMQ has also been validated in meditating and nonmeditating communities and college samples (Baer *et al.*, 2008), revealing adequate to good Cronbach's alpha coefficients (ranging from .72 to .92) in all facets and in all samples, with the exception of the nonreactivity to internal experience facet in the student sample (.67). Most mindfulness facets were significantly related to meditation experience, psychological symptoms, and well-being. Participation in MBSR has been associated with increases in the five facets of the FFMQ (Carmody and Baer, 2008; Carmody *et al.*, 2009).

The validation of the FFMQ to the Portuguese population in a sample of 600 individuals revealed low levels of saturation of two items in two facets that were removed from the Portuguese version. Internal consistency was good (alpha coefficient range from .63 to .89) and the five facets of mindfulness were correlated with other psychopathological constructs, with the exception of the observation facet (Gregório and Pinto-Gouveia, 2013).

Self-Compassion Scale

The Self-Compassion Scale (SCS; Neff, 2003) was developed based on the defining construct that self-compassion involves being kind and understanding towards oneself in times of pain and failure rather than being self-criticizing. It also entails the development that individuals perceive their self-experiences as part of the larger human experience rather than perceiving them as only experienced by themselves, and being mindfully aware of painful feelings and thoughts rather than becoming overly identified with them. The SCS consists of 26 items and is designed to measure three components of self-compassion on separate subscales: self-kindness versus self-judgment, common humanity versus isolation, and mindfulness versus overidentification. Items are rated on a five-point Likert scale ranging from one (*almost never*) to five (*almost always*). Analysis revealed good internal consistency reliability for the five-item self-kindness subscale (.78) and for the five-item self-judgment subscale (.77). Internal consistency reliability for the four-item subscale of common humanity was .80 and for the four-item isolation .79. The four-item mindfulness subscale revealed a .75 internal consistency coefficient and an .81 internal consistency reliability coefficient for the four-item overidentification subscale. An overall model (confirmatory factor analysis) was conducted to evaluate the internal consistency reliability of the scale, revealing good internal consistency (coefficient of .92). Analysis also revealed significant relationships with a variety of scales measuring similar constructs and that SCS significantly predicted mental health outcomes (e.g., depression, anxiety, and life satisfaction). Studies (Birnie *et al.*, 2010; Shapiro *et al.*, 2005) showed that participation in the MBSR program is associated with increases in self-compassion.

The Portuguese version of the SCS (Fontinha, 2009) revealed good internal consistency with a coefficient .91 for the entire scale. Factorial analysis of the different items and subscales resulted in four factors that, according to the results were defined as (a) subscale one—self emotional regulation, (b) subscale two—self-acceptance, (c) subscale three—common humanity, and (d) subscale four—self-appeasement. The Cronbach's alpha coefficients of these subscales were .85, .84, .71, and .79, respectively. Correlation coefficients between subscales were between .37 and .57, and correlation coefficients between subscales and the global scale were between .73 and .80.

Experiences Questionnaire

The Experiences Questionnaire (EQ) was developed by Fresco *et al.* (2007) to assess *decentering*. Decentering has been defined as the ability to observe one's thoughts and feelings as temporary, objective events in the mind, as opposed to as true reflections of the self, with an internal attitude of acceptance and nonjudgment (Fresco *et al.*, 2007). This scale consists of 11 questions rated on a five-point Likert scale with items ranging from one (*never*) to five (*all the time*) to assess individuals' capacity to observe their emotions and thoughts as impermanence, with acceptance and nonjudgment and without becoming identified with negative thoughts and emotions. The questionnaire takes approximately three minutes to complete. Psychometric properties demonstrated good internal consistency of .83. Results also revealed significant and positive correlations with cognitive reappraisal and significant and negative correlations with depressive rumination, experiential avoidance, emotion suppression, and symptoms of depression. Studies (Carmody *et al.*, 2009; Orzech *et al.*, 2009) showed that MBSR and intensive mindfulness training increases participants' capacity for decentering. The validation of this instrument to the Portuguese population in a sample of 201 individuals with ages between 15 and more than 65 years old revealed that the scale has a good internal consistency for the factor of decentering (Cronbach's alpha coefficient .74). Results also revealed significant and negative correlations with the symptoms of psychopathology as measured by the Portuguese version of the Outcome Questionnarie-45 (OQ-45) in both clinical ($n = 53$) and nonclinical groups ($n = 35$) with a mean age of 30 and 25 years old, respectively (Barbosa *et al.*, 2011).

Satisfaction With Life Scale

The Satisfaction With Life Scale (SWLS) was developed by Diener *et al.* (1985) to assess individuals' global judgment of life satisfaction. This scale consists of five questions rated on a seven-point Likert scale with items ranging from one (*strongly disagree*) to seven (*strongly agree*) to assess individuals' subjective experience of quality of life, and takes approximately one minute to complete. SWLS revealed good internal consistency (Cronbach's alpha coefficient of .87) and test-retest reliability after two months (.82). Pavot and Diener (1993), reviewing the research on this scale, found good internal consistency (Cronbach's alpha coefficient range of from .79 to .89) and test-retest reliability after one month (.84). In a sample of older adults, Diener *et al.* (1985) found that SWLS had good internal consistency (Cronbach's alpha coefficient range of from .61 to .81). Participation in MBSR has been associated with increases in satisfaction with life when the SWLS was used with nurses and nurses' aides (McKenzie, Poulin, and Seidman-Carlson, 2006).

The validation of this instrument to the Portuguese population in a sample of 203 individuals with ages between 19 and 89 years revealed that the scale has a good internal consistency (Cronbach's alpha coefficient .77). SWLS was correlated with measures of daily satisfaction, happiness, and both positive and negative affect.

Positive and Negative Affect Schedule

Watson, Clark, and Tellegen (1988) developed the Positive and Negative Affect Schedule (PANAS) to assess the emotional component of subjective well-being. PANAS consists of 20 emotion adjectives that are divided into two ten-item assessments measuring positive-affect (PA) and negative-affect (NA). PA items represent high energy and pleasurable engagement in high ratings and low energy and lethargy in low ratings. NA items represent personal sorrow and feelings such as anger, guilt, nervousness, and fear in high ratings and a sense of peace and calm in low ratings. Items are rated on a five-point Likert scale to indicate the time spent experiencing each emotion. The scale ranges from one (*slightly or not at all*) to five (*extremely*). The scale has six versions, varying with the temporal instruction, measuring how the individual feels in the indicated time frame (i.e., this moment, today, the past few days, the past week, the past year, and generally).

Watson *et al.* (1988) validated PANAS in a sample of undergraduates using the six versions and across three different samples. Results revealed good internal consistency for the various time references with Cronbach's alpha coefficients, ranging between .86 and .90 for the PA scale and between .84 and .87 for the NA scale. For the general period, Cronbach's alpha was .88 for PA and .87 for NA. Test-retest correlations for an eight-week period ranged from .47 to .68 for PA and .39 to .71 for NA (for the general time period, PA stability = .68, NA Stability = .71). PANAS was highly correlated with measures of general distress and dysfunction, depression, and state anxiety.

The validation study of PANAS for the Portuguese population (Galinha and Pais Ribeiro, 2005) resulted in a Portuguese version very similar to the American version of PANAS. It includes the same original categories and shares 13 items of the original 20 items of the American scale. Results indicate a good internal consistency with a Cronbach's alpha coefficient of .86 for the PA scale and of .89 for the NA scale. The correlation between the PA and NA scale was situated near zero ($r = -.10$) revealing orthogonality between the subscales of PA and NA. Participation in the MBSR program has been associated with increased positive affect and decrease in negative affect, using PANAS (e.g., see Anderson *et al.*, 2007; Shapiro *et al.*, 2007).

Psychological Well-Being Scale

The Psychological Well-Being Scale (PWBS) instrument (Ryff, 1989; Ryff and Keynes, 1995) was developed to measure six dimensions of well-being, including self-acceptance, mastery, positive relationships, personal growth, autonomy, and life purpose. It is an 84-item scale with 14 questions for each construct rated on a six-point Likert scale ranging from one (*strongly disagree*) to six (*strongly agree*). Psychometric results (Ryff, 1989) revealed good internal consistency (Cronbach's alpha coefficients ranging between .83 and .91) and strong test-retest reliability (alpha coefficients ranging between .81 and .85) for each of the six constructs.

This scale was not validated to the Portuguese population, but I am using an experimental Portuguese translated version completed by Silva (2004) and released by Dr Ryff from the University of Wisconsin Madison Institute on Aging. Participation in an MBSR program has been associated with increases in psychological well-being as measured by PWB scales (e.g., see Carmody and Baer, 2008) and on environmental mastery and purpose in life scales of the PWB (Carmody *et al.*, 2009).

Perceived Stress Scale

Cohen *et al.* (1983) created the Perceived Stress Scale (PSS) to evaluate the degree to which individuals perceive the situation in their lives as stressful, unpredictable, uncontrollable, and overwhelming. The scale has two versions, one with 14 items and another with ten items. In MBSR studies, the PSS scale with ten items has been most widely used and has revealed that participation in MBSR is associated with decreased perceived stress (Biegel *et al.*, 2009; Carmody, Crawford, and Churchill, 2006; Carmody and Baer, 2008; Shapiro *et al.*, 2007). The PSS-10 is a widely used and well-validated scale. The items are rated on a five-point Likert scale ranging from zero (*never*) to four (*very often*). A high score indicates a greater degree of perceived stress. The psychometric properties of the 14-item scale showed strong internal consistency (Cronbach's alpha coefficient ranging between .84 and .86) and the ten-item scale also showed a strong internal consistency (Cronbach's alpha coefficient of .78).

The validation of PSS-14 to the Portuguese population (Pais Ribeiro and Marques, 2009) resulted in a 13-item scale with a strong internal consistency (alpha coefficient of .88) and the PSS-10 (Mota-Cardoso *et al.*, 2002) revealed an internal consistency of .86. For this study, the Portuguese version of the PSS with 13 items was used, due to the easy acquisition of the translated questionnaire.

Profile of Mood States-Short Form

The Profile of Mood States (POMS) standard is a widely used instrument to assess psychological distress and mood in clinical and nonclinical groups (McNair, Loor, and Droppleman, 1971). It is a five-point Likert scale ranging from one (*not at all*) to five (*extremely*) based on how the testee was feeling the week and day they completed the inventory. It contains 65 adjectives divided into six identified moods that include tension/anxiety, depression/dejection, anger/hostility, vigor/activity, fatigue/inertia, and confusion/bewilderment, and it takes about ten minutes to complete. The Profile of Mood States-Short Form (POMS-SF; Shacham, 1983) uses the same scales as the POMS Standard but contains 37 items and takes about five minutes to complete. Both scales yield a global measure of mood, as well as the stable mood states of tension, anger, vigor, fatigue, and confusion. Psychometric results revealed good internal consistency for POMS-SF (Cronbach's alpha coefficient range from .80 to .91) and POMS original (alpha coefficient range from .74 to .91). These results suggested that the POMS-SF is a good alternative to the POMS original.

The Portuguese version of POMS-SF (Viana *et al.*, 2001) contains 42 items in total and six items per subscale. Psychometric results revealed a strong internal consistency of the six subscales of

POMS-SF with Cronbach's alpha coefficients ranging between .72 and .91. Intercorrelations between scales were all high, not exceeding .60, which showed that all subscales measure independent constructs. The correlations of POMS-SF with education and age were close to zero and correlations with gender were significant in all subscales, with women showing higher scores than did men. Authors presented normative tables for men and women. Participation in an MBSR program has been associated with increased positive mood states, decreased negative mood states, and decrease in total mood disturbance (e.g., see Carlson and Garland, 2005; Speca *et al.*, 2000; Rosenzweig *et al.*, 2003).

World Health Organization Quality of Life-100

The World Health Organization Quality of Life-100 (WHOQOL-100) was developed by the World Health Organization Quality of Life (WHOQOL) Group to evaluate the testee's quality of life (QoL, i.e., "an individual's perception of their position in life in the context of the culture and value systems in which they live, and in relation to their goals, expectations, standards and concerns" (Skevington *et al.*, 2004, p.299) of individuals. It consists of a 100-item questionnaire to evaluate "individuals' subjective perception of their QoL in the context of the physical, cultural, and social environment in which they live" (Canavarro *et al.*, 2009, p.117). It includes six general domains: physical, psychological, level of independence, social relationships, environment, and spirituality. Each domain is divided into a series of areas/facets that summarize a particular domain of QoL. Each of these areas/facets is assessed by four questions in a five-point Likert scale that evaluates intensity (*Not at all—Extremely*), capacity (*Not at all—Completely*), frequency (*Never—Always*), and evaluation (*Very dissatisfied—Very satisfied/Very poor—Very good*). The scores of all facets and domains are transformed to reflect a scale that ranges from 0 to 100 (higher score reflects a better QoL).

In this study I used the Domain 1 Physical section of the instrument, which consists of several questions to assess pain and discomfort, energy and fatigue, and sleep and rest and the Domain 6 Spirituality/Religion/Personal Beliefs from the scale, each of which consists of four questions. Internal reliabilities of the 25 facets (as measured by Cronbach's alpha coefficient) ranged from .65 to .93. Internal consistency of the three facets of the physical domain ranged from .76 to .87; and internal consistency of facet 24 (i.e., Domain 6) was .85. Psychometric results of the development of the WHOQOL-100 in Portugal revealed good internal consistency of the Domain 1 Physical (Cronbach's alpha coefficient of 0.88) and Domain 6 Spirituality (Cronbach's alpha coefficient of .84; Canavarro et al., 2009). Participation in an MBSR program has been associated with increases in the four domains measured by the WHOQOL-100, i.e., physical, psychological, social, and spiritual (Jacobs and Nagel, 2003).

World Health Organization Quality of Life-BREF

The World Health Organization Quality of Life BREF (WHOQOL-BREF; Skevington et al., 2004) was developed by the WHOQOL Group (1998) and consists of a shortened version of the WHOQOL-100. The WHOQOL-BREF consists of 26 items to evaluate the QoL of individuals in four domains, including physical health, psychological, social relations, and environmental quality-of-life concerns. The questionnaire is a five-point Likert interval scale designed to measure the intensity, capacity, frequency, and evaluation of the QoL of individuals. Psychometric properties of WHOQOL-BREF resulted from data collected using a cross-sectional design in 24 centers representing 23 countries. Results revealed good internal consistency for the total sample (Cronbach's alpha coefficient ranged from .82 to .68), and good construct and discriminant validity (Skevington et al., 2004).

The validation of the WHOQOL-BREF in the Portuguese population (Vaz Serra et al., 2006) resulted from data collected from a sample of 604 individuals (315 from the normal population and 289 from the clinical population). Psychometric analysis revealed good internal consistency (Cronbach's alpha coefficient ranged from .87 to .64), significant correlations with the WHOQOL-100, good discriminant validity and construct validity, and showing significant correlations with the Beck's Depression Inventory and the Brief Symptom Inventory. Participation in the MBSR program has been associated with increased QoL after the program (de Vibe and Torbjorn, 2006; Nyklicek and Kuijpers, 2008) and at three and six months' follow-up (de Vibe and Torbjorn, 2006).

Subjective Health Complaint Inventory

The Subjective Health Complaint Inventory (SHCI) was developed by Eriksen et al. (1999) to assess individuals' subjective health complaints. SHCI is a 29-item scale that registers occurrence, intensity, and duration of subjective somatic and psychological complaints experienced by individuals during the past 30 days. It includes five categories/subscales:

musculoskeletal pain, pseudoneurology, gastrointestinal problems, allergy, and flu that are scored on a four-point Likert scale ranging from zero (*never*) to three (*a lot*). The total score ranges from zero (*excellent*) to 87 (*very poor*). Psychometric results showed satisfactory internal consistency: total score of all 29 items yielded a Cronbach's alpha coefficient of .82 for women and .75 for men. A psychometric study of the SHC questionnaire with a sample of older adults revealed good internal consistency with an alpha coefficient of .83 (Thygesen et al., 2009). The Portuguese version of the SHCI (Alves and Figueiras, 2008) revealed good internal consistency in test and retest (alpha coefficient of .87 and .88, respectively). Participation in the MBSR program was associated with increased health using the SHCI (de Vibe and Torbjorn, 2006).

Death Perspective Scales

Spilka et al. (1977) developed several death perspectives scales (DPS) to assess different death perspectives, including death as pain and loneliness (Subscale 1), death as an after-life-or-reward (Subscale 2), indifference towards death (Subscale 3), death as unknown (Subscale 4), death as forsaking dependents plus guilt (Subscale 5), death as courage (Subscale 6), death as failure (Subscale 7), and death as a natural end (Subscale 8). The DPS is made up of eight subscales with four to five questions each, using a six-point Likert scale indicating the agreement or disagreement with each item, ranging from one (*strongly disagree*) to six (*strongly agree*). Internal consistency of these scales ranged from .71 to .92. The correlation coefficients between the subscales ranged from low to moderate in strength. The Portuguese version of the DPS (Barros-Oliveira and Neto, 2004) revealed good internal consistency of all eight factors, with Cronbach's alpha coefficients ranging between .78 and .94. The subscales revealed several significant correlations.

Spiritual Well-Being Questionnaire

The Spiritual Well-Being Questionnaire (SWBQ) was developed by Gomez and Fisher (2003) to measure the global spiritual well-being of individuals as assessed in four different domains, including personal, communal, environmental, and transcendental. The scale comprises 20 items, five items for each of the domains, using a five-point Likert scale ranging from one (*low*) to five (*very high*). Psychometric results revealed good internal consistency of the SWBQ with Cronbach's alpha coefficients for personal, transcendental, environmental, and communal domains of .89, .86, .76, and .79, respectively, and .92 for all items together. The Portuguese version of the SWBQ (Gouveia *et al.*, 2009) revealed good internal consistency of the four domains of the questionnaire (Cronbach's alpha coefficients of .75 for the personal domain, .74 for the communal domain, .89 for the transcendental domain, and .84 for the environmental domain) and for all the items together (alpha coefficient of .88).

Montreal Cognitive Assessment

The Montreal Cognitive Assessment (MOCA) was developed as a screening test for early detection of cognitive impairment. This test is a one-page 30-point test administered in ten minutes. It includes several assessment tasks: (a) short-memory recall (five points); (b) visuospatial abilities task, including the clock-drawing task (three points) and the three-dimensional copy cube (one point); (c) executive functions measured by the Trail Making B task (one point), a phonemic fluency task (one point), and a two-item verbal abstraction task (two points); (d) attention, concentration, and working memory assessments using a sustained attention task (one point), subtraction task (three points), and a digit forward/backwards task (one point); (e) language, evaluated using a three-item confrontation naming task (three points), repetition of two syntactically complex sentences (two points), and the above-mentioned fluency task; and (f) orientation to time and place (six points).

Results revealed good internal consistency of MOCA with Cronbach's alpha coefficients on the standardized items of .83 and good specificity (to exclude normal controls) and sensitivity (to detect mild cognitive impairment and Alzheimer's disease). The MOCA was officially translated to Portuguese (Simões *et al.*, 2007); scores ≥ 26 are considered normal for that test version Freitas *et al.* (2008a, 2008b) analyzed the psychometric charateristics of the experimental version of MOCA in a group of healthy elderly individuals (n = 80) with ages ≥ 50 years old (M=62.91; SD = 9.39; Min = 50; Max = 84). Results suggested good internal consistency (α Cronbach = .71) and good inter-item correlations and good total item correlations with the exception of two items including sustained attention and orientation. The results of MOCA and MMSE presented good correlation (r = .66, p<.01) suggested good concurrent validity.

Simões *et al.* (2008) conducted a validation study with MOCA in three groups: (a) controls showing normal cognitive functioning, functional independency and adequate social behavior), (b) mild cognitive impairment, and (c) mild dementia. Results revealed good test-retest for MoCA r = .85 [p<.01; 33.47 (± 14.65) days] and good internal consistency (α Cronbach .92).

Wechsler Adult Intelligence Scale III

The Wechsler Adult Intelligence Scale III (WAIS III) was developed to provide a measure of general intellectual function in individuals with ages raging from 16 to 89 years old. It includes several subtests to provide a general IQ score and it also provides information on several neuropsychological domains (Strauss *et al.*, 2006). For this study I selected two indexes of the Portuguese version of WAIS III, including the working memory index and the speed processing index to assess working memory and processing speed, respectively.

The *working memory index* includes the arithmetic and digit span subtests. In the arithmetic subtest individuals are asked to solve arithmetic word problems presented orally within a time limit. In the digit span subtest individuals are asked to repeat a number sequence in the same order as presented and in the reverse order as presented. The *speed processing index* includes the digit symbol coding test and the digit symbol incidental learning pairing and free recall subtests. In the coding subtest, individuals are asked to copy symbols paired with numbers in a 120-second limit. In the incidental learning pairing subtest, individuals are given numbers and are requested to recall associated symbols. In the incidental learning free recall subtest, individuals are asked to write as many symbols as they can recall. All the subtests and both indexes revealed good internal consistencies for an older adult population: (a) the working memory index has Cronbach's alpha coefficients of .96 for individuals 65 to 69 years old, .94 for individuals 70 to 74 years old, .93 for individuals 75 to 79 years old, and .92 for individuals ≥ 80 years old; and (b) the speed processing index has a Cronbach's alpha coefficient of .93 for individuals within the different age ranges. Chambers *et al.* (2008) revealed that participants in the MBSR program showed a significant improvement in the digit span backward score pre- and post-intervention compared with the control group, which showed no significant change.

Trail Making Test A and B

The Trail Making Test (TMT) A and B (Army Individual Test Battery, 1944) is primarily a test of visual attention and motor speed, but it also provides information on visual search, executive functions, speed processing, and mental flexibility (Tombaugh, 2004). It consists of two parts: (a) Part A consists of 25 circled numbers, from 1 to 25, distributed over a sheet of paper. Individuals are required to draw lines sequentially connecting the 25 encircled numbers; and (b) Part B includes both encircled numbers (1 to 13) and encircled letters (A to L). Individuals are required to connect the circles in an ascending pattern alternating between numbers and letters (i.e., 1, A, 2, B, 3, C, etc.) as quickly as possible. The score of each part of the test is given by the amount of time spent completing the task.

TMT A and B were translated to Portuguese and normative values have been researched for the Portuguese population (Cavaco *et al.*, 2008). Normative values for the Portuguese population 21 to 65 years of age revealed that the time spent completing TMT A and B increased with age and less education. In general women were slower than were men in completing Part A. The B:A index decreased with increased education.

» Appendix 2 «

Interview Protocol

1. Can you describe your experience of the MBSR program?
2. Can you explain how being part of the program affected you?
3. How has this experience impacted your life?
4. How do you feel being such a good age?
5. How did the program affect the way you are experiencing this stage of life?
6. How do you perceive life and your existence?
7. How did the experience of being part of the program change your perception of life and your existence?
8. Can you explain how you are including the practice of the mindfulness techniques explored during the program in your daily life?
9. How does the practice influence your daily life and sense of well-being?
10. Can you say three words that best describe your experience and impact of the MBSR in your life?

» Appendix 3 «

Treatment of Data

Quantitative data

The quantitative data were collected during the initial and final assessments via psychological and neuropsychological tests. Each participant was given a code number (matching the code number of the interview) and scores from the assessment of each participant were computed by hand and/or on the computer. Participants who had experienced any life event, illness, or changes in medication during the eight weeks of the program were not excluded from the analysis. I included that information in the results section of the dissertation and included these variables in the statistical analysis. Data of each participant was entered in the Statistical Program for Social Sciences (SPSS), and descriptive statistics were computed in SPSS to assess the frequency distribution of observed values and relevant statistics for the quantitative values. A *t*-test was computed in order to assess the significance of differences between mean values observed for both groups and mean value variation of scores as between both groups. A paired *t*-test was computed to evaluate the differences in quantitative variables between pre- and post-intervention in the control group (CG) and treatment group (TG). Correlation coefficients were computed to assess the correlation between practice (formal and informal) and number of sessions attended, and observed variations in the various dependent variables between pre- and post-intervention in the TG. Regression analysis was computed to determine the causal effect between participants' changes in mindful awareness scales and the number of sessions attended, number of days practiced per week with the CDs, and completion of the experiential exercises. Correlation coefficients were also computed to assess correlations between decentering, mindfulness, and acceptance and between these three variables and well-being, psychological and physical symptoms, spiritual well-being, quality of life, and neuropsychological performance. A MANOVA was computed to observe whether mindfulness, decentering, and acceptance mediated changes in well-being, psychological and physical symptoms, quality of life, and spiritual well-being. Tables are included in the following appendices to present relevant quantitative data.

Qualitative data

The qualitative data were collected via the semi-structured interview after the final assessment and also resulted from my personal notes during the intervention program. The audio-recordings of the interviews were transcribed either by me or by a professional transcriber. Before transcribing or reading the transcription of the interviews I meditated and cultivated a state of equanimity, receptivity, deep tranquility, and mindful listening. I brought to mind and body a sense of the participant at the moment of the interview and then began transcribing or reading the transcription of the interview.

The analysis consisted of two general parts. During the first part of the qualitative analysis I meditated and cultivated a mindful presence while systematically listening to and reading the interview transcription of one participant in order to attempt to glean the general meaning and major themes experienced by the participant. During the meditation I cultivated an open presence without bringing to the moment any agenda or expectation and kept an open mind and trust in her ability to detect the meaning of the interviews. I bore witness and accepted whatever arose at each moment while listening and reading the interview scripts. I brought the mind to rest on a state of deep concentration on and attention to the words and the silence between the words, as well as on the conceptual and emotional meaning of the words, allowing spontaneous insights to occur during this process in relation to the material being analyzed. Whatever thoughts or images arose during this process were written down as they occurred. I allowed the data to be set aside for short intervals and then returned to, in order to allow awakening of fresh energy and perspective. This process was repeated until I had obtained a general meaning and the main themes experienced by the participant.

During the second part of the analysis, I used the descriptive methodology that Colaizzi (1978) had used in his own research, taking the following steps: (a) read the entire interview to acquire a feeling of it; (b) read the interview to extract from it words and phrases that are directly associated with the phenomena being studied; (c) extracted the meaning of the significant statements associated with participants' experience; (d) organized the significant statements into clusters of general themes;

(e) referred these themes back to the interview to validate them; (f) wrote down and described the meanings of themes of that one participant and returned the written description to the participant for validation; (g) after completing the above protocol for one participant, repeated the same process for each of the other participants until I had constructed each individual experience of the phenomena; and (h) after completing the individual depictions of the phenomena, looked for recurring themes that appeared in common in several or all interviews. During this last stage, I entered into an immersion process with the data obtained from this analysis and notes from my personal journal until she achieved a composite depiction and a creative synthesis of the phenomena being investigated.

During the phase of merging the two sets of results (i.e., quantitative and qualitative), several strategies were employed, including: (a) identification of content areas represented in both data sets; (b) comparison, contrast, and synthesis of the results in a discussion or table; and (c) identification of differences between quantitative and qualitative sets of results, displaying differences according to dimensions resulting from the analysis and the original research questions (e.g., psychological well-being, spirituality, etc.; Creswell, 2011). During this process, I also used an analytic-synthetic integration of data (Shirazi, 1994) that allowed for the identification and breaking down of the main components of both data strands, followed by the presentation of a synthesis of these components that reflected the complementarities of the dimensions in terms of explaining the phenomena under investigation. During this stage, I also employed several integral skills, including contemplation, mindfulness, compassion, auditory and visual skills, and intuition to address the effects and lived experiences of the participants during the MBSR program. The relationship between the qualitative and quantitative data was examined in Chapter 3 as represented in Figure A3.1.

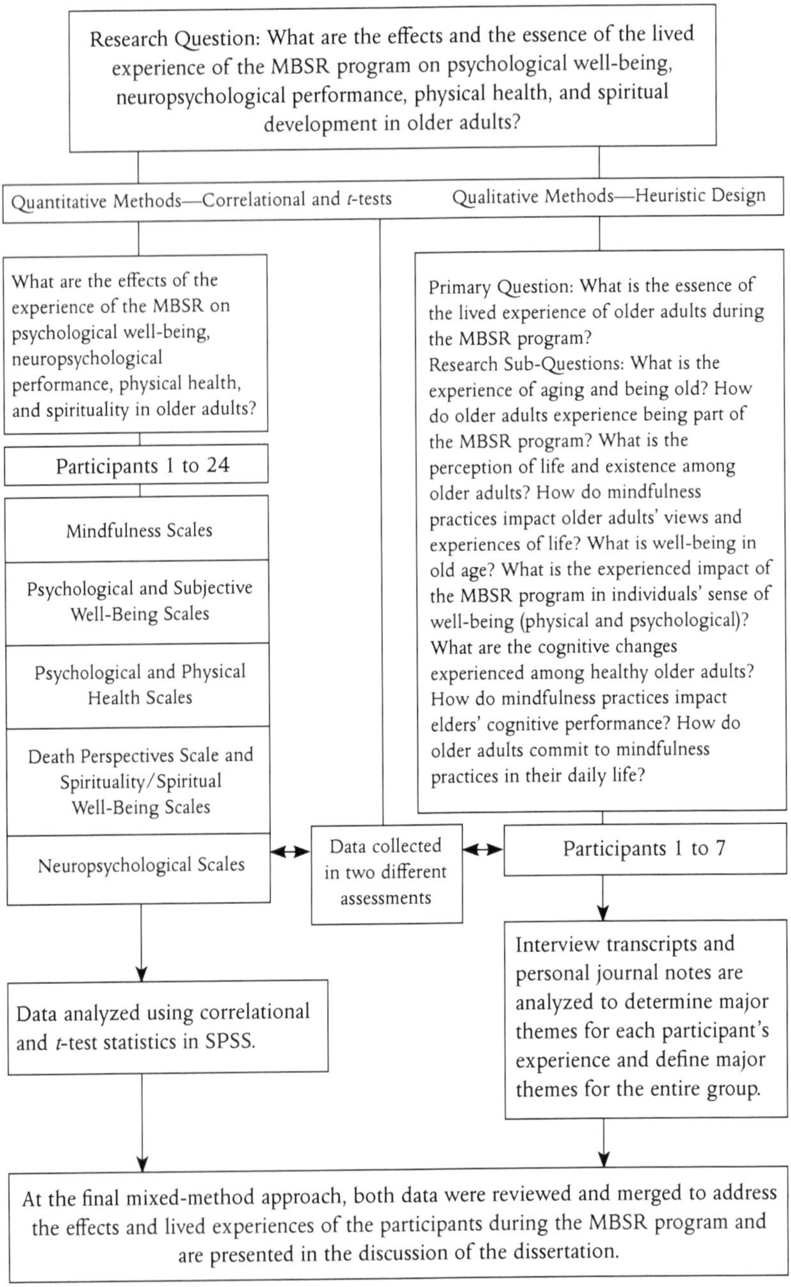

```
                    ┌─────────────────────────────────────────────┐
                    │ Research Question: What are the effects and │
                    │ the essence of the lived experience of the  │
                    │ MBSR program on psychological well-being,   │
                    │ neuropsychological performance, physical    │
                    │ health, and spiritual development in older  │
                    │ adults?                                     │
                    └─────────────────────────────────────────────┘
```

Quantitative Methods—Correlational and *t*-tests   Qualitative Methods—Heuristic Design

Quantitative	Qualitative
What are the effects of the experience of the MBSR on psychological well-being, neuropsychological performance, physical health, and spirituality in older adults?	Primary Question: What is the essence of the lived experience of older adults during the MBSR program?
Participants 1 to 24	Research Sub-Questions: What is the experience of aging and being old? How do older adults experience being part of the MBSR program? What is the perception of life and existence among older adults? How do mindfulness practices impact older adults' views and experiences of life? What is well-being in old age? What is the experienced impact of the MBSR program in individuals' sense of well-being (physical and psychological)? What are the cognitive changes experienced among healthy older adults? How do mindfulness practices impact elders' cognitive performance? How do older adults commit to mindfulness practices in their daily life?
Mindfulness Scales	
Psychological and Subjective Well-Being Scales	
Psychological and Physical Health Scales	
Death Perspectives Scale and Spirituality/Spiritual Well-Being Scales	
Neuropsychological Scales	

Data collected in two different assessments

Participants 1 to 7

Data analyzed using correlational and *t*-test statistics in SPSS.

Interview transcripts and personal journal notes are analyzed to determine major themes for each participant's experience and define major themes for the entire group.

At the final mixed-method approach, both data were reviewed and merged to address the effects and lived experiences of the participants during the MBSR program and are presented in the discussion of the dissertation.

FIGURE A3.1 MIXED AND INTEGRAL METHODOLOGY

External and internal validity

In quantitative and qualitative research several internal and external validity threats may occur that can raise questions regarding the validity of the results of the study (Creswell, 2009). In order to handle possible internal and external threats, I employed certain actions throughout the study in order to increase validity of results.

Validity in quantitative methods

A few possible threats that can arise in quantitative research include selection effect, which occurs when selected participants have certain characteristics that predispose them to have certain outcomes. In order to avoid this effect, the exclusion criteria for this study ensures that participants recruited for the study did not have a personal regular practice of meditation and yoga, and were selected from several places in Porto city that were not places where individuals are more likely to be interested in these practices.

Testing and instrumentation effects that could threaten validity can also occur in quantitative analysis. Testing effect occurs when participants become familiar with the instruments being used and remember responses for later testing. Instrumentation effect occurs when I use different instruments pre and post test, thus impacting the comparison between these stages of evaluation. In order to avoid these effects, I used the same instruments of assessment pre test and post test, and the initial and final assessment interviews were completed within an interval of approximately 12 weeks.

Validity in qualitative methods

Establishing trustworthiness in qualitative research is very important in order to be able to evaluate and demonstrate that results and understandings achieved regarding the phenomena being studied are valid, credible, and reliable (Creswell, 2007, 2009). Two validation strategies were used in this study: member-checking and peer-debriefing.

I used the member-checking strategy in requesting the interviewees to review the analysis of the interview and the description of the themes in order to find out whether participants agreed with the accuracy of the findings and interpretations. Using this strategy during research brought important feedback regarding the interpretation developed of the phenomenon being investigated. Each participant interviewed agreed with their respective analysis and description of the themes.

A peer-debriefer was selected in order to evaluate the methods, meanings, interpretation, and understandings achieved from the interviews. The peer-debriefer selected was Dr Emma Therese Lewis, who holds her Ph.D. in Psychology and who has knowledge and experience with the phenomena being investigated and the qualitative methods being used. From the feedback and discussion that arose from this process, I decided to include more detailed and in-depth narratives of each interviewed participant in the qualitative results that reflected the individual voices of participants in order to provide a more vivid and enriched context that had led to the analysis, the core and secondary themes, and their description.

Conclusion

This study's purpose was to assess and explore the effects and lived experiences of the MBSR program in older adults in terms of psychological well-being, physical health, neuropsychological performance, and spiritual transformation. A sample of 24 participants was recruited from the general population of Portugal 65 years or older. Participants were assessed before the beginning of the MBSR using several quantitative instruments to evaluate their psychological well-being, physical health, neuropsychological performance, and spirituality. During the eight-week program, participants were asked to participate and explore their experience during their mindfulness practices and during the discussion of topics being presented on mindfulness and its application in daily life. After the intervention, participants completed the same quantitative assessment as before the beginning of the program and were interviewed using a semi-structured interview protocol to yield information on their lived experience of program.

Quantitative data were analyzed statistically to observe the effects of mindfulness practice on elders' psychological well-being, physical health, neuropsychological performance, and spiritual development. Qualitative data were explored and analyzed using the heuristic inquiry approach to fully understand the essence of meaning of elders' experience during the MBSR program. Qualitative and quantitative data were combined to provide a comprehensive understanding of the effects and lived experiences of older adults during the MBSR program.

» Appendix 4 «

MAAS Statistical Results

TABLE A4.1 *T*-TEST RESULTS: DIFFERENCES BETWEEN
CG AND TG AT ASSESSMENT 1 AND ASSESSMENT 2

	CG	TG	*t* value and significance level
Assessment 1	M = 60.67 SD = 10.52	M = 59.33 SD = 16.49	$t(22) = .24, p = .81$
Assessment 2	M = 58.8 SD = 10.58	M = 70.75 SD = 14.84	$t(22) = -2.31, p = .03^*$

* $p < .05$ ** $p < .01$.

TABLE A4.2 PAIRED *T*-TEST RESULTS: DIFFERENCES BETWEEN
MEAN MAAS SCORES AT ASSESSMENT 1 AND ASSESSMENT
2 (ASSESSMENT 2—ASSESSMENT 1) FOR CG AND TG

	Mean scores differences	*t* value and significance level
CG	M = −2.08, SD = 1.31	$t(11) = 5.50, p = .00^{**}$
TG	M = 11.41, SD = 9.71	$t(11) = -4.07, p = .00^{**}$

* $p < .05$ ** $p < .01$.

TABLE A4.3 *T*-TEST RESULTS: DELTA VARIATION
BETWEEN PRE- AND POST-INTERVENTION

	CG	TG	*U* value and significance level
Mean value variation	M = −2.08 SD = 1.31	M = 11.41 SD = 9.71	$U = 78.0, p = .00^*$

* $p < .05$ ** $p < .01$.

TABLE A4.4 MAAS: CORRELATIONS WITH LEVELS OF PRACTICE

	$n = 12$	Daily practice CDs	Daily practice informal	Sessions attended
MAAS	Spearman correlation	.74**	.81**	.59*

* $p < .05$ ** $p < .01$.

TABLE A4.5 REGRESSION MODEL COEFFICIENTS FOR MAAS

	Unstandardized coefficients B	Std. Error	Standardized coefficients	t	p
(Constant)	.86	15.15		.06	.96
Daily Practice CDs	−17.07	24.28	−.69	−.70	.50
Daily Practice Informal	29.18	21.86	1.27	1.33	.22
Sessions attended	3.31	19.15	.06	.17	.87

When analyzed together, none of the three levels of practice was sufficiently significant to explain the MAAS scores. Through a systematic analysis looking at the importance of each variable in the model developed, I eliminated the nonsignificant variables. Different procedures (*Forward, Backward, Stepwise,* and *Remove*) were tested, with the same results, conducting to the selection of the significant independent variables. The obtained model revealed the determination coefficient $r^2 = 40.8$ percent, representing the proportion of the dependent variable explained by the model. The adjusted determination coefficient was $ra^2 = 34.9$ percent (see Tables A4.5a and b). Only daily informal practice was significant to explain the variation in MAAS scores. When the variable daily informal practice increased one unit (100 percent), it induced a mean increase of 14.70 in the dependent variable MAAS (*delta*).

TABLE A4.5A MAAS: REGRESSION MODEL COEFFICIENTS FOR SIGNIFICANT VARIABLES

	Unstandardized coefficients		Standardized coefficients	t	p
	B	Std. error			
(Constant)	2.68	4.03		.67	.52
Daily Practice Informal	14.70	5.60	.64	2.62	.03*

* $p < .05$.

TABLE A4.5B MAAS: REGRESSION MODEL COEFFICIENTS FOR EXCLUDED VARIABLES

	Beta in	t	p
Daily Practice CDs	−.65	−.72	.49
Sessions attended	−.004	−.01	.99

The verification of the nonexistence of multicollinearity (i.e., of a correlation between predictor variables in the model) as between the independent variables was conducted using the Durbin–Watson test. For a 5 percent significance level, the critical value for this test is 1.78; whenever the value is higher, the null hypothesis of auto-correlation cannot be rejected. The Durbin–Watson test critical value for this model is 2.73, thus suggesting that there is no multicollinearity.

TABLE A4.6 MAAS: CORRELATIONS WITH MEASURES OF TRAINING AND MEASURES OF WELL-BEING, PSYCHOLOGICAL AND PHYSICAL SYMPTOMS, QUALITY OF LIFE, AND SPIRITUAL WELL-BEING

Measures	r value and significance level
FFMQ	r = .88**
SCS	r = .85**
EQ	r = .74**
SWLS	r = .68**
PANAS PA	r = .63**
PANAS NA	r = −.69**
PWBS	r = .68**
PSS	r = −.92**

cont.

TABLE A4.6 MAAS: CORRELATIONS *CONT.*

Measures	*r* value and significance level
POMS	$r = -.84^{**}$
WHOQOL-BREF Physical	$r = .79^{**}$
WHOQOL-BREF Psychological	$r = .75^{**}$
WHOQOL-BREF Social relations	$r = .41^{**}$
WHOQOL-BREF Environmental	$r = .54^{**}$
WHOQOL-100 Physical	$r = .41^{*}$
WHOQOL-100 Spiritual	$r = .82^{**}$
SHCI	$r = -.76^{**}$
SWBQ	$r = .66^{**}$
Direct Digits	$r = .44^{**}$
Arithmetic	$r = .45^{**}$
Digit Symbol Coding	$r = .45^{**}$
Digit Symbol Incident	$r = .51^{**}$
Free Recall	$r = .53^{**}$

* $p < .05$ ** $p < .01$.

TABLE A4.7 MANOVA RESULTS: RELATION BETWEEN MAAS AND VARIABLES ASSESSING PSYCHOLOGICAL AND PHYSICAL SYMPTOMS, WELL-BEING, QUALITY OF LIFE, AND SPIRITUAL WELL-BEING

Dependent variables (*Delta*)	*F* value and significance level
PANAS PA	9.25**
PANAS NA	3.10*
PWBS (Global Score)	3.48*
PSS	37.41**
POMS (Global Score)	3.62*
SHCI	5.24**
WHOQOL-BREF Physical	9.03**
WHOQOL-BREF Psychological	9.13**
WHOQOL-BREF Social Relations	4.63**
WHOQOL-BREF Environment	11.69**
WHOQOL-100 Physical	9.63**
WHOQOL-100 Spiritual	4.84*

* $p < .05$ ** $p < .01$.

Appendix 5

FFMQ Statistical Results

TABLE A5.1 *T*-TEST RESULTS: DIFFERENCES BETWEEN CG AND TG AT ASSESSMENT 1 AND ASSESSMENT 2

	CG	TG	*t* value and significance level
Assessment 1	M = 107 SD = 22.96	M = 128.8.33 SD = 19.7	$t(22) = -2.50, p = .02$*
Assessment 2	M = 104.25 SD = 22.04	M = 147.17 SD = 20.86	$t(22) = 4.90, p = .00$**

* $p < .05$ ** $p < .01$.

TABLE A5.2 FFMQ SUBSCALES: MEANS, STANDARD DEVIATIONS, AND *T*-TEST STATISTICS AT ASSESSMENT 1 AND ASSESSMENT 2 FOR CG AND TG

FMMQ Dimensions *M (SD)*	CG (*n* = 12)		TG (*n* = 12)		*t*-test or Mann–Whitney *U* and *p*	
	Ass 1	Ass 2	Ass 1	Ass 2	Ass 1	Ass 2
Observation	20.42 (5.21)	19.50 (5.25)	27.42 (6.61)	30.17 (4.82)	$U = 31.5$ $p < .01$	$U = 11.0$ $p < .01$
Description	22.08 (5.62)	22.08 (5.32)	26.42 (6.72)	28.25 (6.89)	$t = -1.71$ $p = .10$	$t = -2.46$ $p < .01$
Act with awareness	21.83 (5.62)	21.00 (5.62)	26.83 (8.27)	30.50 (8.79)	$t = -1.73$ $p = .10$	$t = -3.16$ $p < .05$
Nonjudgment	23.83 (9.08)	24.08 (10.65)	28.17 (8.41)	32.25 (6.17)	$t = -1.21$ $p = .24$	$t = -2.30$ $p < .05$
Nonreaction	18.83 (7.03)	18.08 (7.17)	19.92 (4.01)	23.83 (4.06)	$t = -.46$ $p = .65$	$t = -2.42$ $p < .05$

* $p < .05$ **. $p < .01$.

TABLE A5.3 FFMQ GLOBAL SCORE AND SUBSCALES' SCORES: COMPARISON BETWEEN ASSESSMENT 1 AND ASSESSMENT 2 IN CG AND TG

Control Group (n = 12)	M	SD	t or Wilcoxon Z	p
FFMQ (Mindfulness) ASS2 – ASS1	−2.75	4.35	t = −2.19	.06
FFMQ Observation ASS2 – ASS1	−.92	.90	t = −3.53	.00**
FFMQ Description ASS2 – ASS1	.00	.95	t = .00	1.00
FFMQ Act with awareness ASS2 – ASS1	−.83	1.75	t = −1.65	.13
FFMQ Nonjudgment ASS2 – ASS1	.25	4.20	t = .21	.84
FFMQ Nonreaction ASS2 – ASS1	−.75	1.96	t = −1.33	.21
Treatment Group (n = 12)	**M**	**SD**	**t or Wilcoxon Z**	**p**
FFMQ (Mindfulness) ASS2 – ASS1	18.42	10.26	t = 6.22	.00**
FFMQ Observation ASS2 – ASS1	2.75	3.22	Z = −2.5	.01*
FFMQ Description ASS2 – ASS1	1.83	3.07	t = 2.07	.06
FFMQ Act with awareness ASS2 – ASS1	3.67	4.08	t = 3.12	.01**
FFMQ Nonjudgment ASS2 – ASS1	4.08	3.15	t = 4.50	.00**
FFMQ Nonreaction ASS2 – ASS1	3.92	3.58	t = 3.80	.00**

* $p < .05$ ** $p < .01$.

TABLE A5.4 FFMQ: MEAN VARIATION BETWEEN CG AND TG PRE- AND POST-INTERVENTION

Test and Dimensions	Group n = 24	M	SD	t-test or Mann–Whitney U	p
FFMQ	CG	−2.75	4.35	t = −6.58	.00**
	TG	18.42	10.26		
FFMQ Observation	CG	−.92	.90	U = 1.5	.00**
	TG	2.75	3.22		
FFMQ Description	CG	−2.08	1.31	t = 15.0	.00**
	TG	11.42	9.71		
FFMQ Act with awareness	CG	−.83	1.75	t = 0.0	.00**
	TG	3.67	4.08		
FFMQ Nonjudgment	CG	.25	4.20	t = 15.0	.00**
	TG	4.08	3.15		
FFMQ Nonreaction	CG	−.75	1.96	t = 23.5	.00**
	TG	3.92	3.58		

** $p < .01$.

APPENDIX 5: FFMQ STATISTICAL RESULTS

TABLE A5.5 TG: CORRELATIONS BETWEEN LEVELS OF PRACTICE AND FFMQ GLOBAL AND SUBSCALES

Test and Dimensions	n = 12	Daily practice CDs	Daily practice informal	Sessions attended
FFMQ Global	Spearman Correlation	.69**	.82**	.69*
FFMQ Observation	Spearman Correlation	.17	.24	.42
FFMQ Description	Spearman Correlation	.74*	.81**	.59*
FFMQ Act with awareness	Spearman Correlation	.30	.60*	.42
FFMQ Nonjudgment	Spearman Correlation	.36	.49	.17
FFMQ Nonreaction	Spearman Correlation	.64*	.76*	.56

* $p < .05$ ** $p < .01$.

TABLE A5.6 REGRESSION MODEL COEFFICIENTS FOR FFMQ GLOBAL SCORE

	Unstandardized coefficients B	Std. error	Standardized coefficients	t	p
(Constant)	−1.50	12.23		−.12	.91
Daily Practice CDs	−16.24	19.61	−.62	−.83	.43
Daily Practice Informal	31.00	17.66	1.27	1.76	.12
Sessions attended	11.82	15.47	.20	.76	.47

The model with all IVs revealed a determination coefficient of $r^2 = 63.4$ percent, representing the proportion of the dependent variable explained by the model. The adjusted determination coefficient of $ra^2 = 59.7$ percent.

When analyzed together, none of the scores for the three levels of practice was significant enough to explain the FFMQ scores. Through a systematic analysis of each variable's importance in the model developed, the nonsignificant variables were eliminated in a step-by-step procedure. Different procedures (*Forward, Backward, Stepwise,* and *Remove*) were tested, with the same results, conducting to the selection of the significant independent variables. The obtained model revealed the determination coefficient $r^2 = 40.8$ percent, representing the proportion of the dependent variable explained by the model. The adjusted determination coefficient $ra^2 = 34.9$ percent (see Tables A5.6a and A5.6b).

TABLE A5.6A FFMQ GLOBAL SCORE: REGRESSION MODEL COEFFICIENTS FOR SIGNIFICANT VARIABLES

	Unstandardized coefficients B	Std. error	Standardized coefficients	t	p
(Constant)	6.91	3.35		2.06	.06
Daily Practice Informal	19.38	4.66	.80	4.16	.00**

** $p < .01$.

TABLE A5.6B FFMQ GLOBAL SCORE: REGRESSION MODEL COEFFICIENTS FOR EXCLUDED VARIABLES

	Beta in	t	p
Daily Practice CDs	−.47	−.67	.52
Sessions attended	.14	.58	.58

The verification of the nonexistence of multicollinearity between the independent variables was conducted using the Durbin–Watson test, which allowed for checking the assumption in a multiple regression model. For a 5 percent significance level, the critical value for this test was 1.78; whenever the value was higher, the null hypothesis of autocorrelation could not be rejected. The Durbin–Watson test result for this model is 2.11, thus suggesting that there is no multicollinearity.

APPENDIX 5: FFMQ STATISTICAL RESULTS

TABLE A5.7 FFMQ GLOBAL SCORE: CORRELATIONS WITH MEASURES OF TRAINING AND MEASURES OF WELL-BEING, PSYCHOLOGICAL AND PHYSICAL SYMPTOMS, QUALITY OF LIFE, AND SPIRITUAL WELL-BEING

Measures	r value and significance level
MAAS	$r = .88**$
SCS	$r = .86**$
EQ	$r = .84**$
SWLS	$r = .**$
PANAS PA	$r = .78**$
PANAS NA	$r = -.72**$
PWBS	$r = .75**$
PSS	$r = -.81**$
POMS	$r = -.76**$
WHOQOL-BREF Physical	$r = .73**$
WHOQOL-BREF Psychological	$r = .68**$
WHOQOL-BREF Social relations	$r = .28$
WHOQOL-BREF Environmental	$r = .52**$
WHOQOL-100 Physical	$r = .73**$
WHOQOL-100 Spiritual	$r = .34**$
SHCI	$r = -.73**$
SWBQ	$r = .59**$
Direct Digits	$r = .56**$
Arithmetic	$r = .38$
Digit Symbol Coding	$r = .59**$
Digit Symbol Incident	$r = .56**$
Free Recall	$r = .58**$

* $p < .05$ ** $p < .01$.

TABLE A5.8 MANOVA RESULTS: RELATION BETWEEN FFMQ GLOBAL SCORE AND VARIABLES ASSESSING PSYCHOLOGICAL AND PHYSICAL SYMPTOMS, WELL-BEING, QUALITY OF LIFE, AND SPIRITUAL WELL-BEING

Dependent variables (*Delta*)	F value and significance level
POMS (Global Score)	5.61, $p < .05$
SHCI	4.61, $p < .05$
WHOQOL-BREF Physical	5.90, $p < .05$

» Appendix 6 «

SCS Statistical Results

TABLE A6.1 *T*-TEST RESULTS: DIFFERENCES BETWEEN CG AND TG AT ASSESSMENT 1

		M	SD	*t*-test or Mann–Whitney *U*	*p*
SCS Global	CG	69.25	13.42	$t(22) = -1.07$	.30
	TG	75.58	15.57		
Self-Kindness	CG	13.00	3.02	$t(22) = -.08$	.96
	TG	13.08	5.37		
Self-Judgment	CG	12.25	4.63	$t(22) = .66$	.52
	TG	11.08	3.99		
Common Humanity	CG	12.42	2.54	$t(22) = -.73$	.48
	TG	13.33	3.55		
Isolation	CG	12.08	3.26	$U = 46.0$	.14
	TG	14.08	3.73		
Mindfulness	CG	10.42	3.34	$t(22) = -1.23$	.23
	TG	12.17	3.64		
Reverse Scores	CG	8.83	2.79	$t(22) = -2.26$	.03*
	TG	12.17	4.28		

* $p < .05$ ** $p < .01$.

TABLE A6.2 T-TEST RESULTS: DIFFERENCES BETWEEN CG AND TG AT ASSESSMENT 2

		M	*SD*	*t*-test or Mann–Whitney *U*	*p*
SCS Global	CG	67.50	13.31	$t(22) = -4.04$	.00**
	TG	95.50	19.98		
Self-Kindness	CG	12.25	2.70	$t(22) = -2.33$	.03*
	TG	16.50	5.73		
Self-Judgment	CG	12.08	4.54	$t(22) = -3.05$	.00**
	TG	18.00	4.95		
Common Humanity	CG	12.00	2.49	$t(22) = -3.51$	.00**
	TG	15.83	2.86		
Isolation	CG	12.00	2.80	$U = 25.0$	.00**
	TG	15.92	3.75		
Mindfulness	CG	10.58	3.50	$t(22) = -2.63$	.01*
	TG	14.33	3.47		
Reverse Scores	CG	8.75	2.63	$t(22) = -5.02$	.00**
	TG	14.92	3.34		

* $p < .05$ ** $p < .01$.

TABLE A6.3 SCS GLOBAL SCORE AND SUBSCALES' SCORES: COMPARISON BETWEEN ASSESSMENT 1 AND ASSESSMENT 2 IN CG AND TG

Control Group (*n* = 12)	*M*	*SD*	*t* / Wilcoxon *Z*	*p*
SCS Global ASS2 – ASS1	−1.75	2.38	$t = -2.55$	.03*
SC Self-Kindness ASS2 – ASS1	−.75	1.60	$t = -1.62$	.13
SC Self-Judgment ASS2 – ASS1	−.17	.72	$Z = -.82$	0.41
SC Common Humanity ASS2 – ASS1	−.42	.90	$t = -1.60$	0.14
SC Isolation ASS2 – ASS1	−.08	1.17	$Z = -.25$	0.80
SC Mindfulness ASS2 – ASS1	.17	.94	$t = .62$	0.55
SC Reverse Scores ASS2 – ASS1	−.08	.90	$t = -.32$	0.75
Treatment Group (*n* = 12)	*M*	*SD*	*t* / Wilcoxon *Z*	*p*
SCS Global ASS2 – ASS1	19.92	12.25	$t = 5.63$	.00**
SC Self-Kindness ASS2 – ASS1	3.42	4.48	$t = 2.64$	.02*
SC Self-Judgment ASS2 – ASS1	6.92	4.62	$t = 5.19$	.00**
SC Common Humanity ASS2 – ASS1	2.50	2.43	$t = 3.56$	.00**

cont.

TABLE A6.3 SCS GLOBAL SCORE AND SUBSCALES'
SCORES: COMPARISON BETWEEN ASSESSMENT 1
AND ASSESSMENT 2 IN CG AND TG *CONT.*

SC Isolation ASS2 − ASS1	1.83	3.54	$t = 1.80$	.10
SC Mindfulness ASS2 − ASS1	2.17	3.19	$t = 2.36$	.04*
SC Reverse Scores ASS2 − ASS1	2.75	2.22	$t = 4.30$	.00**

* $p < .05$. ** $p < .01$.

TABLE A6.4 SCS: MEAN VARIATION BETWEEN CG
AND TG PRE- AND POST-INTERVENTION

Dimensions	Group	*M*	*SD*	*t*-test or Mann–Whitney *U*	*p*
SCS Global	CG	−1.75	2.38	$t = -6.01$	.00**
	TG	19.92	12.25		
SCS Self-Kindness	CG	−.75	1.60	$t = -3.03$	.01*
	TG	3.42	4.48		
SCS Self-Judgment	CG	−.17	.72	$U = 10.00$	.00**
	TG	6.92	4.62		
SCS Common Isolation	CG	−.42	.90	$t = -3.90$	.00**
	TG	2.50	2.43		
SCS Isolation	CG	−.08	1.17	$t = -1.78$	.10
	TG	1.83	3.54		
SCS Mindfulness	CG	.17	.94	$t = -2.09$	.06
	TG	2.17	3.19		
SCS Reverse Scores	CG	−.08	.90	$U = 16.00$	.00**
	TG	2.75	2.22		

* $p < .05$ ** $p < .01$.

TABLE A6.5 SCS GLOBAL SCORES: CORRELATIONS WITH MEASURES OF TRAINING AND MEASURES OF WELL-BEING, PSYCHOLOGICAL AND PHYSICAL SYMPTOMS, QUALITY OF LIFE, AND SPIRITUAL WELL-BEING

Measures	r value and significance level
MAAS	$r = .85^{**}$
FFMQ	$r = .86^{**}$
EQ	$r = .83^{**}$
SWLS	$r = .83^{**}$
PANAS PA	$r = .69^{**}$
PANAS NA	$r = -.67^{**}$
PWBS	$r = .79^{**}$
PSS	$r = -.83^{**}$
POMS	$r = -.82^{**}$
WHOQOL-BREF Physical	$r = .70^{**}$
WHOQOL-BREF Psychological	$r = .64^{**}$
WHOQOL-BREF Social relations	$r = .39$
WHOQOL-BREF Environmental	$r = .40^{**}$
WHOQOL-100 Physical	$r = .40$
WHOQOL-100 Spiritual	$r = .76^{**}$
SHCI	$r = -.68^{**}$
SWBQ	$r = .80^{**}$
Direct Digits	$r = .44^{**}$
Arithmetic	$r = .42^{**}$
Digit Symbol Coding	$r = .38$
Digit Symbol Incident	$r = .43^{**}$
Free Recall	$r = .58^{**}$

* $p < .05$ ** $p < .01$.

TABLE A6.6 MANOVA RESULTS: RELATION BETWEEN SCS AND VARIABLES ASSESSING PSYCHOLOGICAL AND PHYSICAL SYMPTOMS, WELL-BEING, QUALITY OF LIFE, AND SPIRITUAL WELL-BEING

Dependent variables (*Delta*)	F value and significance level
SWLS	10.14, $p < .01$
PANAS PA	8.5, $p < .01$
PWBS (Global Score)	9.98, $p < .01$
POMS (Global Score)	5.56, $p < .05$
SWBQ (Global Score)	16.82, $p < .01$

TABLE A6.7 SCS: CORRELATIONS WITH LEVELS OF PRACTICE

	Daily practice CDs	Daily practice informal	Sessions attended
SCS Global	.47	.43	.55
SCS Self-Kindness	.44	.29	.37
SCS Self-Judgement	.19	.31	.76**
SCS Common Humanity	.15	.24	.53
SCS Isolation	.51	.61*	.22
SCS Mindfulness	.30	.19	.21
SCS Reverse Scores	.35	.33	.55

* $p < .05$ ** $p < .01$.

Appendix 7

EQ Statistical Results

TABLE A7.1 *T*-TEST RESULTS: DIFFERENCES BETWEEN
CG AND TG AT ASSESSMENT 1 AND ASSESSMENT 2

	CG	TG	*t* value and significance level
Assessment 1	M = 32.08 SD = 6.19	M = 34.75 SD = 8.21	$t(22) = -.90, p = .38$
Assessment 2	M = 31.67 SD = 5.88	M = 40.92 SD = 8.15	$t(22) = -3.19, p = .00**$

* $p < .05$ ** $p < .01$.

TABLE A7.2 PAIRED *T*-TEST RESULTS: DIFFERENCES BETWEEN
MEAN EQ SCORES AT ASSESSMENT 1 AND ASSESSMENT 2
(ASSESSMENT 2—ASSESSMENT 1) FOR CG AND TG

	Mean scores differences	*t* value and significance level
CG	M = −.42, SD = 1.24	$t(11) = -1.16, p = .27$
TG	M = 6.20, SD = 2.25	$t(11) = 9.50, p = .00**$

* $p < .05$ ** $p < .01$.

TABLE A7.3 *T*-TEST RESULTS: DELTA VARIATION
BETWEEN PRE- AND POST-INTERVENTION

	CG	TG	*t* value and significance level
Mean value variation	M = −.42 SD = 1.24	M = 6.17 SD = 2.25	$t(22) = -8.88, p = .00**$

* $p < .05$ ** $p < .01$.

TABLE A7.4 EQ: CORRELATIONS WITH MEASURES OF TRAINING AND MEASURES OF WELL-BEING, PSYCHOLOGICAL AND PHYSICAL SYMPTOMS, QUALITY OF LIFE, AND SPIRITUAL WELL-BEING

Measures	r value and significance level
MAAS	$r = .74^{**}$
FFMQ	$r = .84^{**}$
SCS	$r = .84^{**}$
SWLS	$r = .83^{**}$
PANAS PA	$r = .85^{**}$
PANAS NA	$r = -.77^{**}$
PWBS	$r = .80^{**}$
PSS	$r = -.80^{**}$
POMS	$r = -.65^{**}$
WHOQOL-BREF Physical	$r = .64^{**}$
WHOQOL-BREF Psychological	$r = .67^{**}$
WHOQOL-BREF Social relations	$r = .28$
WHOQOL-BREF Environmental	$r = .55^{**}$
WHOQOL-100 Physical	$r = .64$
WHOQOL-100 Spiritual	$r = .53^{**}$
SHCI	$r = -.75^{**}$
SWBQ	$r = .67^{**}$
Direct Digits	$r = .65^{**}$
Arithmetic	$r = .42^{**}$
Digit Symbol Coding	$r = .45^{**}$
Digit Symbol Incident	$r = .50^{**}$
Free Recall	$r = .65^{**}$

TABLE A7.5 MANOVA RESULTS: RELATION BETWEEN EQ AND VARIABLES ASSESSING PSYCHOLOGICAL AND PHYSICAL SYMPTOMS, WELL-BEING, QUALITY OF LIFE, AND SPIRITUAL WELL-BEING

Dependent variables (*Delta*)	*F* value and significance level
SWLS	4.45, $p < .01$
PANAS PA	5.58, $p < .01$
PANAS NA	8.10, $p < .01$
PWBS (Global Score)	15.70, $p < .01$
PSS	3.84, $p < .05$
POMS (Global Score)	2.99, $p < .05$
SHCI	4.21, $p < .05$
WHOQOL-BREF Environment	4.34, $p < .05$
WHOQOL-100 Physical	3.20, $p < .05$

TABLE A7.6 EQ: CORRELATIONS WITH LEVELS OF PRACTICE

	Daily practice CDs	Daily practice informal	Sessions attended
EQ	.54	.67*	.64*

* $p < .05$ ** $p < .01$.

Appendix 8

SWLS Statistical Results

TABLE A8.1 *T*-TEST RESULTS: DIFFERENCES BETWEEN
CG AND TG AT ASSESSMENT 1 AND ASSESSMENT 2

	CG	TG	*t* value and significance level
Assessment 1	M = 23.00 SD = 5.56	M = 20.17 SD = 7.22	$t(22) = 1.08, p = .29$
Assessment 2	M = 22.00 SD = 6.08	M = 25.42 SD = 7.15	$t(22) = -1.08, p = .22$

* $p < .05$ ** $p < .01$.

TABLE A8.2 PAIRED *T*-TEST RESULTS: DIFFERENCES BETWEEN
MEAN SWLS SCORES AT ASSESSMENT 1 AND ASSESSMENT
2 (ASSESSMENT 2—ASSESSMENT 1) FOR CG AND TG

	Mean Scores Differences	*t* value and significance level
CG	M = −1.00, SD = 1.70	$t(11) = -2.03, p = .07$
TG	M = 5.25, SD = 3.14	$t(11) = 5.8, p = .00$**

* $p < .05$ ** $p < .01$.

TABLE A8.3 *T*-TEST RESULTS: DELTA VARIATION
BETWEEN PRE- AND POST-INTERVENTION

	CG	TG	*t* value and significance level
Mean value variation	M = 5.25 SD = 3.14	M = −1.00 SD = 1.71	$t(22) = -6.66, p = .00$**

* $p < .05$ ** $p < .01$.

TABLE A8.4 SWLS: CORRELATIONS WITH LEVELS OF PRACTICE

	Daily practice CDs	Daily practice informal	Sessions attended
SWLS	.39	.12	.32

* $p < .05$ ** $p < .01$.

Appendix 9

PANAS Statistical Results

TABLE A9.1 *T*-TEST RESULTS: DIFFERENCES BETWEEN
CG AND TG AT ASSESSMENT 1 AND ASSESSMENT 2

PA	CG	TG	*t* value and significance level
Assessment 1	M = 15.33 SD = 4.89	M = 22.5 SD = 7.82	$t(22) = -2.69, p = .01$*
Assessment 2	M = 14.42 SD = 26.17	M = 26.17 SD = 9.50	$t(22) = -3.85, p = .00$**
NA			
Assessment 1	M = 16.00 SD = 8.77	M = 19.50 SD = 7.55	$t(22) = -1.05, p = .31$
Assessment 2	M = 17.92 SD = 9.34	M = 13.75 SD = 4.54	$t(22) = 1.40, p = .19$

* $p < .05$ ** $p < .01$.

TABLE A9.2 PAIRED *T*-TEST RESULTS: DIFFERENCES
BETWEEN MEAN PANAS SCORES AT ASSESSMENT 1 AND
ASSESSMENT 2 (ASSESSMENT 2—ASSESSMENT 1) FOR CG AND TG

PA	Mean scores differences	*t* value and significance level
CG	M = −.92, SD = 1.51	$t(11) = .21, p = .06$
TG	M = 3.68, SD = 2.64	$t(11) = 4.81, p = .00$**
NA		
CG	M = 1.92, SD = 1.51	$t(11) = 4.41, p = .00$**
TG	M = −5.57, SD = 5.15	$t(11) = -3.86, p = .00$**

* $p < .05$ ** $p < .01$.

TABLE A9.3 *T*-TEST RESULTS: DELTA VARIATION
BETWEEN PRE- AND POST-INTERVENTION

PA	TG	CG	*t* value and significance level
Mean value variation	M = 3.67 SD = 2.64	M = −.92 SD = 1.5	$t(22) = -5.23, p = .00$**
NA			
Mean value variation	M = −5.75 SD = 5.15	M = 192 SD = 1.51	$t(22) = 4.95, p = .00$**

* $p < .05$ ** $p < .01$.

TABLE A9.4 PANAS: CORRELATIONS WITH LEVELS OF PRACTICE

	Daily practice CDs	Daily practice informal	Sessions attended
PANAS PA	.61*	.40	.40
PANAS NA	−.57	−.44	−.18

* $p < .05$ ** $p < .01$.

» Appendix 10 «
PWBS Statistical Results

TABLE A10.1 *T*-TEST RESULTS: DIFFERENCES BETWEEN CG AND TG AT ASSESSMENT 1 AND ASSESSMENT 2

	TG	CG	*t* value and significance level
Assessment 1	M = 365.92 SD = 46.82	M = 362.17 SD = 39.55	$t(22) = .21, p = .83$
Assessment 2	M = 400.08 SD = 50.50	M = 357.75 SD = 41.11	$t(22) = -2.25, p = .01*$

* $p < .05$ ** $p < .01$.

TABLE A10.2 PAIRED *T*-TEST RESULTS: DIFFERENCES BETWEEN MEAN PWBS SCORES AT ASSESSMENT 1 AND ASSESSMENT 2 (ASSESSMENT 2—ASSESSMENT 1) FOR CG AND TG

	Mean scores differences	*t* value and significance level
CG	M = –4.42, SD = 5.44	$t(11) = -2.82, p = .01*$
TG	M = 34.17, SD = 20.53	$t(11) = 5.77, p = .00**$

* $p < .05$ ** $p < .01$.

TABLE A10.3 *T*-TEST RESULTS: DELTA VARIATION BETWEEN PRE- AND POST-INTERVENTION

	CG	TG	*t* value and significance level
Mean value variation	M = –4.42 SD = 5.44	M = 34.17 SD = 20.52	$t(22) = -6.30, p = .00**$

* $p < .05$ ** $p < .01$.

TABLE A10.4 MEANS, STANDARD DEVIATIONS, AND STATISTICAL *T*-TEST FOR PWBS SUBSCALES AT ASSESSMENT 1 AND ASSESSMENT 2 FOR CG AND TG

PWBS Subscales M(SD)	CG (n = 12) Ass 1	CG (n = 12) Ass 2	TG (n = 12) Ass 1	TG (n = 12) Ass 2	t-test or Mann–Whitney U p Ass 1	t-test or Mann–Whitney U p Ass 2
Autonomy	63.08 (8.25)	62.25 (8.44)	59.17 (9.24)	63.83 (10.05)	t = 1.10 p = .29	t = −.42 p = .68
Environmental Mastery	61.83 (6.55)	60.58 (7.69)	56.17 (10.03)	58.42 (10.17)	t = 1.64 p = .12	t = .59 p = .56
Personal Growth	58.17 (6.64)	57.44 (6.47)	64.17 (9.39)	71.00 (8.59)	U = 40.00 p = .06	t = −4.40 p = .00**
Relations With Others	60.42 (6.99)	59.42 (7.65)	65.00 (16.70)	68.67 (17.81)	U = 59.50 p = .47	t = −1.64 p = .12
Purpose in Life	58.67 (9.30)	59.08 (10.18)	65.92 (15.63)	71.50 (16.35)	t = −1.36 p = .19	t = −2.23 p = .04*
Self-Acceptance	61.17 (8.48)	60.17 (7.25)	59.00 (12.35)	66.67 (12.64)	t = .50 p = .62	t = −1.55 p = .14

*p < .05 ** p < .01.

TABLE A10.5 PWBS SUBSCALES: MEAN DIFFERENCES BETWEEN ASSESSMENT 1 AND ASSESSMENT 2 IN CG AND TG

Control Group (n = 12)	M	SD	t / Wilcoxon Z	p
PWBS (Psychological Well-Being) ASS2 − ASS1	−4.42	5.44	t(11) = −2.82	.02*
PWBS Autonomy ASS2 − ASS1	−.83	1.75	t(11) = −1.65	.13
PWBS Environmental Mastery ASS2 − ASS1	−1.25	2.60	t(11) = −1.67	.12
PWBS Personal Growth ASS2 − ASS1	−.83	2.89	Z = −.95	.34
PWBS Relations With Others ASS2 − ASS1	−1.00	2.73	Z = −1.33	.18
PWBS Purpose in Life ASS2 − ASS1	.42	3.03	t(11) = .48	.64
ASS2 PWBS Self-Acceptance ASS2 − ASS1	−1.00	2.95	t(11) = −10.17	.27

APPENDIX 10: PWBS STATISTICAL RESULTS

Treatment Group ($n = 12$)	M	SD	t / Wilcoxon Z	p
PWBS (Psychological Well-Being) ASS2 – ASS1	34.17	20.53	$t(11) = 5.77$	.00**
PWBS Autonomy ASS2 – ASS1	4.67	3.39	$t(11) = 4.76$	.00**
PWBS Environmental Mastery ASS2 – ASS1	2.25	4.86	$t(11) = 1.60$	.14
PWBS Personal Growth ASS2 – ASS1	6.83	4.15	$t(11) = 5.70$	.00**
PWBS Relations with Others ASS2 – ASS1	3.67	5.42	$t(11) = 2.35$	.04*
PWBS Purpose in Life ASS2 – ASS1	5.58	3.00	$t(11) = 6.45$	.00**
ASS2 PWBS Self-Acceptance ASS2 – ASS1	7.67	4.01	$t(11) = 6.63$	.00**

* $p < .05$ ** $p < .01$.

TABLE A10.6 PWBS SUBSCALES: MEAN VARIATION BETWEEN TG AND CG

Subscales	Group $n = 24$	M	SD	t-test or Mann–Whitney U	p
PWBS Autonomy	CG	–.83	1.75	$U = 9.50$	.00**
	TG	4.67	3.39		
PWBS Environmental Mastery	CG	–1.25	2.60	$U = 35.50$	.03*
	TG	2.25	4.86		
PWBS Personal Growth	CG	–.83	2.89	$t(22) = -5.25$	.00**
	TG	6.83	4.15		
PWBS Relations with Others	CG	–1.00	2.73	$U = 28.50$	.01*
	TG	3.67	5.42		
PWBS Purpose in Life	CG	.42	3.03	$t(22) = -4.20$	.00**
	TG	5.58	3.00		
PWBS Self-Acceptance	CG	–1.00	2.95	$t(22) = -6.03$	.00**
	TG	7.67	4.01		

* $p < .05$ ** $p < .01$.

TABLE A10.7 PWBS: CORRELATIONS WITH LEVELS OF PRACTICE

	Daily practice CDs	Daily practice informal	Sessions attended
PWBS Global Score	.45	.36	.19
PWBS Autonomy	.46	.22	.35
PWBS Environmental Mastery	.81**	.56	.52
PWBS Personal Growth	.33	.60*	.48
PWBS Relations with Others	.46	.38	.30
PWBS Purpose in Life	.45	.26	.45
PWBS Self-Acceptance	.24	.23	.38

* $p < .05$ ** $p < .01$.

» Appendix 11 «

POMS Statistical Results

TABLE A11.1 *T*-TEST RESULTS: DIFFERENCES BETWEEN
CG AND TG AT ASSESSMENT 1 AND ASSESSMENT 2

	TG	CG	*t* value and significance level
Assessment 1	M = 121.40 SD = 27.07	M = 112.50 SD = 13.90	$t(22) = -1.02, p = .33$
Assessment 2	M = 104.00 SD = 15.50	M = 121.42 SD = 27.07	$t(22) = 2.09, p = .05^*$

* $p < .05$ ** $p < .01$.

TABLE A11.2 PAIRED *T*-TEST RESULTS: DIFFERENCES
BETWEEN MEAN POMS SCORES AT ASSESSMENT 1 AND
ASSESSMENT 2 (ASSESSMENT 2—ASSESSMENT 1) FOR CG AND TG

	Mean scores differences	*t* / Wilcoxon Z value and significance level
CG	M = 4.92, SD = 4.44	$t(11) = 5.07, p = .00^{**}$
TG	M = −17.33, SD = 19.42	$Z = -2.79, p = .00^{**}$

* $p < .05$ ** $p < .01$.

TABLE A11.3 *T*-TEST RESULTS: DELTA VARIATION
BETWEEN PRE- AND POST-INTERVENTION

	CG	TG	*t* value and significance level
Mean value variation	M = 4.92 SD = 4.44	M = −17.33 SD = 19.42	$t(22) = 3.87, p = .00^{**}$

* $p < .05$ ** $p < .01$.

TABLE A11.4 MEANS, STANDARD DEVIATIONS, AND *T*-TEST STATISTICS FOR POMS SUBSCALES AT ASSESSMENT 1 AND ASSESSMENT 2 FOR CG AND TG

POMS Subscales M (SD)	CG (n = 12) Ass 1	CG (n = 12) Ass 2	TG (n = 12) Ass 1	TG (n = 12) Ass 2	t-test or Mann–Whitney U p Ass 1	t-test or Mann–Whitney U p Ass 2
Tension	7.83 (3.69)	9.50 (3.97)	9.08 (4.36)	6.08 (2.94)	t = −.76 p = .46	t = 2.10 p = .04
Depression	4.58 (2.39)	6.25 (2.73)	8.42 (10.68)	4.17 (6.97)	t = −1.21 p = .25	t = 2.40 p = .03
Hostility	3.92 (3.12)	4.08 (3.23)	5.67 (4.44)	3.00 (3.10)	t = 1.12 p = .28	t = .97 p = .35
Vigor	13.42 (3.75)	13.92 (3.92)	13.42 (3.94)	15.92 (3.87)	t = .00 p = 1	t = .84 p = .41
Fatigue	6.42 (4.52)	7.17 (4.67)	7.00 (5.38)	2.67 (2.53)	t = −.29 p = .78	t = 2.94 p = .00
Confusion	3.92 (2.91)	4.42 (3.06)	4.42 (3.06)	5.83 (3.35)	t = −1.50 p = .15	t = .81 p = .42

* $p < .05$ ** $p < .01$.

TABLE A11.5 POMS GLOBAL SCORE AND SUBSCALES: MEAN DIFFERENCES BETWEEN ASSESSMENT 1 AND ASSESSMENT 2 IN CG AND TG

Control Group (n = 12)	M	SD	t / Wilcoxon Z	p
POMS Global Score ASS2 – ASS1	−4.92	4.44	t(11) = 3.84	.00**
POMS Tension ASS2 – ASS1	1.67	1.16	t(11) = 5.00	.00**
POMS Depression ASS2 – ASS1	1.67	1.83	t(11) = 3.16	.01**
POMS Hostility ASS2 – ASS1	.16	1.34	t(11) = 0.43	.67
POMS Vigor ASS2 – ASS1	.50	67.4	t(11) = 2.57	.03*
POMS Fatigue ASS2 – ASS1	.75	.97	t(11) = 2.69	.02*

APPENDIX 11: POMS STATISTICAL RESULTS

POMS Confusion ASS2 – ASS1	.50	.80	$t(11) = 2.17$	.05
Treatment Group ($n = 12$)	***M***	***SD***	***t* / Wilcoxon *Z***	***p***
POMS Global Score ASS2 – ASS1	−17.33	19.42	$Z = -2.79$	.01**
POMS Tension ASS2 – ASS1	−3.00	2.63	$t(11) = -3.95$	.00**
POMS Depression ASS2 – ASS1	−4.25	5.10	$Z = -2.30$	.02*
POMS Hostility ASS2 – ASS1	−2.66	3.73	$Z = -2.25$	.02*
POMS Vigor ASS2 – ASS1	2.50	1.83	$t(11) = 4.72$	.00**
POMS Fatigue ASS2 – ASS1	−4.33	5.68	$t(11) = -2.64$	.02*
POMS Confusion ASS2 – ASS1	−2.50	3.45	$t(11) = -2.51$	.03*

* $p < .05$ ** $p < .01$.

TABLE A11.6 POMS GLOBAL SORE AND SUBSCALES: MEAN VARIATION BETWEEN TG AND CG

	Group $n = 24$	***M***	***SD***	***t*-test or Mann–Whitney *U***	***p***
POMS Global Score	CG	−1.00	1.71	$t(22) = -6.06$	.00**
	TG	5.25	3.14		
POMS Tension	CG	1.67	1.16	$t(22) = 5.63$	.00**
	TG	−3.00	2.63		
POMS Depression	CG	1.67	1.83	$U = 17.0$	.00**
	TG	−4.25	5.10		
POMS Hostility	CG	.17	1.34	$U = 36.0$	.04*
	TG	2.67	3.73		
POMS Vigor	CG	.50	.67	$U = 16.0$	.00**
	TG	2.50	1.83		
POMS Fatigue	CG	.75	.97	$t(22) = 3.06$	.01**
	TG	−4.33	5.68		
POMS Confusion	CG	.50	.80	$U = 18.0$	.00*
	TG	−2.50	3.45		

* $p < .05$ ** $p < .01$.

TABLE A11.7 POMS: CORRELATIONS WITH LEVELS OF PRACTICE

	Daily practice CDs	Daily practice informal	Sessions attended
POMS Global Score	−.30	−.41	−.14
POMS Tension	−.69*	−.78**	−.39
POMS Depression	−.45	−.63*	−.05
POMS Hostility	−.48	−.51	−.02
POMS Vigor	.86**	.79	.47
POMS Fatigue	−.04	−.20	−.20
POMS Confusion	−.73**	−.418	−.15

* $p < .05$ ** $p < .01$

» Appendix 12 «

PSS Statistical Results

TABLE A12.1 *T*-TEST RESULTS: DIFFERENCES BETWEEN
CG AND TG AT ASSESSMENT 1 AND ASSESSMENT 2

	TG	CG	*t* value and significance level
Assessment 1	M = 26.00 SD = 7.12	M = 27.58 SD = 4.03	$t(22) = .67, p = .51$
Assessment 2	M = 17.00 SD = 5.15	M = 26.00 SD = 7.12	$t(22) = 6.53, p = .00^{**}$

* $p < .05$ ** $p < .01$.

TABLE A12.2 PAIRED *T*-TEST RESULTS: DIFFERENCES
BETWEEN MEAN PSS SCORES AT ASSESSMENT 1 AND
ASSESSMENT 2 (ASSESSMENT 2—ASSESSMENT 1) FOR CG AND TG

	Mean scores differences	*t* value and significance level
CG	M = 3.92, SD = 2.68	$t(11) = 5.07, p = .00^{**}$
TG	M = –9.00, SD = 8.01	$t(11) = -3.89, p = .00^{**}$

* $p < .05$ ** $p < .01$.

TABLE A12.3 *T*-TEST RESULTS: DELTA VARIATION
BETWEEN PRE- AND POST-INTERVENTION

	CG	TG	*t* value and significance level
Mean value variation	M = 3.92 SD = 2.68	M = –9.00 SD = 8.01	$t(22) = -2.30, p = .00^{**}$

* $p < .05$ ** $p < .01$.

TABLE A12.4 PSS: CORRELATIONS WITH LEVELS OF PRACTICE

	Daily practice CDs	Daily practice informal	Sessions attended
PSS	–.86**	–.82**	–.58*

* $p < .05$ ** $p < .01$.

» Appendix 13 «

WHOQOL-BREF Statistical Results

TABLE A13.1 WHOQOL-BREF: MEANS AND STANDARD DEVIATIONS FOR CG AND TG AT ASSESSMENT 1 AND ASSESSMENT 2

WHOQOL-BREF Subscales M (SD)	Control Group ($n = 12$) Assessment 1	Assessment 2	Treatment Group ($n = 12$) Assessment 1	Assessment 2
Physical	75.67 (10.99)	73.00 (10.66)	71.00 (11.31)	79.92 (10.42)
Psychological	70.92 (10.42)	68.25 (10.95)	61.00 (19.76)	76.25 (17.85)
Social Relations	70.17 (11.05)	71.75 (10.16)	61.42 (19.01)	66.08 (16.71)
Environment	68.92 (11.74)	68.83 (11.02)	67.33 (10.42)	75.08 (9.98)

TABLE A13.2 T-TEST RESULTS: DIFFERENCES BETWEEN CG AND TG AT ASSESSMENT 1

		M	SD	t-test or Mann–Whitney U	p
ASS1 WHOQOL BREF Physical	CG TG	75.67 71.00	10.99 15.08	$t(22) = 0.87$	.40
ASS1 WHOQOL BREF Psychological	CG TG	70.92 61.00	10.42 19.76	$t(22) = 1.54$	.14
ASS1 WHOQOL BREF Social Relations	CG TG	70.17 61.42	11.05 19.01	$U = 50.5$	.21
ASS1 WHOQOL BREF Environment	CG TG	68.92 67.33	11.74 10.42	$U = 67.0$	.77

* $p < .05$ ** $p < .01$.

APPENDIX 13: WHOQOL-BREF STATISTICAL RESULTS

TABLE A13.3 *T*-TEST RESULTS: DIFFERENCES BETWEEN CG AND TG AT ASSESSMENT 2

		M	*SD*	*t*-test or Mann–Whitney *U*	*p*
ASS2 WHOQOL-BREF Physical	CG	73.00	10.66	$t(22) = -1.54$	.14
	TG	79.92	11.31		
ASS2 WHOQOL-BREF Psychological	CG	68.25	10,.95	$t(22) = -1.32$	.20
	TG	76.25	17.85		
ASS2 WHOQOL-BREF Social Relations	CG	71.75	10.16	$U = 58.0$	.41
	TG	66.08	16.71		
ASS2 WHOQOL-BREF Environment	CG	68.83	11.02	$U = 48.5$	.17
	TG	75.08	9.98		

TABLE A13.4 WHOQOL-BREF: DIFFERENCES BETWEEN ASSESSMENT 1 AND ASSESSMENT 2 FOR CG AND TG

Control Group (*n* = 12)	*M*	*SD*	*t* / Wilcoxon *Z*	*p*
WHOQOL-BREF Physical ASS2 – ASS1	−2.67	4.31	$t(11) = -2.14$	.055
WHOQOL-BREF Psychological ASS2 – ASS1	−2.67	3.31	$t(11) = -2.79$	.02*
WHOQOL-BREF Social Relations ASS2 – ASS1	1.58	5.49	$Z = 1.00$	.32
WHOQOL-BREF Environment ASS2 – ASS1	−.08	2.78	$t(11) = -0.10$	.92
Treatment Group (*n* = 12)	*M*	*SD*	*t* / Wilcoxon *Z*	*p*
WHOQOL-BREF Physical ASS2 – ASS1	8.92	9.34	$t(11) = 3.31$	.01**
WHOQOL-BREF Psychological ASS2 – ASS1	15.25	13.91	$t(11) = 3.80$	.00**
WHOQOL-BREF Social Relations ASS2 – ASS1	4.67	12.29	$t(11) = 1.32$	.22
WHOQOL-BREF Environment ASS2 – ASS1	7.75	9.42	$Z = 2.14$	.03*

* $p < .05$ ** $p < .01$.

TABLE A13.5 *T*-TEST RESULTS: DELTA VARIATION
BETWEEN PRE- AND POST-INTERVENTION

		M	*SD*	*t*-test or Mann–Whitney *U*	*p*
WHOQOL-BREF Physical	CG	−2.67	4.31	*U* = 16.0	.00**
	TG	8.92	9.34		
WHOQOL-BREF Psychological	CG	−2.67	3.31	*U* = 3.5	.00**
	TG	15.25	13.91		
WHOQOL-BREF Social Relations	CG	1.58	5.49	*U* = 65.0	.61
	TG	4.67	12.29		
WHOQOL-BREF Environment	CG	−.08	2.78	*U* = 31.0	.01**
	TG	7.75	9.42		

* $p < .05$ ** $p < .01$.

TABLE A13.6 WHOQOL-BREF: CORRELATIONS
WITH LEVELS OF PRACTICE

	Daily practice CDs	Daily practice informal	Sessions attended
WHOQOL-BREF Physical	.58*	.51	.31
WHOQOL-BREF Psychological	.65*	.49	.17
WHOQOL-BREF Social Relations	.52	.57	.18
WHOQOL-BREF Environment	.52	.41	.08

* $p < .05$ ** $p < .01$.

» Appendix 14 «

WHOQOL-100 Statistical Results

TABLE A14.1 WHOQOL-100: MEANS AND STANDARD DEVIATIONS FOR CG AND TG AT ASSESSMENT 1 AND ASSESSMENT 2

WHOQOL-100 Subscales M (SD)	Control Group ($n = 12$) Assessment 1	Assessment 2	Treatment Group ($n = 12$) Assessment 1	Assessment 2
Physical	49.92 (5.47)	50.58 (13.06)	55.58 (16.37)	62.42 (17.31)
Spiritual	64.67 (22.58)	63.67 (22.34)	69.39 (20.24)	80.33 (15.25)

TABLE A14.2 T-TEST RESULTS: DIFFERENCES BETWEEN CG AND TG AT ASSESSMENT 1

		M	SD	Mann–Whitney U	p
ASS1 WHOQOL-100 Physical	CG	49.92	5,47	$U = 61.5$	.54
	TG	55.58	16.37		
ASS1 WHOQOL-100 Spiritual	CG	70.92	22.58	$U = 65.5$	.70
	TG	61.00	20.24		

* $p < .05$ ** $p < .01$.

TABLE A14.3 T-TEST RESULTS: DIFFERENCES BETWEEN CG AND TG AT ASSESSMENT 2

		M	SD	t-test or Mann–Whitney U	p
ASS2 WHOQOL-100 Physical	CG	50.58	13.06	$U = 30.5$	.01*
	TG	62.42	17.31		
ASS2 WHOQOL-100 Spiritual	CG	63.67	22.34	$t(22) = -2.14$	.04*
	TG	80.33	15.25		

* $p < .05$ ** $p < .01$.

TABLE A14.4 WHOQOL-100: DIFFERENCES BETWEEN ASSESSMENT 1 AND ASSESSMENT 2 FOR CG AND TG

Control Group	M	SD	t-test or Wilcoxon Z	p
WHOQOL-100 Physical ASS2 – ASS1	.67	9.74	Z = 0.68	.50
WHOQOL-100 Spiritual ASS2 – ASS1	–1.00	3.46	Z = –1.00	.32
Treatment Group	M	SD	t-test or Wilcoxon Z	p
WHOQOL-100 Physical ASS2 – ASS1	6.83	6.73	Z = 2.82	.00**
WHOQOL-100 Spiritual ASS2 – ASS1	10.94	14.89	$t(11) = 4.30$	.03*

* $p < .05$ ** $p < .01$.

TABLE A14.5 T-TEST RESULTS: DELTA VARIATION BETWEEN PRE- AND POST-INTERVENTION

		M	SD	t-test or Mann–Whitney U	p
WHOQOL-100 Physical	CG	.67	9.74	U = 19.0	.00**
	TG	6.83	6.73		
WHOQOL-100 Spiritual	CG	–1.00	3.35	U = 27.5	.00**
	TG	10.92	14.90		

* $p < .05$ ** $p < .01$.

TABLE A14.6 WHOQOL-100: CORRELATIONS WITH LEVELS OF PRACTICE

	Daily practice CD	Daily practice informal	Sessions attended
WHOQOL-100 Physical	.47	.43	.30
WHOQOL-100 Spiritual	.56	.56	.23

* $p < .05$ ** $p < .01$.

» Appendix 15 «
SHCI Statistical Results

TABLE A15.1 *T*-TEST RESULTS: DIFFERENCES BETWEEN CG AND TG AT ASSESSMENT 1 AND ASSESSMENT 2

	TG	CG	*t* value and significance level
Assessment 1	M = 19.50 SD = 9.66	M = 11.58 SD = 7.79	$t(22) = -2.21, p = .04*$
Assessment 2	M = 14.83 SD = 7.02	M = 13.75 SD = 7.72	$t(22) = -.37, p = .72*$

* $p < .05$ ** $p < .01$.

TABLE A15.2 PAIRED *T*-TEST RESULTS: DIFFERENCES BETWEEN MEAN SHCI SCORES AT ASSESSMENT 1 AND ASSESSMENT 2 (ASSESSMENT 2—ASSESSMENT 1) FOR CG AND TG

	Mean scores differences	*t* value and significance level
CG	M = 2.17, SD = 2.08	$t(11) = 3.61, p = .00**$
TG	M = −4.67, SD = 5.31	$t(11) = -3.04, p = .01*$

* $p < .05$ ** $p < .01$.

TABLE A15.3 *T*-TEST RESULTS: DELTA VARIATION BETWEEN PRE- AND POST-INTERVENTION

	CG	TG	*U* value and significance level
Mean value variation	M = 2.17 SD = 2.08	M = −4.67 SD = 5.31	$U = 16.5, p = .00**$

* $p < .05$ ** $p < .01$.

TABLE A15.4 SHCI: CORRELATIONS WITH LEVELS OF PRACTICE

	Daily practice CD	Daily practice informal	Sessions attended
PSS	−.60*	−.81**	−.24

* $p < .05$ ** $p < .01$.

» APPENDIX 16 «

Death Perspectives Statistical Results

TABLE A16.1 DPS: MEANS AND STANDARD DEVIATIONS FOR
CG AND TG AT ASSESSMENT 1 AND ASSESSMENT 2

DPS Subscales M (SD)	Control Group ($n = 12$) Assessment 1	Control Group ($n = 12$) Assessment 2	Treatment Group ($n = 12$) Assessment 1	Treatment Group ($n = 12$) Assessment 2
Pain and Loneliness	18.42 (8.56)	17.75 (8.35)	14.75 (5.82)	21.58 (10.29)
Afterlife/Reward	21.58 (10.29)	21.08 (9.72)	24.55 (11.51)	24.58 (9.18)
Indifferent	16.50 (6.04)	16.25 (6.02)	16.17 (7.04)	16.83 (6.73)
Unknown	25.50 (7.85)	24.67 (7.61)	24.75 (8.59)	25.00 (8.20)
Dependents/ Guilt	13.08 (3.75)	13.42 (3.55)	12.58 (5.95)	13.33 (5.96)
Courage	18.42 (6.07)	19.00 (6.86)	20.25 (8.82)	21.83 (6.71)
Failure	16.67 (6.43)	16.08 (5.25)	20.17 (4.78)	19.67 (4.46)
Natural End	20.17 (4.78)	19.67 (4.46)	21.00 (3.10)	20.83 (3.10)

TABLE A16.2 T-TEST RESULTS: DIFFERENCES BETWEEN CG AND TG AT ASSESSMENT 1

		M	SD	t-test or Mann–Whitney U	p
ASS1 DP1 Pain and Loneliness	CG	18.42	8.57	t(22) = 1.09	.28
	TG	14.92	7.08		
ASS1 DP2 Afterlife or reward	CG	21.58	10.30	U = 51.5	.24
	TG	24.58	11.51		
ASS1 DP3 Indifferent	CG	16.50	6.04	t(22) = .12	.90
	TG	16.17	7.04		
ASS1 DP4 Unknown	CG	25.50	7.85	t(22) = .22	.83
	TG	24.75	8.59		
ASS1 DP5 Dependents and Guilt	CG	13.08	3.75	t(22) = .26	.81
	TG	12.58	5.95		
ASS1 DP6 Courage	CG	18.42	6.07	t(22) = −.59	.56
	TG	20.25	8.82		
ASS1 DP7 Failure	CG	16.67	6.43	t(22) = 1.32	.20
	TG	13.42	5.55		
ASS1 DP8 Natural End	CG	20.17	4.78	U = 68.0	.81
	TG	21.00	3.10		

* $p < .05$ ** $p < .01$.

TABLE A16.3 T-TEST RESULTS: DIFFERENCES BETWEEN CG AND TG AT ASSESSMENT 2

		M	SD	t-test or Mann–Whitney U	p
ASS2 DP1 Pain and Loneliness	CG	17.75	8.35	t(22) = 1.02	.32
	TG	14.75	5.82		
ASS2 DP2 Afterlife or reward	CG	21.08	9.72	t(22) = −.91	.37
	TG	24.58	9.18		
ASS2 DP3 Indifferent	CG	16.25	6.02	t(22) = −.22	.83
	TG	16.83	6.73		
ASS2 DP4 Unknown	CG	24.67	7.61	t(22) = −.10	.92
	TG	25.00	8.20		
ASS2 DP5 Dependents and Guilt	CG	13.42	3.55	t(22) = .04	.97
	TG	13.33	5.96		
ASS2 DP6 Courage	CG	19.00	6.86	t(22) = −1.02	.32
	TG	21.83	6.71		
ASS2 DP7 Failure	CG	16.08	5.95	t(22) = 1.03	.32
	TG	13.50	6.38		
ASS2 DP8 Natural End	CG	19.67	4.46	t(22) = −.74	.47
	TG	20.83	3.10		

TABLE A16.4 DPS: DIFFERENCES BETWEEN ASSESSMENT
1 AND ASSESSMENT 2 FOR CG AND TG

Control Group (n = 12)	M	SD	t / Wilcoxon Z	p
DP1 Pain and Loneliness ASS2 − ASS1	−.67	2.23	$t(11) = -1.04$	.32
DP2 Afterlife or reward ASS2 − ASS1	−.50	1.88	$t(11) = -.92$	.38
DP3 Indifferent ASS2 − ASS1	−.25	2.09	$t(11) = -.41$	.69
DP4 Unknown ASS2 − ASS1	−.83	1.95	$t(11) = -1.48$	.17
DP5 Dependents and Guilt ASS2 − ASS1	.33	1.56	$t(11) = .74$	.47
DP6 Courage ASS2 − ASS1	.58	1.68	$t(11) = 1.21$	.25
DP7 Failure ASS2 − ASS1	−.58	1.83	$t(11) = -1.10$	.29
DP8 Natural End ASS2 − ASS1	−.50	1.31	$t(11) = -1.32$	.21
Treatment Group (n = 12)	M	SD	t / Wilcoxon Z	p
DP1 Pain and Loneliness ASS2 − ASS1	−.17	7.58	$t(11) = -.08$	.94
DP2 Afterlife or reward ASS2 − ASS1	.00	6.25	$Z = .41$	.69
DP3 Indifferent ASS2 − ASS1	.67	6.96	$t(11) = .33$	.75
DP4 Unknown ASS2 − ASS1	.25	6.20	$t(11) = .14$	.89
DP5 Dependents and Guilt ASS2 − ASS1	.75	5.21	$t(11) = .50$	.63
DP6 Courage ASS2 − ASS1	1.58	4.62	$t(11) = 1.19$	.26
DP7 Failure ASS2 − ASS1	.08	5.09	$t(11) = .06$	.96
DP8 Natural End ASS2 − ASS1	−.17	3.22	$Z = -.18$	.86

TABLE A16.5 *T*-TEST RESULTS: DELTA VARIATION
BETWEEN PRE- AND POST-INTERVENTION

		M	SD	*t*-test or Mann–Whitney *U*	*p*
DP1 Pain and Loneliness	CG	−.67	2.23	*U* = 70.5	.83
	TG	−.17	7.58		
DP2 Afterlife or reward	CG	−.50	1.88	$t(22) = -.265$	.80
	TG	.00	6.25		
DP3 Indifferent	CG	−.25	2.09	$t(22) = -.437$	.67
	TG	.67	6.96		
DP4 Unknown	CG	−.83	1.95	*U* = 61.0	.57
	TG	.25	6.20		
DP5 Dependents and Guilt	CG	.33	1.56	$t(22) = -.266$	.79
	TG	.75	5.21		
DP6 Courage	CG	.58	1.68	$t(22) = -.705$	.49
	TG	1.58	4.62		
DP7 Failure	CG	−.58	1.83	$t(22) = -.427$	.68
	TG	.08	5.09		
DP8 Natural End	CG	−.50	1.31	*U* = 53.0	.74
	TG	−.17	3.26		

» APPENDIX 17 «
SWBQ Statistical Results

TABLE A17.1 *T*-TEST RESULTS: DIFFERENCES BETWEEN
CG AND TG AT ASSESSMENT 1 AND ASSESSMENT 2

	TG	CG	*t* value and significance level
Assessment 1	M = 14.89 SD = 1.95	M = 14.15 SD = 2.42	$t(22) = -.83, p = .42$
Assessment 2	M = 15.89 SD = 1.44	M = 14.13 SD = 2.35	$t(22) = -.37, p = .03$*

* $p < .05$ ** $p < .01$.

TABLE A17.2 PAIRED *T*-TEST RESULTS: DIFFERENCES BETWEEN
MEAN SWBQ SCORES AT ASSESSMENT 1 AND ASSESSMENT 2
(ASSESSMENT 2—ASSESSMENT 1) FOR CG AND TG

	Mean scores differences	*t* value and significance level
CG	M = –.03, SD = .21	$t(11) = -.41, p = .69$
TG	M = 1.08, SD = 1.03	$t(11) = 3.65, p = .00$**

* $p < .05$ ** $p < .01$.

TABLE A17.3 *T*-TEST RESULTS: DELTA VARIATION
BETWEEN PRE- AND POST-INTERVENTION

	CG	TG	*U* value and significance level
Mean value variation	M = .00 SD = .00	M = 1.08 SD = 1.00	$U = 30.00, p = .00$**

* $p < .05$ ** $p < .01$.

TABLE A17.4 SWBQ: CORRELATIONS WITH LEVELS OF PRACTICE

	Daily practice CDs	Daily informal practice	Sessions attended
SWBQ GLB Spiritual Well-Being	.13	.16	.11
SWBQ1 Personal	.14	.45	.09**
SWBQ2 Community	−.42	−.54	.00**
SWBQ3 Environment	.31	.35	.17
SWBQ4 Transcendental	.31	.36	.17

* $p < .05$ ** $p < .01$.

TABLE A17.5 SWBQ: MEANS, STANDARD DEVIATIONS, AND STATISTICAL SIGNIFICANCE FOR CG AND TG AT ASSESSMENT 1 AND ASSESSMENT 2

SWBQ Subscales $M (SD)$	CG ($n = 12$) Ass 1	CG Ass 2	TG ($n = 12$) Ass 1	TG Ass 2	t-test or Mann–Whitney U p Ass 1	Ass 2
Personal	3.53 (.56)	3.54 (.52)	3.53 (.65)	3.80 (.49)	$U = 68.5$ $p = .84$	$t = −1.26$ $p = .22$
Community	3.75 (.74)	3.75 (.72)	3.73 (.57)	3.94 (.34)	$t = .09$ $p = .93$	$U = 57.5$ $p = .39$
Environment	3.58 (.59)	3.63 (.59)	3.58 (.55)	3.63 (.59)	$t = −1.95$ $p = .07$	$U = 29.0$ $p < .05$
Transcendental	3.77 (.77)	3.72 (.77)	3.77 (.80)	3.88 (.67)	$t = .52$ $p = .61$	$t = −.56$ $p = .58$

* $p < .05$ ** $p < .01$.

TABLE A17.6 PAIRED *T*-TEST RESULTS: DIFFERENCES BETWEEN MEAN SWBQ SCORES AT ASSESSMENT 1 AND ASSESSMENT 2 (ASSESSMENT 2—ASSESSMENT 1) FOR CG AND TG

Control Group	*M*	*SD*	*t* / Wilcoxon Z	*p*
SWBQ1 Personal ASS2 – ASS1	.01	.17	Z = .00	1.00
SWBQ2 Community ASS2 – ASS1	.00	.12	Z = .00	1.00
SWBQ3 Environment ASS2 – ASS1	.05	.12	Z = 1.34	.18
SWBQ4 Transcendental ASS2 – ASS1	–.05	.12	*t*(11) = –1.39	.19
Treatment Group	*M*	*SD*	*t* / Wilcoxon Z	*p*
SWBQ1 Personal ASS2 – ASS1	.27	.54	*t*(11) = 1.56	.12
SWBQ2 Community ASS2 – ASS1	.22	.54	*t*(11) = 1.38	.19
SWBQ3 Environment ASS2 – ASS1	.22	.30	*t*(11) = 2.50	.03*
SWBQ4 Transcendental ASS2 – ASS1	.28	.44	*t*(11) = 2.24	.05*

* $p < .05$ ** $p < .01$.

TABLE A17.7 SWBQ SUBSCALES: MEAN DIFFERENCES, STANDARD DEVIATIONS, AND STATISTICAL SIGNIFICANCE BETWEEN TG AND CG

SWBQ Dimensions	Groups	*M*	*SD*	*t*-test or Mann–Whitney *U*	*p*
Personal	CG	.00	.00	U = 48.0	.07
	TG	.33	.65		
Community	CG	.00	.00	U = 72.0	1.00
	TG	.00	.60		
Environment	CG	.00	.00	U = 66.0	.31
	TG	.08	.29		
Transcendental	CG	.00	.00	U = 66.0	.31
	TG	.08	.29		

* $p < .05$ ** $p < .01$.

» Appendix 18 «

Working Memory Index Statistical Results

TABLE A18.1 DIRECT DIGITS *T*-TEST RESULTS: DIFFERENCES BETWEEN CG AND TG AT ASSESSMENT 1 AND ASSESSMENT 2

	TG	CG	*t* value and significance level
Assessment 1	M = 9.08 SD = 1.78	M = 8.27 SD = 1.78	$t(22) = -1.10, p = .28$
Assessment 2	M = 10.25 SD = 2.5	M = 8.45 SD = 1.92	$t(22) = -2.16, p = .04$*

* $p < .05$ ** $p < .01$.

TABLE A18.2 INVERSE DIGITS *T*-TEST RESULTS: DIFFERENCES BETWEEN CG AND TG AT ASSESSMENT 1 AND ASSESSMENT 2

	TG	CG	*t* value and significance level
Assessment 1	M = 5.42 SD = 2.61	M = 4.82 SD = 1.17	$U = 64.00, p = .90$
Assessment 2	M = 6.42 SD = 2.11	M = 5.00 SD = 1.27	$t(22) = -1.93, p = .07$

* $p < .05$ ** $p < .01$.

TABLE A18.3 ARITHMETIC *T*-TEST RESULTS: DIFFERENCES BETWEEN CG AND TG AT ASSESSMENT 1 AND ASSESSMENT 2

	TG	CG	*t* value and significance level
Assessment 1	M = 12.17 SD = 3.16	M = 9.36 SD = 2.62	$t(22) = -2.31, p = .03$*
Assessment 2	M = 12.83 SD = 3.38	M = 9.27 SD = 2.37	$U = 24.00, p = .01$**

* $p < .05$ ** $p < .01$.

TABLE A18.4 WORKING MEMORY INDEX: DIFFERENCES BETWEEN ASSESSMENT 1 AND ASSESSMENT 2 FOR CG AND TG

Control Group ($n=12$)	M	SD	t / Wilcoxon Z	p
Direct Digits ASS2 – ASS1	.18	.41	$t(10) = 1.49$	.17
Inverse Digits ASS2 – ASS1	.18	.60	$Z = 1.00$	.32
Arithmethic ASS2 – ASS1	–.09	.54	$Z = -.58$	.56
Treatment Group ($n = 12$)	M	SD	t / Wilcoxon Z	p
Direct Digits ASS2 – ASS1	1.17	1.27	$t(11) = 3.19$	.01**
Inverse Digits ASS2 – ASS1	1.00	1.76	$t(11) = 1.97$	.07
Arithmethic ASS2 – ASS1	.67	1.44	$t(11) = 1.61$	.14

* $p < .05$ ** $p < .01$.

TABLE A18.5 *T*-TEST RESULTS: DELTA VARIATION BETWEEN PRE- AND POST-INTERVENTION

	CG	TG	U value and significance level
Direct Digits	$M = .18$ $SD = .41$	$M = 1.17$ $SD = 1.27$	$U = 22.5, p = .00$**
Inverse Digits	$M = .18$ $SD = 1.00$	$M = 1.00$ $SD = 1.76$	$U = 40.5, p = .10$
Arithmetic	$M = .09$ $SD = .54$	$M = .67$ $SD = 1.14$	$U = 32.5, p = .04$*

* $p < .05$ ** $p < .01$.

TABLE A18.6 CORRELATIONS BETWEEN LEVELS OF PRACTICE AND WORKING MEMORY INDEX

	Daily practice CDs	Daily practice informal	Sessions attended
Direct Digits	.14	.34	.17
Inverse Digits	.16	.00	.40
Arithmethic	.45	.17	.30

* $p < .05$ ** $p < .01$.

» Appendix 19 «

Processing Speed Index Statistical Results

TABLE A19.1 DIGIT SYMBOL CODING *T*-TEST RESULTS: DIFFERENCES BETWEEN CG AND TG AT ASSESSMENT 1 AND ASSESSMENT 2

	TG	CG	*t* value and significance level
Assessment 1	M = 48.67 SD = 15.07	M = 44.64 SD = 15.30	$t(22) = .63, p = .54$
Assessment 2	M = 55.58 SD = 16.57	M = 45.82 SD = 15.07	$t(22) = -1.47, p = .15$

* $p < .05$ ** $p < .01$.

TABLE A19.2 DIGIT SYMBOL INCIDENT *T*-TEST RESULTS: DIFFERENCES BETWEEN CG AND TG AT ASSESSMENT 1 AND ASSESSMENT 2

	TG	CG	*t* value and significance level
Assessment 1	M = 8.17 SD = 5.42	M = 4.91 SD = 3.62	$t(22) = -1.68, p = .54$
Assessment 2	M = 9.75 SD = 5.08	M = 5.27 SD = 4.02	$t(22) = -2.33, p = .04$*

* $p < .05$ ** $p < .01$.

TABLE A19.3 PROCESSING SPEED INDEX: DIFFERENCES BETWEEN ASSESSMENT 1 AND ASSESSMENT 2 FOR CG AND TG

Control Group ($n = 12$)	M	SD	*t*/Wilcoxon Z	*p*
Digit Symbol Coding ASS2 – ASS1	1.18	1.17	$t(10) = 3.36$	0.01**
Digit Symbol Incident ASS2 – ASS1	.36	.67	$t(10) = 1.79$	.10
Treatment Group ($n = 12$)	M	SD	*t*/Wilcoxon Z	*p*
Digit Symbol Coding ASS2 – ASS1	6.92	6.83	$t(11) = 3.51$	.01**
Digit Symbol Incident ASS2 – ASS1	1.58	2.94	$t(11) = 1.87$	.09

* $p < .05$ ** $p < .01$.

TABLE A19.4 T-TEST RESULTS: DELTA VARIATION
BETWEEN PRE- AND POST-INTERVENTION

	CG	TG	U value and significance level
Digit Symbol Coding	M = .18 SD = .41	M = 6.92 SD = 6.81	$U = 14.00, p = .00$**
Digit Symbol Incident	M = .36 SD = .67	M = 1.58 SD = 2.93	$U = 40.5, p = .10$

* $p < .05$ ** $p < .01$.

TABLE A19.5 CORRELATIONS BETWEEN LEVELS OF
PRACTICE AND PROCESSING SPEED INDEX

	Daily practice CDs	Daily practice informal	Sessions attended
Digit Symbol Coding	.11	.32	−.45
Digit Symbol Incident	.76**	.74**	.51

* $p < .05$ ** $p < .01$.

» Appendix 20 «

Memory Statistical Results

TABLE A20.1 FREE RECALL *T*-TEST RESULTS: DIFFERENCES BETWEEN CG AND TG AT ASSESSMENT 1 AND ASSESSMENT 2

	TG	CG	*t* value and significance level
Assessment 1	M = 6.75 SD = 1.36	M = 6.45 SD = 1.86	$t(22) = .44, p = .67$
Assessment 2	M = 7.58 SD = 1.38	M = 6.55 SD = 1.75	$t(22) = -1.58, p = .13$

* $p < .05$ ** $p < .01$.

TABLE A20.2 FREE RECALL: DIFFERENCES BETWEEN ASSESSMENT 1 AND ASSESSMENT 2 FOR CG AND TG

	Mean scores differences	*t* value and significance level
CG	M = .09, SD = .54	$t(11) = .56, p = .59$
TG	M = .83, SD = .94	$t(11) = 3.08, p = .01$*

* $p < .05$ ** $p < .01$.

TABLE A20.3 FREE RECALL *T*-TEST RESULTS: DELTA VARIATION BETWEEN PRE- AND POST-INTERVENTION

	CG	TG	*U* value and significance level
Free Recall	M = 77.90 SD = .54	M = .83 SD = .94	$U = 33.5, p = .00$**

* $p < .05$ ** $p < .01$.

TABLE A20.4 CORRELATIONS BETWEEN LEVELS OF PRACTICE AND FREE RECALL

	Daily practice CDs	Daily practice informal	Sessions attended
Free Recall	.35	.47	–.46

TABLE A20.5 TRAIL MAKING *T*-TEST RESULTS: DIFFERENCES BETWEEN CG AND TG AT ASSESSMENT 1 AND ASSESSMENT 2

	TG	CG	*t* value and significance level
Assessment 1	M = 70.50 SD = 1.36	M = 77.90 SD = 53.07	$U = 59.5, p = .97$
Assessment 2	M = 61.75 SD = 24.61	M = 76.80 SD = 52.62	$U = 56.00, p = .79$

* $p < .05$ ** $p < .01$.

TABLE A20.6 TRAIL MAKING: DIFFERENCES BETWEEN ASSESSMENT 1 AND ASSESSMENT 2 FOR CG AND TG

	Mean scores differences	*t* value or Z value and significance level
CG	M = −1.10, SD = 2.59	$Z = -1.14, p = .25$
TG	M = −8.75, SD = 29.72	$t(11) = -1.02, p = .33$

* $p < .05$ ** $p < .01$.

TABLE A20.7 TRAIL MAKING *T*-TEST RESULTS: DELTA VARIATION BETWEEN PRE- AND POST-INTERVENTION

	CG	TG	*U* value and significance level
Trail Making	M = −1.10 SD = 2.56	M = −8.75 SD = 29.72	$U = 40.00, p = .19$

* $p < .05$ ** $p < .01$.

TABLE A20.8 CORRELATIONS BETWEEN LEVELS OF PRACTICE AND TRAIL MAKING

	Daily practice CDs	Daily practice informal	Sessions attended
Trail Making	−.01	−.19	−.31

* $p < .05$ ** $p < .01$.

Glossary

Alpha coefficient (or Cronback's alpha): One specific method of estimating the internal consistency of a measure revealing how closely related a set of items are as a group and if the items measure an underlying construct.

Correlation coefficient: A coefficient that provides a measure of strength of linear association between two variables.

Decentering: The ability to observe one's thoughts and feelings as temporary, objective events in the mind, as opposed to as true reflections of the self, with an internal attitude of acceptance and nonjudgment (Fresco *et al.*, 2007).

Delta variable: A variable *delta* was created in this study's analysis by calculating the difference between Assessment 2 and Assessment 1 and was used to analyze statistically the mean value of variation of scores in order to assess the evolution of the treatment and control groups in the various dependent variables.

Dichotomous variables: Nominal variables that have only two categories or levels.

Digit symbol coding: A subtest of the Wechsler Adults Intelligence Scale III that contributes to the score of the speed processing index. In this subtest individuals are asked to copy symbols paired with numbers in a 120-second limit.

Digit symbol incident: A subtest of the Wechsler Adults Intelligence Scale III that contributes to the score of the speed processing index. In this subtest individuals are given numbers and are requested to recall associated symbols direct digits.

Factor MAAS: Mean variation of the Mindfulness Attention Awareness Scale.

Free recall: A subtest of the Wechsler Adults Intelligence Scale III that contributes to the score of the speed processing index. In this subtest individuals are asked to write as many symbols as they can recall learned during the digit symbol coding subtest of the speed processing index.

Global model: A global test score computed in MANOVA that reveals whether group means differ for any if the variables included in the model.

MAAS delta: MAAS *delta* was created in this study's analysis by calculating the difference between Assessment 2 and Assessment 1 and was used to analyze statistically the mean value of variation of scores in order to assess the evolution of the TG and CG in MAAS.

Mann–Whitney *U* test: The Mann–Whitney *U* test is used to compare differences between two independent groups when the dependent variable is either ordinal or continuous, but not normally distributed.

MANOVA: Multivariate analysis of variance or multiple analysis of variance is a statistical test procedure for comparing multivariate (population) means of several groups.

Mean variation value: The mean difference between pre- and post-intervention.

MEDLINE: Online database that contains journal citations and abstracts for biomedical and life science literature from around the world.

Nonparametric test (Wilcoxon sign test): A nonparametric statistical hypothesis test used when comparing two related samples, matched samples, or repeated measurements on a single sample to assess whether their population mean ranks differ. It is used as an alternative to the *t*-test for matched pairs, or the *t*-test for dependent samples when the population cannot be assumed to be normally distributed (e.g., Mann–Whitney *U* test, Wilcoxon sign test).

Observed values: Values obtained from test statistics.

Paired *t*-test: A paired *t*-test measures whether means from a within-subjects test group vary over two test conditions. The paired *t*-test is commonly used to compare a sample group's scores before and after an intervention

Parametric *t*-test: A statistical test that is used to determine if there is a significant difference between the mean of two groups in a given variable. It is used when the population distribution is approximately normal.

PANAS; PANAS PA; PANAS NA: The Positive and Negative Affect Schedule (PANAS) used to assess the emotional component of subjective well-being. PANAS consists of 20 emotion adjectives that are divided into two 10-item assessments measuring positive-affect (PA) and negative-affect (NA).

Quantitative values: Measures of values or counts and are expressed as numbers.

Regression analysis: A statistical test used to predict change in a dependent variable on the basis of change in one or more independent variables.

Reverse scores: Items in a psychological test that are scored backwards.

SCS global: Total score of the Self-Compassion Scale (SCS) that includes the sum of all the different subscales.

Trail Making Test: The Trail Making Test (TMT) A and B is primarily a test of visual attention and motor speed, but it also provides information on visual search, executive functions, speed processing, and mental flexibility.

References

Aldwin, C. M., Park, C. L., and Spiro, A., III. (2007) *Handbook of Health Psychology and Aging*. New York, NY: The Guilford Press.

Alexander, C. N., Langer, E. J., Newman, R. I., Chandler, H. M., and Davies, J. L. (1989) 'Transcendental meditation, mindfulness, and longevity: An experimental study with the elderly.' *Journal of Personality and Social Psychology, 57*, 950–964. doi: 10.1037/0022-3514.57.6.950

Alves, N. C., and Figueiras, M. J. (2008) Adaptação experimental da Escala de Queixas Subjectivas de Saúde para a população portuguesa.' [Experimental adaptation of the Subjective Health Complaints to the Portuguese population]. *Análise Psicológica, 2* (XXVI), 281–293. Available at www.scielo.oces.mctes.pt/scielo.php?pid=S0870-82312008000200009&script=sci_arttext, accessed on 7 May 2014.

Anderson, N. D., Lau, M. L., Segal, Z. V., and Bishop, S. R. (2007) 'Mindfulness-based stress reduction and attentional control.' *Clinical Psychology and Psychotherapy, 14*, 449–463. doi: 10.1002/cpp.544

Andresen, J. (2000) 'Meditation meets behavioral medicine: The story of experimental research on meditation.' *Journal of Consciousness Studies, 11–12*, 17–73.

Armstrong, T. (2007) *The Human Odyssey: Navigating the Twelve Stages of Life*. New York, NY: Sterling.

Army Individual Test Battery (1944) *Manual of Directions and Scoring*. Washington, DC: War Department, Adjutant General's Office.

Arnhoff, F. N., Leon, H., and Lorge, I. (1964) 'Cross-cultural acceptance of stereotypes towards aging.' *Journal of Social Psychology, 63*, 41–58.

Aronson, H. B. (1986) *Love and Sympathy in Theravada Buddhism*. Jawahar Nagar, Delhi: Motilal Banarsidass.

Ashman, O., Shiomura, K., and Levy, B. R. (2006) 'Influence of culture and age on control beliefs: The missing link of interdependence.' *International Journal of Aging and Human Development, 62*(2), 143–157.

Astin, J. (1997) 'Stress reduction through mindfulness meditation. Effects on psychological symptomatology, sense of control, and spiritual experiences.' *Psychotherapy and Psychosomatics, 66*, 97–106.

Baddeley, A. (1992) 'Working memory.' *Science, 255*(5044), 556–559.

Baer, R. A. (2003) 'Mindfulness training as a clinical intervention: A conceptual and empirical review.' *Clinical Psychology Science and Practice, 10*(2), 125–143. doi: 10.1093/clipsy/bpg015

Baer, R. A., Smith, G. T., Hopkins, J., Krietemeyer, J., and Toney, L. (2006) 'Using self-report assessment methods to explore facets of mindfulness.' *Assessment, 13*(1), 27–45.

Baer, R. A., Smith, G. T., Lykins, E., Button, D., Krietemeyer, J., Sauer, S., *et al.* (2008) 'Construct validity of the Five Facet Mindfulness Questionnaire in meditating and nonmeditating samples.' *Assessment, 15*, 329–342.

Baer, R. A., Walsh, E., and Lykins, E. L. B. (2009) 'Assessment of mindfulness.' In F. Didonna (ed.) *Clinical Handbook of Mindfulness*. New York, NY: Springer Science.

Baltes, P. B. and Baltes, M. M. (1990) *Successful Aging: Perspectives from the Behavioral Sciences*. New York, NY: Cambridge University Press.

Barbosa, E., Mendes, I., Salgado, J., and Santos, A. (2011, July) 'Versão Portuguesa do questionário de experiências.' [Portuguese version of the experience questionnaire]. Poster session presented at the XV International Conference of Psychological Assessment, Lisbon, Portugal.

Barks, C. (1995) *The Essential Rumi*. New York, NY: HarperCollins.

Barnhofer, T. and Crane, C. (2009) 'Mindfulness-based Cognitive Therapy for Depression and Suicidality.' In F. Didonna (ed.) *Clinical Handbook of Mindfulness*. New York, NY: Springer Science.

Barreto, H., Moreira, A. R., and Ferreira, C. (2008) *Wechsler Adult Intelligence Scale (WAIS-III)*: Versão Portuguesa [WAIS-III: Portuguese version]. Lisboa, Portugal: Cegoc.

Barros-Oliveira, J. and Neto, F. (2004) 'Validação de um instrumento sobre diversas perspectivas da morte. [Validation of an instrument assessing several perspectives of death].' *Análise Psicológica*, 2(22), 355–367. Available at www.scielo.oces.mctes.pt/pdf/aps/v22n2/v22n2a04.pdf, accessed on 29 January 2014.

Batchelor, S. (1998) *Buddhism Without Beliefs*. New York, NY: Riverhead Books.

Bédard, M., Felteau, M., Mazmanian, D., Fedyk, K., et al. (2003) 'Pilot evaluation of mindfulness-based intervention to improve quality of life among individuals who sustained traumatic brain injuries.' *Disability and rehabilitation*, 25(3), 722–731.

Begley, S. (2007) *Train Your Mind, Change Your Brain: How a New Science Reveals our Extraordinary Potential to Transform Ourselves*. New York, NY: Ballantine.

Berg, C. A., Smith, T. W., Henry, N. J. M., and Pearce, G. E. (2007) 'A developmental approach to psychosocial risk factors and successful aging.' In C. M. Aldwin, C. L. Park, and A. Spiro, III (eds) *Handbook of Health Psychology and Aging*. New York, NY: Guilford Press.

Bhikkhu, B. (1997a) 'Insight by the nature method.' In R. Bucknell and C. Kang (eds) *The Meditative Way*. Abingdon, UK: Routledge Press.

Bhikkhu, B. (1997b) 'A spectrum of meditative practices.' In R. Bucknell, and C. Kang (eds) *The Meditative Way*. Abingdon, UK: Routledge Press.

Biegel, G. M., Brown, K. W., Shapiro, S. L., and Schubert, C. M. (2009) 'Mindfulness-based stress reduction for the treatment of adolescent psychiatric outpatients: A Randomized Clinical Trial.' *Journal of Consulting and Clinical Psychology*, 77(5), 855–866. doi: 10.1037/a0016241

Birnie, K., Speca, M., and Carlson, L. E. (2010) 'Exploring self-compassion and empathy in the context of mindfulness-based stress reduction (MBSR).' *Stress and Health* 26(5), 359–371. doi: 10.1002/smi.1305

Birren, J. E. and Schaie, K. W. (1996) *Handbook of the Psychology of Aging*. New York, NY: Van Nostrand.

Birren, J. E. and Svensson, C. M. (2005) 'Wisdom in history.' In R. J. Sternberg and J. Jordan (eds) *A Handbook of Wisdom: Psychological Perspectives*. New York, NY: Cambridge University Press.

Bishop, S. R. (2002) 'What do we really know about mindfulness-based stress reduction?' *Psychosomatic Medicine*, 64(1), 71–84. Available at http://people.ucalgary.ca/~lcarlso/mindfulness/bishop%20review.pdf, accessed on 7 May 2014.

Bishop, S. R., Lau, M., Carlson, L., Anderson, N. D., et al. (2004) 'Mindfulness: A proposed operational definition.' *Clinical Psychology: Science and Practice*, 11(3), 230–241. doi: 10.1093/clipsy.bph077

Blackledge, J. T. (2007) 'Disrupting verbal processes: Cognitive defusion in acceptance and commitment therapy and other mindfulness-based psychotherapies.' *The Psychological Record*, 57(4), 555–576.

REFERENCES

Boddhi, B. (2000) *A Comprehensive Manual of Abhidhamma*. Seattle, WA: BPS Pariyatti.

Bond, J., Coleman, P., and Peace, S. (1993) *Ageing in Society: An Introduction to Social Gerontology*. London, UK: Sage.

Braud, W. (1998) 'Integral inquiry: Complementary ways of knowing, being, and expression.' In W. Braud and R. Anderson (eds) *Transpersonal Research Methods for the Social Sciences*. Thousand Oaks, CA: Sage.

Braud, W. and Anderson, R. (1998) *Transpersonal Research Methods for the Social Sciences*. Thousand Oaks, CA: Sage.

Brazier, C. (2003) *Buddhist Psychology: Liberate the Mind, Embrace Life*. London, UK: Constable and Robinson.

Breteler, M. M., van Swieten, J. C., Bots, M. L., Grobbee, D. E., et al. (1994) 'Cerebral white matter lesions, vascular risk factors, and cognitive function in a population-based study: The Rotterdam study.' *Neurology, 44*(7), 1246–1252.

Brewi, J. and Brennan, A. (1999) *Mid-life Spirituality and Jungian Archetypes*. York Beach, ME: Nicolas-Hays.

Bridges, L. J., Denham, S. A., and Ganiban, J. M. (2004) 'Definitional issues in emotion regulation research.' *Child Development, 75*(2), 340–345. doi: 10.1111/j.1467-8624.2004.00675.x

Brown, K. W. and Cordon, S. (2009) 'Towards a phenomenology of mindfulness: Subjective experience and emotional correlated.' In F. Didonna (ed.) *Clinical Handbook of Mindfulness*. New York, NY: Springer Science.

Brown, K. W. and Ryan, R. M. (2003) 'The benefits of being present: Mindfulness and its role in psychological well-being.' *Journal of Personality and Social Psychology, 84*, 822–848. doi: 10.1037/0022-3514.84.4.822

Brown, K. W., Ryan, R. M., and Creswell, J. D. (2007) 'Mindfulness: Theoretical foundations and evidence for its salutary effects.' *Psychological Inquiry, 18*(4), 211–237.

Bucknell, R. and Kang, C. (1997) *The Meditative Way*. Abingdon, UK: Routledge Press.

Butler, R. N. (1969) 'Age-ism: Another form of bigotry.' *The Gerontologist, 9*, 243–246. doi: 10.1093/geront/9.4_Part_1.243

Butler, R. N., Lewis, M. I., and Sunderland, T. (eds) (1991) *Aging and Mental Health: Positive Psychosocial and Biomedical Approaches*. Englewood Cliffs, NJ: Macmillan.

Byock, I. R. (1996) 'The nature of suffering and the nature of opportunity at the end of life.' *Clinics in the Geriatric Medicine, 12*(2), 237–254.

Cahn, B. R. and Polich, J. (2006) 'Meditation states and traits: EEG, ERP, and neuroimaging studies.' *Psychological Bulletin, 132*(2), 180–211. doi: 10.1037/0033-2909.132.2.180

Campos, J. J., Frankel, C. B., and Camras, L. (2004) 'On the nature of emotion regulation.' *Child Development, 75*(2), 377–394. doi: 10.1111/j.1467-8624.2004.00681.x

Canavarro, M. C., Vaz Serra, A., Simões, M. R., Rijo, D., et al. (2009) 'Development and psychometric properties of the World Health Organization Quality of Life Assessment Instrument (WHOQOL-100) in Portugal.' *International Journal of Behavioural Medicine, 16*, 116–124. doi: 10.1007/s12529-008-9024-2

Caplan, M., Hartelius, G., and Rardin, M. A. (2003) 'Contemporary viewpoints on transpersonal psychology.' *The Journal of Transpersonal Psychology, 35*(2), 143–162.

Carlson, L. E. and Brown, K. W. (2005) 'Validation of the Mindful Attention and Awareness Scale in a cancer population.' *Journal of Psychosomatic Research, 58*(1), 29–33. doi: 10.1016/j.jpsychores.2004.04.366

Carlson, L. E. and Garland, S. N. (2005) 'Impact of mindfulness-based stress reduction (MBSR) on sleep, mood, stress, and fatigue symptoms in cancer outpatients.' *International Journal of Behavioral Medicine, 12*(4), 278–285.

Carlson, L. E., Labelle, L. E., Garland, S. N., Hutchins, M. L., and Birnie, K. (2009) 'Mindfulness-based interventions in oncology.' In F. Didonna (ed.) *Clinical Handbook of Mindfulness*. New York, NY: Springer Science.

Carmody, J. and Baer, R. A. (2008) 'Relationships between mindfulness practice and levels of mindfulness, medical and psychological symptoms and well-being in a mindfulness-based stress reduction program.' *Journal of Behavioral Medicine, 31*, 23–33. doi: 10.1007/s10865-007-9130-7

Carmody, J., Baer, R. A., Lykins, E. L. B., and Olendzki, N. (2009) 'An empirical study of the mechanisms of mindfulness on a mindfulness-based stress reduction program.' *Journal of Clinical Psychology, 65*(6), 613–626. doi: 10.1002/jclp.20579

Carmody, J., Crawford, S., and Churchill, L. (2006) 'A pilot study of mindfulness-based stress reduction for hot flashes.' *Menopause, 13*, 760–769. doi: 10.1097/01.gme.0000227402.98933.d0

Carmody, J., Reed, G., Kristeller, J., and Merriam, P. (2008) 'Mindfulness, spirituality, and health-related symptoms.' *Journal of Psychosomatic Research, 64*, 393–403. doi: 10.1016/j.jpsychores.2007.06.015

Cavaco, S., Pinto, C., Gonçalves, A., Pereira, A., and Malaquias, C. (2008) 'Trail Making Test: Dados normativos dos 21 aos 65 anos.' [Trail Making Test: Normative data for individuals with 21 to 65 years of age]. *Psychologica, 49*, 222–238.

Chambers, R., Gullone, E., and Allen, N. B. (2009) 'Mindful emotion regulation: An integrative view.' *Clinical Psychology Review, 29*, 560–572. doi: 10.1016/j.cpr.2009.06.005

Chambers, R. H., Lo, B. C. Y., and Allen, N. A. (2008) 'The impact of intensive mindfulness training on attentional control, cognitive style, and affect.' *Cognitive Therapy and Research, 32*, 303–322. doi: 10.1007/s10608-007-9119-0

Chew-Graham, C. A., Baldwin, R., and Burns, A. (2008) *Integrated Management of Depression in the Elderly.* Cambridge, UK: Cambridge University Press.

Chodzko-Zajko, W., Proctor, D., Fiatarone Singh, M., Minson, *et al.* (2009) American College of Sports Medicine. Position Stand. Exercise and Physical Activity for Older Adults. *Medicine and Science in Sports and Exercise 41*, 1510–1530.

Cohen, S., Kamarck, T., and Mermelstein, R. (1983) 'A global measure of perceived stress.' *Journal of Health and Social Behavior, 24*, 385–396.

Colaizzi, P. (1978) 'Psychological research as the phenomenologist views it.' In R. Valle and M. King (eds) *Existential-phenomenological Alternatives for Psychology.* New York, NY: Oxford Press.

Coleman, P. (1993) 'Psychological Ageing.' In J. Bond, P. Coleman, and S. Peace (eds) *Ageing in Society: An Introduction to Social Gerontology.* London, UK: Sage.

Corless, I. B., Germino, B. B., and Pittman, M. (1994) *Dying, Death, and Bereavement: Theoretical Perspectives and Other Ways of Knowing.* Boston, MA: Jones and Barlett.

Craik, F. I. M. (1999) 'Memory, and Aging.' In D. Park and N. Schwartz (eds) *Cognitive Aging: A Primer.* New York, NY: Psychology Press.

Creswell, J. W. (2007) *Qualitative Inquiry and Research Design: Choosing Among Five Approaches.* Thousand Oaks, CA: Sage.

Creswell, J. W. (2009) *Research Design: Qualitative, Quantitative, and Mixed Methods Approaches.* Thousand Oaks, CA: Sage.

Creswell, J. W. (2011) *Designing and Conducting Mixed Methods Research.* London, UK: Sage.

Cumming, E. and Henry, W. H. (1961) *Growing Old: The Process of Disengagement.* New York, NY: Basic Books.

Darowski, E. S., Helder, E., Zacks, R. T., Hambrick, D. Z., and Hasher, L. (2008) 'Age related differences in cognition: The role of distraction control.' *Neuropsychology, 22*(5), 638–644. doi: 10.1037/0894-4105.22.5.638

Davidson, R. J., Kabat-Zinn, J., Schumacher, J., Rosenkranz, M., *et al.* (2003) 'Alterations in brain and immune function produced by mindfulness meditation.' *Psychosomatic Medicine, 65*(4), 564–570. doi: 10.1097/01.PSY.0000077505.67574.E3

Davis, M. C., Zautra, A. J., Johnson, L. A., Murray, K. E., and Okvat, A. (2007) 'Psychosocial stress, emotional regulation, and resilience.' In C. M. Aldwin, C. L. Park, and A. Spiro, III (eds) *Handbook of Health Psychology and Aging*. New York, NY: Guilford Press.

De Groot, J. C., de Leeuw, F. E., Oudkerk, M., van Gijn, J., Hoifman, A., Jolles, J., and Breteler, M. M. (2000) 'Cerebral white matter lesions and cognitive function: The Rotterdam study.' *Annals of Neurology*, 47, 145–151.

Deberry, S., Davis, S., and Reinhard, K. E. (1989) 'A comparison of meditation-relaxation and cognitive/behavioral techniques for reducing anxiety and depression in a geriatric population.' *Journal of Geriatric Psychiatry*, 22, 231–247.

Depaola, S. J., Griffin, M., Young, J. R., and Neimeyer, R. A. (2003) 'Death anxiety and attitudes toward the elderly among older adults: The role of gender and ethnicity.' *Death Studies*, 27, 335–354. doi: 10.1080/07481180390199091

de Vibe, M. and Torbjorn, M. (2006) 'Training in mindfulness for patients with stress and chronic illness.' *Tidsskrift for den Norske lægeforening: tidsskrift for praktisk medicin, ny række*, 126(15),1898–1902.

Didonna, F. (2009) *Clinical Handbook of Mindfulness*. New York, NY: Springer Science.

Diener, E., Emmons, R., Larsen, R., and Griffin, S. (1985) 'The Satisfaction With Life Scale.' *Journal of Personality Assessment*, 49, 71–75.

Douglass, B. G. and Moustakas, C. (1985) 'Heuristic inquiry: The internal search to know.' *Journal of Human Psychology*, 25(3), 39–55. doi: 10.1177/0022167885253004

Ekman, P. (2008) *Emotional Awareness: Overcoming the Obstacles to Psychological Balance and Compassion*. New York, NY: Henry Holt.

Ekman, P., Davidson, R. J., Ricard, M., and Wallace, B. A. (2005) 'Buddhist and psychological perspectives on emotions and well-being.' *Current Directions in Psychological Science*, 14(2), 59–63. doi: 10.1111/j.0963-7214.2005.00335.x

Epstein, M. (1995) *Thoughts Without a Thinker: Psychotherapy from a Buddhist Perspective*. New York, NY: HarperCollins.

Eriksen, H. R., Ihlebaek, C., and Ursin, H. (1999) 'A scoring system for subjective health complaints (SHC)' *Scandinavian Journal of Public Health*, 27, 63–72. doi: 10.1177/14034948990270010401

Erikson, E. (1980) *Identity and the Life Cycle*. New York, NY: W.W. Norton.

Erikson, J. M. (1997) 'Gerotranscendence.' In E. H. Erickson (ed.) *The Life Cycle Completed*. New York, NY: W.W. Norton.

Ernst, S., Welke, J., Heintze, C., Gabriel, R., *et al.* (2008) 'Effects of mindfulness-based stress reduction on quality of life in nursing home residents: A feasibility study.' *Forschende Komplementärmedizin*, 15, 74–81. doi: 10.1159/ 000121479

Eyetsemitan, F. E. (2007) 'Perceptions of aging in different cultures.' In M. Robinson, W. Novelli, C. Pearson, and L. Norris (eds) *Global Health and Global Aging*. San Francisco, CA: Jossey-Bass.

Eysenck, M. W. and Keane, M. T. (1995) *Cognitive Psychology: A Student's Handbook*. East Sussex, UK: Psychology Press.

Fenner, P. (1987) 'Cognitive theories of the emotion in Buddhism and Western Psychology.' *Psychologia*, 30, 217–227.

Fernàndez-Ballesteros, R. (2006) 'Geropsychology: An applied field for the 21st Century.' *European Psychologist*, 11(4), 312–323. doi: 10.1027/1016-9040.11.4.312

Field, M. J. and Cassel, C. K. (1997) *Approaching death: Improving care at the end of life*. Washington, DC: National Academy Press. Available at www.nap.edu/openbook.php?record_id=5801&page=R3, accessed on 7 May 2014.

Finch, J. F., Okun, M. A., Barrera M. Jr., Zautra, A. J., and Reich, J. W. (1989) 'Positive and negative social ties among older adults: Measurement models and the predictions of psychological distress and well-being.' *American Journal of Community Psychology*, 15(5), 585–605.

Follette, V. M. and Vijay, A. (2009) 'Mindfulness for trauma and posttraumatic stress.' In F. Didonna (ed.) *Clinical Handbook of Mindfulness*. New York, NY: Springer Science.

Fontinha, J. M. G. M. (2009) *"Faz a ti mesmo aquilo que farias aos outros": Estilo de vinculação como determinante da compaixão e auto-compaixão*. ["Do to yourself what you would do to others": Attachment style as a determinant of compassion and self-compassion]. Unpublished Doctoral Dissertation. University of Lisbon, Lisbon, Portugal.

Fortner, B. V. and Neimeyer, R. A. (1999) 'Death anxiety in older adults: A quantitative review.' *Death Studies, 23,* 387–407.

Fortner, B. V., Neimeyer, R. A., and Rybarczyk, B. (2000) 'Correlates of death anxiety in older adults: A comprehensive overview.' In A. Tomer (ed.) *Death Attitudes and the Older Adults: Theories, Concepts, and Applications*. Philadelphia, PA: Brunner-Routledge.

Fowler, J. W. (1981) *Stages of Faith: The Psychology of Human Development and the Quest for Meaning*. San Francisco, CA: Harper.

Fowler, J. W. (1986) 'Dialogue towards a future.' In C. Dykstra and S. Parks (eds) *Faith Development and Fowler*. Birmingham, AL: Religious Education Press.

Frankl, V. (2004a) *The Doctor and the Soul*. London, UK: Souvenir Press.

Frankl, V. (2004b) *Man's Search for Meaning*. London, UK: Rider.

Freitas, S., Simões, M. R., and Santana, I. (2008a, June). Montreal Cognitive Assessment (MoCA): Validation studies in a sample of normal population. (Montreal Cognitive Assessment (MoCA): Estudos de validação numa amostra da população normal.) Work presented at the 22nd Group Meeting for Studies of the Cerebral Aging and Dementia. Luso, Portugal.

Freitas, S., Simões, M. R., and Santana, I. (2008b, June). Montreal Cognitive Assessment (MoCA): Validation study in a sample of normal population. (Montreal Cognitive Assessment (MoCA): Estudo de validação numa amostra da população normal.) Work presented at XIII Multidisciplinaty Congress – Psychology and Education. Coimbra, Portugal.

Freitas, S., Simões, M. R., Martins, C., Vilar, M., and Santana, I. (2010). Adaptation studies for the Montreal Cognitive Assessment (MOCA) to the Portuguese population (Estudos de adaptação do Montreal Cognitive Assessment (MOCA) para a população Portuguesa) *Avaliação Psicológica 9*(3), 345–357.

Fresco, D. M., Moore, M. T., van Dulmen, M., Segal, Z. V., et al. (2007) 'Initial psychometric properties of the Experiences Questionnaire: Validation of a self-report measure of decentering.' *Behavior Therapy, 38,* 234–246.

Galinha, I. C. and Pais Ribeiro, J. L. (2005) 'Contribuição para o estudo da versão portuguesa da Positive and Negative Affect Schedule (PANAS): II—Estudo psicométrico.' [Contribution to the study of the Portuguese version of the Positive and Negaitve Affect Schedule (PANAS): II—Psychometric study]. *Análise Psicológica, 2*(23), 219–227.

Garland, E. and Gaylord, S. (2009) 'Envisioning a future contemplative science of methods and new content for the next wave of research.' *Complementary Health Practice Review, 14*(1), 3–9. doi: 10.1177/1533210109333718

George, L. K., Ellison, C. G., and Larson, D. B. (2002) 'Explaining the relationships between religious involvement and health.' *Psychological Inquiry, 13*(3), 190–200. doi: 10.1207/S15327965PLI1303_04

Gesser, G., Wong, P. T. P., and Reker, G. T. (1987) 'Death attitudes across the life-span: The development and validation of the death attitude profile.' *Omega, 2,* 113–128.

Giles, H., Noels, K. A., Williams, A., Ota, H., Lim, T., Ng, S. H., Ryan, E. B., and Somera, L. (2003) 'Intergenerational communication across cultures: Young people's perceptions of conversations with family elders, non-family elders, and same-age peers.' *Journal of Cross-Cultural Gerontology, 18,* 1–31.

Goleman, D. J. (1988) *The Meditative Mind: The Varieties of Meditative Experience*. New York, NY: G. P. Putman's Sons.

Goleman, D. J. (2003) *Destructive Emotions*. New York, NY: Bantam Books.

Golub, S. A. and Langer, E. J. (2007) 'Challenging assumptions about adult development: Implications for the health of older adults.' In C. M. Aldwin, C. L. Park, and A. Spiro, III (eds) *Handbook of Health Psychology and Aging*. New York, NY: Guilford Press.

Gomez, R. and Fisher, J. W. (2003) 'Domains of spiritual well-being and development and validation of the Spiritual Well-Being Questionnaire.' *Personality and Individual Differences*, 35, 1975–1991. doi: 10.1016/S0191-8869(03)00045-X

Gouveia, M. J., Marques, M., and Pais Ribeiro, J. L. (2009) 'Versão Portuguesa do Questionário de Bem-Estar Espiritual (SWBQ): Análise confirmatória da sua estrutura factorial.' [Portuguese version of the Spiritual Well-Being Questionnaire: Confirmatory analysis of its factorial structure]. *Psicologia, Saúde, and Doenças, 10*(2), 285–293. Available at www.scielo.oces.mctes.pt/scielo.php?pid=S1645-00862009000200012&script=sci_arttext, accessed on 7 May 2014.

Greenland, S. K. (2010) *The Mindful Child*. New York, NY: Free Press.

Gregório, S. and Pinto-Gouveia, J. (2011) *Mindful Attention and Awareness: Relationships with Psychopathology and Emotion Regulation*. Manuscript submitted for publication.

Gregório, S. and Pinto-Gouveira, J. (2013). Mindful attention and awareness: relationships with psychopathology and emotion regulation. *Spanish Journal of Psychology 16*(79), 1–10. doi: 10.1017/sjp.2013.79.

Grossman, P., Niemann, L., Schmidt, S., and Walach, H. (2004) 'Mindfulness-based stress reduction and health benefits: A meta-analysis.' *Journal of Psychosomatic Research*, 57, 35–43. doi: 10.1016/S0022-3999(03)00573-7

Gruenewald, T. L. and Kemeny, M. E. (2007) 'Psychoneuroimmunological processes in aging and health.' In C. M. Aldwin, C. L. Park, and A. Spiro, III (eds) *Handbook of Health Psychology and Aging*. New York, NY: Guilford Press.

Hansson, R. and Stroebe, M. S. (2007) *Bereavement in Late Life: Coping, Adaptation, and Developmental Influences*. Washington, DC: American Psychological Association.

Harris, M. (1976) 'History and significance of the emic/etic distinction.' *Annual Review of Anthropology*, 5, 329–350.

Hart, W. (1997) *The Art of Living: Vipassana Meditation as Taught by S. N. Goenka*. Maharashtra, India: Vipassana Research Institute.

Harvey, I. S. (2005) *The Role of Spirituality in the Self-management of Chronic Illness Among Older Adults*. Unpublished Doctoral Dissertation, University of Pittsburgh, Kansas.

Hayes, S. C. (2003) 'Mindfulness: Method and process.' *Clinical Psychology: Science and Practice*, 10(2), 161–165. doi: 10.1093/clipsy.bpg018

Hayes, S. C. and Feldman, G. (2004) 'Clarifying the construct of mindfulness in the context of emotion regulation and the process of change in therapy.' *Clinical Psychology: Science and Practice*, 11(3), 255–262. doi: 10.1093/clipsy.bph080

Hayes, S. C., Strosahl, K., and Wilson, K. G. (1999) *Acceptance Commitment Therapy: An Experiential Approach to Behavior Change*. New York, NY: Guilford Press.

Hill, P. C. and Pargament, K. I. (2008) 'Advances in the conceptualization and measurement of religion and spirituality: Implications for physical and mental health research.' *Psychology of Religion and Spirituality*, 1, 3–17. doi: 10.1037/1941-1022.S.1.3

Hill, P. C., Pargament, K. I., Hood, R. W., McCullough, M. E., et al. (2000) 'Conceptualizing religion and spirituality: Points in commonality, points of departure.' *Journal for the Theory of Social Behaviour*. 30(1), 51–77. doi: 10.1111/ 1468-5914.00119

Ho, D.Y. (1994) 'Filial Piety, authoritarian moralism, and cognitive conservatism in Chinese societies.' *Genetic, Social, and General Psychology Monographs, 120*, 347–365.

Hoppes, K. (2006) 'The application of mindfulness-based cognitive intervention in the treatment of co-occuring addictive and mood disorders.' *CNS Spectrum*, 11, 829–851.

Huppert, F. A., Baylis, N., Kenerne, B. (2005) *The Science of Well-being*. New York, NY: Oxford University Press.

Imara, M. (1975) 'Dying as the last stage of growth.' In E. Kübler-Ross (ed.) *Death: The Final Stage of Growth*. New York, NY: Touchstone.

Jacobs, B. and Nagel, L. (2003) 'The impact of a brief mindfulness-based stress reduction program on perceived quality of life.' *International Journal of Self-Help and Self-Care, 2*(2), 155–168.

Jager, C. A., Budge, M. M., and Clark, R. (2003) 'Utility of TICS-M for assessment of cognitive function in older adults.' *International Journal of Geriatric Psychiatry, 18*(4), 318–324.

Jewell, A. (2004) *Aging, Spirituality, and Well-being*. London, UK: Jessica Kingsley Publishers.

Jordan, T. (2002) *Self-awareness, meta-awareness, and Witness Self*. Available at www.perspectus.se/tjordan/selfawarenessUS.pdf, accessed on 29 January 2014.

Jung, C. G. (1939a) 'Conscious, Unconscious, and Individuation.' In A. Storr (ed.) *The Essential Jung*. London, UK: HarperCollins.

Jung, C. G. (1939b) 'Psychology and Religion.' In A. Storr (ed.) *The Essential Jung*. London, UK: HarperCollins.

Jung, C. G. (1971) 'The Stages of Life.' In J. Campbell (ed.) *The Portable Jung*. New York, NY: Penguin Books.

Jyoti, N. (2010) 'Mindfulness: A lived experience of existential-phenomenological themes.' *Existential Analysis, 20*(1), 147–162.

Kabat-Zinn, J. (1982) 'An out-patient program in behavioural medicine for chronic pain patients based on the practice of mindfulness meditation: Theoretical considerations and preliminary results.' *General Hospital Psychiatry, 4*, 33–47. doi: 10.1016/0163-8343(82)90026-3

Kabat-Zinn, J. (1990) *Full Catastrophe Living: Using the Wisdom of your Body and Mind to Face Stress, Pain, and Illness*. New York, NY: Delta Trade Paperbacks.

Kabat-Zinn, J. (1994) *Wherever You Go, There You Are: Mindfulness Meditation in Everyday Life*. New York, NY: Hyperion.

Kabat-Zinn, J. (2005) *Coming to our Senses*. New York, NY: Hyperion.

Kabat-Zinn, J., Lipworth, L., and Burney, R. (1985) 'The clinical use of mindfulness meditation for the self-regulation of chronic pain.' *Journal of Behavioral Medicine, 8*, 163–190. doi: 10.1007/BF00845519

Kabat-Zinn, J., Massion, A. O., Kristeller, J., Peterson, L. G. *et al.* (1992) 'Effectiveness of a meditation-based stress reduction program in the treatment of anxiety disorders.' *American Journal of Psychiatry, 149*, 936–943.

Kabat-Zinn, J., Wheeler, E., Light, T., Skillings, Z. *et al.* (1998) 'Influence of a mindfulness meditation-based stress reduction intervention on rates of skin clearing in patients with moderate to severe psoriasis undergoing phototherapy (UVB) and photochemotherapy (PUVA).' *Psychosomatic Medicine, 50*, 625–632.

Kaplan, K. H., Goldenberg, D. L., and Galvin-Nadeau, M. (1993) 'The impact of a meditation-based stress reduction program on fibromyalgia.' *General Hospital Psychiatry, 15*(5), 284–289. doi: 10.1016/0163-8343(93)90020-O

Kelleher, K. (1992) 'The afternoon of life: Jung's view of the tasks of the second half of life.' *Perspectives in Psychiatric Care, 28*(2), 25–28.

Keller, J. W., Sherry, D., and Piotrowski, C. (1984) 'Perspectives on death: A developmental study.' *The Journal of Psychology, 116*, 37–47.

Kempermann, G. (2006) 'Adult Neurogenesis.' In P. B. Baltes and P. A. F. Reuter-Lorenz (eds.) *Lifespan Development and the Brain: The Perspective of Biocultural Co-Constructivism*. New York, NY: Cambridge University Press.

Khong, B. S. L. (2009) 'Expanding the understanding of mindfulness: Seeing the tree and the forest.' *The Humanistic Psychologist, 37*, 117–136. doi: 10.1080/08873260902892006

King, U. (2004) 'The dance of life: Spirituality, ageing and human flourishing.' In A. Jewell (ed.) *Ageing, Spirituality and Well-being*. London, UK: Jessica Kingsley Publishers.

Koenig, H. G., McCullough, M. E., and Larson, D. B. (2001) *Handbook of Religion and Health*. New York, NY: Oxford University Press.

Kornfield, J. (2008) *The Wise Heart*. London, UK: Rider Books.

Krasner, M. (2004) 'Mindfulness-based interventions: A coming of age?' *Families, Systems, and Health, 22*, 207–212. doi: 10.1037/1091-7527.22.2.207

Krishnamurti, J. (1998) 'Listening to the silence.' In H. Palmer (ed.) *Inner Knowing: Consciousness, Creativity, Insight, and Intuition*. New York, NY: Jeremy P. Tarcher/Putnam.

Kristeller, J. L. and Hallett, C. B. (1999) 'An exploratory study of a meditation-based intervention for binge eating disorder.' *Journal of Health Psychology, 4*, 357–363. doi: 10.1177/135910539900400305

Kübler-Ross, E. (2009) *On Death and Dying: What the Dying Have to Teach Doctors, Nurses, Clergy and Their Own Families*. Abingdon, Oxon: Routledge.

Kumar, S. (2010) 'Ascending the spiral staircase of grief.' In M. Kerman (ed.) *Clinical Pearls of Wisdom*. New York, NY: W.W. Norton.

Laing, R. D. (1967) *Politics of Experience*. London, UK: Penguin.

Lajoie, D. H. and Shapiro, S. L. (1992) 'Definitions of transpersonal psychology: The first twenty-three years.' *The Journal of Transpersonal Psychology, 24*(1), 79–98.

Langer, E. J., Heffernan, D., and Kiester, M. (1988) *Reducing Burnout in an Institutional Setting: An Experimental Investigation*. Unpublished manuscript, Harvard University, Cambridge, MA.

Lantz, M. S., Buchalterm E. N., and McBee, L. (1997) 'The Wellness Group: A novel intervention for coping with disruptive behavior in elderly nursing home residents.' *The Gerontologist, 37*(4), 551–555. doi: 10.1093/geront/37.4.551

Lazar, S. W., Kerr, C. E., Wasserman, R. H., Gray, J. R., *et al.* (2005) 'Meditation experience is associated with increased cortical thickness.' *Neuroreport, 16*(17),1893–1897.

Leigh, J., Bowen, S., and Marlatt, G. A. (2005) 'Spirituality, mindfulness, and substance abuse.' *Addictive Behaviors, 30*, 1335–1341. doi: 10.1016/j.addbeh.2005.01.010

Levinson, D. J. (1978) *The Season of a Man's Life*. New York, NY: Alfred A. Knopf.

Levy, B. R. (2003) 'Mind matters: cognitive and physical effects of aging self-stereotypes.' *Journal of Gerontology, 58B*(4), 203–211.

Levy, B. R., Hausdorff, J., Hencke, R., and Wei, J. Y. (2000) 'Reducing cardiovascular stress with positive self-stereotype of aging.' *Journals of Gerontology: Psychological Sciences, 55*(4), 205–213. doi: 10.1093/geronb/55.4.P205

Levy, B. R. and Langer, E. (1994) 'Aging free from negative stereotypes: Successful memory in China and among the American deaf.' *Journal of Personality and Social Psychology, 66*, 989–997.

Levy, B. R., Slade, M. D., Kundel, S. R., and Kasl, S. V. (2002) 'Longevity increased by positive self-perceptions of aging.' *Journal of Personality and Social Psychology, 83*(2), 261–270. doi: 10.1037/0022-3514.83.2.261

Lher, U. (1991) 'Aging: A challenge for psychology, and psychologists.' Invitational lecture at the 1st European Congress of Psychology, Amsterdam, Netherlands.

Lichtenberg, P. A., Ross, T., Millis, S. R., and Manning, C. A. (1995) 'The relationship between depression and cognition in older adults: A cross-validation study.' *Journal of Gerontology B: Psychological Sciences, 50B*(1), 25–32. doi: 10.1093/geronb/50B.1.P25

Lief, J. L. (2001) *Making Friends with Death: A Buddhist Guide to Encountering Mortality*. Boston, Massachusetts: Shambala Publications.

Lindberg, D. A. (2005) 'Integrative review of research related to meditation, spirituality, and the elderly.' *Geriatric Nursing, 26*(6), 372–377.

Linehan, M. M. (1993) *Cognitive-behavioral Treatment of Borderline Personality Disorder*. New York, NY: Guilford.

Löckenhoff, C. E., Fruyt, F., Terracciano, A., McCrane, R. R., *et al.* (2009) 'Perceptions of aging across 26 cultures and their culture-level associates.' *Psychology and Aging, 24*(4), 941–954. doi: 10.1037/a0016901

Long, J. B. (1975) 'The Death that Ends Death in Hinduism and Buddhism.' In E. Kübler-Ross (ed.) *Death: The Final Stage of Growth*. New York, NY: Touchstone.

Lopez, O. L., Jaqust, W. J., Dulberg, C., Becker, J. T., et al. (2003) 'Risk factors for mild cognitive impairment in the Cardiovascular Health Study Cognition Study: Part 2.' *Archives of Neurology*, 60(10), 1394–1399.

Lutz, A., Dunne, J. D., and Davidson, R. (2007) 'Meditation and the Neuroscience of Consciousness: An Introduction.' In P. Zelazo, M. Moscovitch, and E. Thompson (eds) *Cambridge Handbook of Consciousness*. Available at http://brainimaging.waisman.wisc.edu/~lutz/Meditation_Neuroscience_2005_AL_JDD_RJD_2.pdf, accessed on 29 January 2014.

MacKenzie, M. J., Carlson, L. E., Munoz, M., and Speca, M. (2007) 'A qualitative study of self-perceived effects of mindfulness-based stress reduction (MBSR) in a psychosocial oncology setting.' *Stress and Health: Journal of the International Society for the Investigation of Stress*, 23(1), 59–69. doi: 10.1002/smi.1120

MacKinlay, E. (2001) *The Spiritual Dimension of Aging*. London, UK: Jessica Kingsley Publishers.

MacKinlay, E. (2004) 'The Spiritual Dimension of Aging.' In A. Jewell (ed.) *Aging, Spirituality and Well-being*. London, UK: Jessica Kingsley Publishers.

Madnawat, A. V. S. and Kachhawa, P. S. (2007) 'Age, gender, and living circumstances discriminating older adults on death anxiety.' *Death Studies*, 31, 763–769. doi: 10.1080/07481180701490743

Martins, C. (2008) *Compassion and its Application in Research*. Unpublished manuscript, Institute of Transpersonal Psychology, Palo Alto, CA.

Martins, C. (2012) 'Be.' Unpublished poem.

Masuda, A., Hayes, S. C., Sackett, C. F., and Twohig, M. P. (2004) 'Cognitive defusion and self-relevant negative thoughts: Examining the impact of a ninety-year-old technique.' *Behavior Research and Therapy*, 42(4), 477–485. doi: 10.1016/j.brat. 2003.10.008

McBee, L. (2008) *Mindfulness-based elder care: A CAM Model for Frail Elders and their Caregivers*. New York, NY: Springer.

McBee, L. (2009) 'Mindfulness-based Elder Care: Communicating mindfulness to frail elders and their caregivers.' In F. Didonna (ed.) *Clinical Handbook of Mindfulness*. New York, NY: Springer Science.

McBee, L., Westreich, L., and Likourezos, A. (2004) 'A psychoeducational relaxation group for pain and stress management in the nursing home.' *Journal of Social Work in Long-Term Care*, 3(1), 15–28. doi: 10.1300/J181v03n01_03

McCann, R. M., Cargile, A. C., Giles, H., and Bui, C. T. (2004) 'Communicative ambivalence towards elders: Data from North Vietnam, South Vietnam, and the U.S.A.' *Journal of Cross-Cultural Gerontology*, 19, 275–297.

McDowd, J. M. (1997) 'Inhibition in attention, and aging.' *Journal of Gerontology: Psychological Sciences*, 52B(6), 265–273. doi: 10.1093/geronb/52B.6.P265

McFadden, S. H. (1995) 'Religion, and well-being in aging persons in an aging society.' *Journal of Social Issues*, 51, 161–175. doi: 10.1111/j.1540-4560.1995.tb01329.x

McGlashan, A. (1988) *The Savage and Beautiful Country*. Einsiedeln, Switzerland: Daimon Verlag.

Mckenzie, C. S., Poulin, P. A., and Seidman-Carlson, R. (2006) 'A brief mindfulness-based stress reduction intervention for nurses and nurse aides.' *Applied Nursing Research*, 19, 105–109.

Mckenzie, E. R., Rajagopal, D. E., Meibohm, M., and Lavizzo-Mourey, R. (2000) 'Spiritual support and psychological well-being: Older adults' perceptions of the religion and health connection.' *Alternative Therapies in Health and Medicine*, 6(6), 37–45. doi: 10.1016/j.apnr.2005.08.002

McMordie, W. R. and Kumar, A. (1984) 'Cross-cultural research on the Templer/McMordie Death Anxiety Scale.' *Psychological Reports*, 54, 959–963. doi: 10.2466/pr0.1984.54.3.959

McNair, D. M., Loor, M., and Droppleman, L. F. (1971) *Manual for the Profile of Mood States*. San Diego, CA: Educational and Industrial Testing Service.

Meisenhelder, J. B. and Chandler, E. N. (2002) 'Spirituality and health outcomes in the elderly.' *Journal of Religion and Health, 41*(3), 243–252. doi: 10.1023/A: 1020236903663

Merleau-Ponty, M. (1962) *Phenomenology of Perception* (C. Smith, Trans.) London, UK: Routledge and Kegan Paul.

Mertens, D. M. (2005) *Research and Evaluation in Education and Psychology: Integrating Diversity with Quantitative, Qualitative, and Mixed Methods.* Thousand Oaks, CA: Sage.

Metzer, R. (1998) *The Unfolding Self.* Novato, CA: Origin Press.

Miller, J. J., Fletcher, K., and Kabat-Zinn, J. (1995) 'Three-year follow up and clinical implications of a mindfulness meditation-based stress reduction intervention in the treatment of anxiety disorders.' *General Hospital Psychiatry, 17,* 192–200. doi: 10.1016/0163-8343(95)00025-M

Mills, N. and Allen, J. (2000) 'Mindfulness of movement as a coping strategy in multiple sclerosis: A pilot study.' *General Hospital Psychiatry, 22,* 425–431. doi: 10.1016/S0163-8343(00)00100-6

Mind and Life Institute (undated) Information available at www.mindandlife.org, accessed 29 January 2014.

Missine, L. (2004) 'The Search for Meaning of Life in Old Age.' In A. Jewell (ed.) *Aging, Spirituality and Well-being.* London, UK: Jessica Kingsley Publishers.

Moberg, D. O. (2008) 'Spirituality and aging: Research and implications.' *Journal of Religion, Spirituality, and Aging, 20*(1–2), 95–133. doi: 10.1080/155280308019 22038

Moody, H. R. (2000) *Conscious Aging: A New Level of Growth in Later Life.* Available at www.hrmoddy.com/art4.html, accessed 29 January 2014.

Morone, N. E., Greco, C. M., and Weiner, D. K. (2008) 'Mindfulness meditation for the treatment of chronic low back pain in older adults: A randomized controlled pilot study.' *Pain, 134,* 310–319. doi: 10.1016/j.pain.2007.04.038

Morone, N. E., Lynch, C. S., Greco, C. M., Tindle, H. A., and Weiner, D. K. (2008) '"I feel like a new person." The effects of mindfulness meditation on older adults with chronic pain: A qualitative narrative analysis of diary entries.' *Journal of Pain, 9,* 841–848. doi: 10.1016/j.jpain.2008.04.003

Moscovici, S. (1988) 'Notes towards a description of social representations.' *Journal of European Social Psychology, 18,* 211–250. doi: 10.1002/ejsp.2420180303

Mota-Cardoso, R., Araújo, A., Ramos, R. C., Gonçalves, G., and Ramos, M. (2002) *O stress nos professores portugueses: Estudo IPSSO 2000.* [Stress in Portuguese teachers: Study IPSSO 2000]. Porto, Portugal: Porto Editora.

Moustakas, C. (1990) *Heuristic Research: Design, Methodology, and Applications.* Newbury Park, CA: Sage.

Moye, J. and Hanlon, S. (1996) 'Relaxation training for nursing home patients: Suggestions for simplifying and individualizing treatment.' *Clinical Gerontologist, 16*(3), 37–47. doi: 10.1300/J018v16n03_05

Mullin, G. (1998) *Living in the Face of Death.* Ithaca, NY: Snow Lion.

Murphy, R. (1995) 'The effects of mindfulness meditation vs progressive relaxation training on stress egocentrism anger and impulsiveness among inmates.' *Dissertation Abstracts International: Section B: The Sciences and Engineering, 55*(8), 3596–3604.

Nasreddine, A. S., Phillips, N. A., Bedirian, V., Charbonneau, S. C. *et al.* (2005) 'The Montreal Cognitive Assessment, MOCA: A brief screening tool for mild cognitive impairment.' *Brief Methodological Reports, 53,* 695–699.

Neale, N. I. (2006) *Mindfulness Meditation: An Integration of Perspectives from Buddhism, Science, and Clinical Psychology.* Unpublished Doctoral Dissertation, California Institute of Integral Studies, San Francisco, CA.

Neff, K. D. (2003) 'The development and validation of a scale to measure self-compassion.' *Self and Identity, 2,* 223–250. doi: 10.1080/15298860390209035

Neimeyer, R. A. (1997–1998) 'Death anxiety research: The state of the art.' *Omega, 36,* 97–120.

Newhill, C. E., Bell, M. M., Eack, S. M., and Mulvey, E. P. (2010) 'Confirmatory factor analysis of the emotion dysregulation measure.' *Journal of the Society for Social Work and Research*, *1*(3), 159–168. doi: 10.5243/jsswr.2010.12

Nyanaponika, T. (1992) *The Heart of Buddhist Meditation*. Kandy, Sri Lanka: Buddhist Publication Society.

Nyklicek, I. and Kuijpers, K. F. (2008) 'Effects of mindfulness-based stress reduction intervention on psychological well-being and quality of life: Is increased mindfulness indeed a mechanism?' *Annual of Behavioral Medicine*, *35*, 331–340. doi: 10.1007/s12160-008-9030-2

Oken, B. S., Zajdel, D., Kishimaya, S., Flegal, K., *et al*. (2006) 'Randomized, controlled, six-month trial of yoga in healthy seniors: Effects on cognition and quality of life.' *Alternative Therapy Health Medicine*, *12*(1), 40–47.

Olendzki, A. (2009) 'Mindfulness and Meditation.' In F. Didonna (ed.) *Clinical Handbook of Mindfulness*. New York, NY: Springer Science.

Orzech, K. M., Shapiro, S. L., Brown, K. and McKay, M. (2009) 'Intensive mindfulness training related changes in cognitive and emotional experience.' *The Journal of Positive Psychology: Dedicated to furthering research and promoting good practice*, *4*, 212–222. doi: 10.1080/17439760902819394

Ostir, G. V., Markides, K. S., Peek, M. K., and Goodwin, J. S. (2001) 'The association between emotional well-being and the incidence of stroke in older adults.' *Psychosomatic Medicine*, *63*(2), 210–215.

Pagnoni, G., and Cekic, M. (2007) 'Age effects on gray matter volume and attentional performance in zen meditation.' *Neurobiology and Aging*, *28*(10), 1623–1627. doi: 10.1016/j.neurobiolaging.2007.06.008

Pais Ribeiro, J. L. and Marques, T. (2009) 'A avaliação do stresse: a propósito de um estudo de adaptação da escala de percepção de stresse. [Evaluation of stress: A study for the adaptation of the Perception of Stress Scale].' *Psicologia, Saúde, and Doença*, *10*(2), 237–248.

Palladino, P. and DeBeni, R. (1999) 'Working memory in aging maintenance, and suppression.' *Aging Clinical and Experimental Research*, *11*(5), 301–306.

Patton, J. F. (2006) 'Jungian spirituality: A developmental context for late-life growth.' *American Journal of Hospice and Palliative Medicine*, *23*, 304–308. doi: 10.1177/1049909106289087

Pavot, W. and Diener, E. (1993) 'Review of the Satisfaction With Life Scale.' *Psychological Assessment*, *5*(2), 164–172. doi: 10.1037/1040-3590.5.2.164

Plante, T. G. and Sherman, A. C. (2001) *Faith and Health: Psychological Perspectives*. New York, NY: Guilford Press.

Polanyi, M. (1983) *The Tacit Dimension*. Gloucester, MA.: Peter Smith.

Powell, L. H., Shahabi, L., and Thoresen, C. E. (2003) 'Religion and spirituality: Linkages to physical health.' *American Psychologist*, *58*, 36–52. doi: 10.1037/0003-066X.58.1.36

Pressman, S. D. and Cohen, S. (2005) 'Does positive affect influence health?' *Psychological Bulletin*, *131*, 925–971. doi: 10.1037/0033-2909.131.6.925

Prewitt, S. H. (2000) *The Experiences of Older Women with Fibromyalgia in a Mindfulness-Based Stress Reduction and Relaxation Program: A Qualitative Study*. Unpublished Doctoral Dissertation, University of Kentucky, Lexington.

Rabbitt, P., Ibrahim, S., Lunn, M., Scott, M., *et al*. (2008) 'Age-associated losses of brain volume predict longitudinal cognitive declines over 8 to 20 years.' *Neuropsychology*, *22*(1), 3–9. doi: 10.1037/0894-4105.22.1.3

Radhakrishnan, S. and Moore, C. A. (1957) *A Sourcebook in Indian philosophy*. Princeton, NJ: Princeton University Press.

Ram Dass (2000) *Still Here: Embracing Aging, Changing, and Dying*. New York, NY: Riverhead Books.

REFERENCES

Ramel, W., Goldin, P. R., Carmona, P. E., and McQuaid, R. (2004) 'The effects of mindfulness meditation on cognitive processes and affect in patients with past depression.' *Cognitive Therapy and Research*, 28, 433–455. doi: 10.1023/B:COTR.0000045557.15923.96

Reed, P. G. (1987) 'Spirituality and well-being in terminally ill hospitalized adults.' *Research in Nursing and Health*, 10, 335–344. doi: 10.1002/nur.4770100507

Reed, P. G. (1991) 'Towards a nursing theory of self-transcendence.' *Advances in Nursing Research*, 13(4), 64–77.

Rizvi, S. L., Welch, S. S., and Dimidjian, S. (2009) 'Mindfulness and Borderline Personality Disorder'. In F. Didonna (ed.) *Clinical Handbook of Mindfulness*. New York, NY: Springer Science.

Robba, S. (2006) *Conscious Aging: A Personal Experience*. Unpublished Master's Dissertation, Institute of Transpersonal Psychology, Palo Alto, CA.

Rook, K. S., Mavandali, S., Sorkin, D. H., and Zetel, L. A. (2007) 'Optimizing Social Relationships as a Resource for Health and Well-being in Later Life.' In C. M. Aldwin, C. L. Park, and A. Spiro, III (eds) *Handbook of Health Psychology and Aging*. New York, NY: Guilford Press.

Rosenzweig, S., Reibel, D. K., Greeson, J. M., Brainard, G. C., and Hojat, M. (2003) 'Mindfulness-based stress reduction lowers psychological distress in medical students.' *Teaching and Learning in Medicine*, 15(2), 88–92.

Rowe, J. W. and Kahn, R. L. (1997) 'Successful aging.' *The Gerontologist*, 37(4), 433–440. doi: 10.1093/geront/37.4.433

Rusting, R. L. (1992) 'Why do we age?' *Scientific American*, 12, 86–95.

Ruumet, H. (1997) 'Pathways of the soul: A helical model pf psychospiritual development.' *Presence: The Journal of Spiritual Directors International*, 3(3), 6–24.

Ryan, R. M. and Deci, E. L. (2001) 'On happiness and human potentials: A review of research on hedonic and eudaimonic well-being.' *Annual Review of Psychology*, 52, 141–166.

Ryff, C. (1989) 'Happiness is everything, or is it? Explorations on the meaning of psychological well-being.' *Journal of Personality and Social Psychology*, 57, 1069–1081. doi: 10.1037/0022-3514.57.6.1069

Ryff, C. D. and Keynes, C. L. M. (1995) 'The structure of psychological well-being revisited.' *Journal of Personality and Social Psychology*, 69, 719–727. doi: 10.1037/0022-3514.69.4.719

Schachter-Shalomi, Z. (1995) *From Age-ing to Sage-ing: A Profound New Vision of Growing Older*. New York, NY: Grand Central.

Schaefer, C. (2006) *Grandmothers Counsel the World*. Boston, MA: Trumpeter Books.

Schumaker, J. F., Warren, W. G., and Groth-Marnat, G. (1991) 'Death anxiety in Japan and Australia.' *The Journal of Social Psychology*, 131, 511–518.

Seeman, T. E. (2000) 'Health promoting effects of friends and family on health outcomes in older adults.' *American Journal of Health Promotion*, 14(6), 362–370.

Segal, Z. V., Williams, J. M. G., and Teasdale, J. D. (2002) *Mindfulness-based Cognitive Therapy for Depression: A New Approach to Preventing Relapse*. New York, NY: Guilford.

Selby, J. (2003) *Seven Masters, One Path*. New York, NY: Harper Collins

Shacham, S. (1983) 'A shortened version of the Profile of Mood States.' *Journal of Personality Assessment*, 47(3), 305–306. doi: 10.1207/s15327752jpa4703_14

Shah, C. S. (2000) *Neurophysiology of Meditation*. Available at www.boloji.com/index.cfm?md=Content&sd=Articles&ArticleID=1267, accessed on 7 May 2014.

Shapiro, D. H. and Shwartz, G. E. (1999) 'Intentional systemic mindfulness: An integrative model for self-regulation and health.' *Advances in Mind–Body Medicine*, 15, 128–134.

Shapiro, L. S., Astin, J. A., Bishop, S. R., and Cordova, M. (2005) 'Mindfulness-based stress reduction for health care professionals: Results from a randomized trial.' *International Journal of Stress Management*, 12(2), 164–176. doi: 10.1037/1072-5245.12.2.164

Shapiro, S. and Carlson. L. E. (2009) *The Art and Science of Mindfulness: Integrating Mindfulness into Psychology and the Helping Professions.* Washington, DC: American Psychological Association.

Shapiro, S., Carlson, L. E., Astin, J. A., and Freedman, B. (2006) 'Mechanisms of mindfulness.' *Journal of Clinical Psychology, 62*(3), 373–386. doi: 10.1002/jclp.20237

Shapiro, S. L., Brown, K. W., Biegel, G. M. (2007) 'Teaching self-care to caregivers: Effects of mindfulness-based stress reduction on the mental health of therapists in training.' *Training and Education in Professional Psychology, 1*(2), 105–115. doi: 10.1037/1931-3918.1.2.105

Shapiro, S. L., Schwartz, G. E., and Bonner, G. (1998) 'Effects of mindfulness-based stress reduction on medical and premedical students.' *Journal of Behavioral Medicine, 21*, 581–599. doi: 10.1023/A:1018700829825

Shauna, S. and Carlson, L. E. (2009) *The Art and Science of Mindfulness: Integrating Mindfulness into Psychology and the Helping Professions.* Washington, DC: American Psychological Association.

Shirazi, B. (1994) *Integrative Methods: The Spectrum Approach.* Unpublished manuscript.

Siegel, D. J. (2007) *The Mindful Brain.* New York, NY: W.W. Norton.

Silva, M. E. D. (2004) 'Bem estar psicológico: Versão experimental.' [Psychological well-being: Experimental version]. Unpublished manuscript.

Simões, A. (1992) 'Ulterior validação de uma escala de satisfação com a vida (SWLS)' [Validation of the Satisfaction With Life Scale]. *Revista Portuguesa de Pedagógia, 26*(3), 503–515.

Simões, M. R., Firmino, H., Vilar, M., and Martins, M. (2007) *Montreal Cognitive Assessment (MOCA): Experimental version.* Available at www.mocatest.org, accessed on 29 January 2014.

Simões, M. R., Freitas, S., Santana, I., Firmino, H., Martins, C., Nasreddine, Z., & Vilar, M. (2008). Montreal Cognitive Assessment (MoCA): Final Portuguese version. Montreal Cognitive Assessment (MoCA): Versão final portuguesa. Serviço de Avaliação Psicológica, Faculdade de Psicologia e de Ciências da Educação da Universidade de Coimbra. Coimbra, Portugal.

Singh, K. D. (1998) *The Grace in Dying: A Message of Hope, Comfort, and Spiritual Transformation.* New York, NY: HarperCollins.

Skevington, S. M., Lotfy, M., and O'Connell, K. A. (2004) 'The World Health Organization's WHOQOL-BREF quality of life assessment: Psychometric properties and results of the international field trial a report from the WHOQOL group.' *Quality of Life Research, 13*, 299–310. doi: 10.1023/B:QURE.0000018486.91360.00

Smith, A. (2004) 'Clinical uses of mindfulness training for older people.' *Behavioral and Cognitive Psychotherapy, 32*, 423–430. doi: 10.1017/S1352465804001602

Smith, A. (2006) '"Like waking up from a dream": Mindfulness Training for Older People with Anxiety and Depression.' In R. A. Baer (ed.) *Mindfulness-based Treatment Approaches: Clinician's Guide to Evidence Base and Applications.* San Diego, CA: Elsevier Academic Press.

Smith, H. and Novak, P. (2003) *Buddhism: A Concise Introduction.* New York, NY: HarperCollins.

Sogyal Rinpoche (1993) *The Tibetan Book of Living and Dying.* San Francisco: HarperCollins.

Speca, M., Carlson, L. E., Goodey, E., and Angen, M. (2000) 'A randomized, wait-list controlled clinical trial: The effect of a mindfulness meditation-based stress reduction program on mood and symptoms of stress in cancer outpatients.' *Psychosomatic Medicine, 62*, 613–622.

Spilka, B., Stout, L., Minton, B., and Sizemore, D. (1977) 'Death and personal faith: A psychometric investigation.' *Journal for the Scientific Study of Religion, 16*(2), 169–178.

Steele, C. M. (1997) 'A threat in the air: How stereotypes share the intellectual identities performance of women and African-Americans.' *American Psychologist, 52*, 613–629.

Strada, E. (2004) *The Nature and Application of Spiritual Care for the Dying: Perspectives from Mahayana Buddhism and the Western Hospice Tradition.* Unpublished Doctoral Dissertation, California Institute of Integral Studies, San Francisco, CA.

Strauss, E., Sherman, E. M. S. and Spreen, O. (2006) *A Compendium of Neuropsychological Tests: Administration, Norms, and Commentary*. New York, NY: Oxford University Press.

Sung, K. (2001) 'Elder respect: Exploration of ideals and forms in East Asia.' *Journal of Aging Studies*, 15, 13–26. doi: 10.1016/S0890-4065(00)00014-1

Teasdale, J. D., Moore, R. G., Hayhurst, H., Pope, M., Williams, S., and Segal, Z. V. (2002) 'Metacognitive awareness and prevention relapse in depression: Empirical evidence.' *Journal of Consulting and Clinical Psychology*, 70(2), 275–287. doi: 10.1037//0022-006X.70.2.275

Thera, N. (1965) *The Heart of Buddhist Meditation*. San Francisco, CA: Red Wheel/Weiser.

Thygesen, E., Lindstrom, T. C., Saevareid, H. I., and Engedal, K. (2009) 'The subjective health complaints inventory: A useful instrument to identify various aspects of health and ability to cope in older people?' *Scandinavian Journal of Public Health*, 37, 690–696. doi: 10.1177/1403494809344104

Tombaugh, T. N. (2004) '"Trail making test A and B: Normative data stratified by age and education.' *Archives in Clinical Neuropsychology*, 19, 203–214. doi: 10.1016/S0887-6177(03)00039-8

Toms, J. and Toms, M. (1998) *True Work: The Sacred Dimension of Earning a Living*. Princeton, NJ: Princeton University Press.

Tornstam, L. (1997) 'Gerotranscendence: The contemplative dimension of aging.' *Journal of Aging Studies*, 11(2), 143–154. doi: 10.1016/S0890-4065(97) 90018-9

Tornstam, L. (2005) *Gerotranscendence: A Developmental Theory of Positive Aging*. New York, NY: Springer.

Treadway, M. T. and Lazar, S. W. (2009) 'The Neurobiology of Mindfulness.' In F. Didonna (ed.) *Clinical Handbook of Mindfulness*. New York, NY: Springer Science.

Turner, K. (2010) *The Promotion of Successful Aging through Mindfulness Skills Training*. Unpublished Doctoral Dissertation, University of Pennsylvania, Philadelphia.

U.S. Centers for Disease Control and Prevention (2003) *Public Health and Aging: Trends in Aging—United States and Worldwide*. Available at www.cdc.gov/mmwr/preview/mmwrhtml/mm5206a2.htm, accessed on 29 Janaury 2014.

Varela, F. J. (1997) *Sleeping, Dreaming, and Dying*. Boston: Wisdom.

Varela, F. J. and Depraz, N. (2003) 'Imagining: Embodiment, Phenomenology, and Transformation.' In B. A. Wallace (ed.) *Buddhism and Science: Breaking (New Ground*. New York, NY: Columbia University Press.

Vaughan, F. (1977) 'Transpersonal perspectives in psychotherapy.' *Journal of Humanistic Psychology*, 17(2), 69–81. doi: 10.1177/002216787701700208

Vaughan, F. (1998) 'Mental, Emotional, and Body-based Intuition.' In H. Palmer (ed.) *Inner knowing: Consciousness, Creativity, Insight, and Intuition*. New York, NY: Jeremy P. Tarcher/Putnam.

Vaz Serra, A., Canavarro, M. C., Simões, M., Pereira, M., et al. (2006) 'Estudos psicométricos do instrumento de avaliação da qualidade de vida da Organização Mundial de Saúde (WHOQOL-BREF) para Português de Portugal.' [Psychometric studies of an instrument to evaluate the quality of life from the World Health Organization (WHOQOL-BREF) to Portuguese from Portugal]. *Psiquiatria Clínica*, 27(1), 41–49.

Verbraak, A. (2000) *Gerotranscendence: An Examination of a Proposed Extension to Erik Erikson's Theory of Identity Development*. Unpublished Doctoral Dissertation, University of Kent, Canterbury, UK.

Viana, M. F., De Almeida, P. L., and Santos, R. C. (2001) 'Adaptação Portuguesa da versão reduzida do Perfil de Estados de Humor—POMS.' [Adaptation of the Portuguese version of the Short Version of Profile of Mood States]. *Análise Psicológica*, 1(19), 77–92.

Wagner, K. D. and Lorion, R. P. (1984) 'Correlates of death anxiety in elderly persons.' *Journal of Clinical Psychology*, 4(5), 1235–1241.

Walsh, R. and Vaughan, F. (1993) *Paths Beyond Ego*. New York, NY: Jeremy P. Tarcher/Putnam.

Washburn, M. (1988) *The Ego and the Dynamic Ground*. Albany: State University of New York Press.

Watson, D., Clark, L., and Tellegen, A. (1988) 'Development and validation of brief measures of positive and negative affect: The PANAS scales.' *Journal of Personality and Social Psychology, 54*, 1063–1070.

Welch, D. and Salva, V. (2006) *Peaceful Warrior*. E.U.A.: Sobini Films.

Welwood, J. (1985) *Awakening the Heart: East/West Approaches to Psychotherapy and the Healing Relationship*. Boston: Shambala.

WHOQOL Group (1998) 'The World Health Organization Quality of Life Assessment (WHOQOL): Development and general psychometric properties.' *Social Sciences and Medicine, 46*(12),1569–1585. doi: 10.1016/S0277-9536(98)00009-4

Wilber, K. (1980) *The Atman Project: A Transpersonal View of Human Development*.

Wink, P. and Dillon, M. (2008) 'Religiousness, spirituality, and psychosocial functioning in late adulthood: Findings from a longitudinal study.' *Psychology of Religion and Spirituality, 1*, 102–105.

Wink, P. and Scott, J. (2005) 'Does religiousness buffer against the fear of death and dying in late adulthood? Findings from a longitudinal study.' *The Journals of Gerontology, 60B*(4), 207–214. doi: 10.1093/geronb/60.4.P207

Wolever, R. Q. and Best, J. L. (2009) 'Mindfulness-based approaches to eating disorders.' In F. Didonna (ed.) *Clinical Handbook of Mindfulness*. New York, NY: Springer Science.

Woods, S. L. (2009) 'Training professionals in mindfulness: The heart of teaching.' In F. Didonna (ed.) *Clinical Handbook of Mindfulness*. New York, NY: Springer Science.

Wulff, D. M. (1996) 'Psychology of Religion: An Overview.' In E. P. Shafranske (ed.) *Religion and the Clinical Practice of Psychology*. Washington, DC: American Psychological Association.

Yaffe, K., Barnes, D., Nevitt, M., Lui, L., and Covinsky, K. (2001) 'A prospective study of physical activity and cognitive decline in elderly women.' *Archives of International Medicine, 161*, 1703–1708.

Yalom, I. (1980) *Existential Psychotherapy*. New York, NY: Basic Books.

Yalom, I. (1985) *Group Psychotherapy*. New York, NY: Basic Books.

Subject Index

acceptance
  effect of MBSR program on 61, 156–8, 187
  increase in 110–2, 117–8, 120, 123–5, 129–30, 135–7, 142, 149–50
  meaning of (mindfulness context) 32, 134–5
  mixed-method results 173–6
Acceptance and Commitment Therapy (ACT) 205
aging
  attitudes towards 50
  biological dimensions of 43–4
  conscious 43
  cultural differences 49–51
  mixed-method results 173–6
  psychosocial dimensions of 44
  self-perceptions of 113, 119, 126, 132, 144, 150, 157, 162–3, 197
  spirituality and 45–9, 52–3
  successful 42–3, 187
  Western concept of 43
  see also older adults
Amara Association for Dignity in Life and Death, Portugal 56
anxiety
  ACT treatment of 205
  death 55–8
  MBSR treatment of 23, 61–2, 112
  in older adults 44, 61–2
applications of the study 207–9
Army Individual Test Battery
  description of 222–3

summary of results 106–7
attention
  control 37–8
  increase in 117, 129–30, 155
  self-regulation of 29–31
attitude, self-regulation of 29–31
awareness
  increase in 112, 131, 143, 148, 156
  see also choiceless awareness; consciousness; meta-awareness (reperceiving); metacognitive awareness

bare attention 37–8
Be (poem) 152–3
"beginner's mind" 31
being with self 142, 156, 196
"being" versus "doing" 51
bereavement 58–9, 110–2, 137, 147, 149, 157, 199, 208
borderline personality disorder 205
brain injury, MBSR application 23
brain plasticity 40, 2
Buddhist philosophy
  on death and dying 53–6
  mindfulness in 24, 34–40
  observing own emotions 155, 189–90
  supported by study results 196–8
  see also Eastern cultures

cancer, MBSR application 23, 25, 200
Catholic upbringing 130
Catholic values 139
CDs 77, 138, 182, 201, 205
Center for Mindfulness, University of Massachusetts 77
change, openness versus resistance 177–9
choiceless awareness 31
civil status 84
clear comprehension (in Buddhism) 38
cognitive performance see neuropsychological performance
cognitive therapy, mindfulness-based (MBCT) 26, 204–5
compassion
  assessment of 88–90
  increase in 120, 126, 131, 138, 150, 167
  mixed-method results 173–6
compassionate knowing 67–8, 79
compliance 83
confidence 112, 124
consciousness
  in Buddhism 35
  development of 48, 124, 156
  see also awareness
construct validity 211
content validity 211
control group/treatment group differences 83–4
conventional reality 35
creative synthesis phase 72
creativity 168

cultural differences
 in aging 49–51
 in attitudes towards death 53–4, 58

daily practice
 mixed-method results 173–6
 participants' 83, 115, 121, 168–9, 201–2
death and dying
 attitudes of older adults 57–8, 127, 163, 197
 Buddhist perspective 53–6
 as developmental stage 56–7
 fear of 56–8
 perspective (assessment of) 73, 101–2
 perspective (mixed-method results) 173–6
 in Western cultures 53–4
 see also DPS (Death Perspective Scales)
decentering 29, 33, 90–1, 143, 155, 173–6, 187
delimitations of study 206
demographic changes 18
depression
 MBCT treatment of 204–5
 MBSR treatment of 27, 61–2, 110–2, 147
 in older adults 44, 61–2
design *see* methodology
development
 death and dying as stage of 56–7
 late-life 45–9, 114, 120, 126, 132–3, 145, 150–1, 197
Dialectical Behavior Therapy (DBT) 205
discernment 38, 112, 116, 119–20, 125, 126, 131, 137, 167
"doing" versus "being" 51
DPS (Death Perspective Scales)
 description of 220
 statistical results 266–9
 summary of results 101–2
dying *see* death and dying

Eastern cultures, older adults in 49–50

eating disorders, MBSR treatment of 23
economic factors 108
educational background 82, 84, 130
Eightfold Path (Buddhist) 37
emic viewpoint 72
emotional regulation 32–3, 41, 62, 114–5, 147, 157
empathy 186
EQ (Experiences Questionnaire)
 description of 214
 statistical results 245–7
 summary of results 90–1
etic viewpoint 72
eudaimonic well-being 188
explication phase 72

Factors of Enlightenment (Buddhist) 37
faith
 development of 48
 see also religion
FFMQ (Five Facet Mindfulness Questionnaire)
 description of 212–3
 statistical results 235–9
 summary of results 86–8
fibromyalgia 17, 187
flexibility 30–1, 33, 142–3
focusing, by researcher 70–1
food/diet 113, 126
formal practices 200–3
Four Noble Truths (Buddhist) 35–7, 54
future research 208–9

gender 84
"gerotranscendence" 47
grief 58–9, 110–2, 137, 147, 149, 157, 199, 208
growth 114, 126, 150, 163, 165, 178, 187

"harvesting" tasks 46–7
hedonic well-being 188
helping others 150, 166, 180–1
 see also compassion
heuristic research 69–72
holistic approach 18–20
home practice 200–3

illumination phase 72
immersion phase 71
immune system 23
impermanence 36, 54–5, 62, 118, 125, 129–30, 137, 143, 149, 158–9
implications of the study 207–9
incubation phase 71
individuation 45, 48
indwelling 70
informal practices 200–3
Inner Kids ABC program 205
insecurity, reduction in 122–3
insights, researcher's 71–2
integral inquiry method 65
integral skills 67
integrity, attaining sense of 47, 58
intention
 integral skill of 67
 self-regulation of 29–31
interconnectedness 69, 114, 120, 123, 127, 133, 139, 151, 164, 196
interviews
 individual depictions 109–52
 protocol for 224
 selection of participants for 78–80
intuition, of researcher 70

journal-keeping 80, 177–82
Jung, Carl 45–6

Karuna Hospice Services, Australia 56
knowing
 compassionate 67–8, 79
 tacit 70

language limitations 129, 207
late-life development 45–9, 114, 120, 126, 132–3, 145, 150–1, 197
life review 47
limitations of study 206–7
loss 58–9, 110–2, 137, 147, 149, 157, 199, 208

MAAS (Mindfulness Awareness Attention Scale)
 description of 211–2

statistical results 231–4
summary of results 85–6
MBCT (mindfulness-based cognitive therapy) 26, 204–5
MBSR (mindfulness-based stress reduction)
adaptation to older adults 182, 204–5
applications of 23–4
development of 22–3
learned principles from 171, 175
mental health therapists 186
and spirituality 25–6
studies with older adults 26–9
training in 203
meaning
finding 51–3, 114, 120, 164, 180–2, 198
in suffering 57, 113, 119, 126–7, 149–50, 157, 165
meditation
definition of 21
effects of 19, 24–5, 200
memory
assessment of 105–6
improvement in 168
statistical results 277–8
see also neuropsychological performance; Working Memory Index (WAIS III)
meta-awareness (repercieving) 30–1, 61, 143
metacognitive awareness 33–4, 187
methodology
heuristic research 69–72
integral inquiry method 65
integral skills in 67
limitations of previous studies 17–8, 29, 184
mixed-method design 66–9, 228
procedure 76–80
qualitative research methods 69–72, 229–30
quantitative research methods 72–4, 229–30

recruitment of participants 74–5
research questions 65, 71, 183, 228
mid-life crisis 45
mindfulness
assessment of 73, 85–8
in Buddhist philosophy 24
definitions of 17, 21–2, 201–2
effect of MBSR program on 154–6, 184–7
mixed-method results 173–6
practice of 29–34
research into 17–8
and spirituality 24–6
teaching of 76–8
mindfulness-based cognitive therapy (MBCT) 26, 204–5
mixed-method
design 66–9, 228
results 173–6
MOCA (Montreal Cognitive Assessment)
description of 221–2
summary of results 84
mood, assessment of 73
motivation, increased 112–3
multiple sclerosis, MBSR application 23

neuroplasticity 40–2
neuropsychological performance
assessment of 74–5, 103–7
effect of MBSR program on 194–5
improvement in 167–8
mixed-method results 173–6
see also memory
nirvana 35
nursing homes, MBSR treatment in 28
nutrition 113, 126

observing own emotions 155, 189–90
older adults
attitudes towards 50
attitudes towards death of 57–8, 127, 163, 197
brain plasticity of 40–2

challenges faced by 18
in Eastern cultures 49–50
experience of MBSR program 203–4
"harvesting" tasks 46–7
late-life development 45–9, 114, 120, 126, 132–3, 145, 150–1, 197
MBSR adapted to 182, 204–5
MBSR studies on 26–9
perception of own age 113, 119, 126, 132, 144, 150, 157, 162–3, 197
spiritual eldering 46–7
stereotyping of 50–1, 62
in Western cultures 49–50
see also aging
ontology 40
openness 30–1, 123, 177–9, 187

pain, MBSR treatment of 17, 23, 26–8, 118, 138–9, 158, 187
PANAS (Positive and Negative Affect Schedule)
description of 215–6
statistical results 249–50
summary of results 93–4
panic disorders, MBSR treatment of 23
participants
characteristics of 82–4
individual depictions 109–52
previous meditation experience 141
recruitment of 74–5
selected for interview 78–80
peacefulness 119, 125, 131, 137, 144, 148, 160
personal practice 20, 202–3
physical changes (in aging) 43–4
physical exercise 113, 126, 161, 191
physical health
assessment of 73–4, 82–3, 100–1
effect of MBSR program on 190–2
improvement in 113, 131–2, 138, 144, 148, 160–2

» 299 «

physical health *cont.*
  mixed-method results 173–6
  spirituality and 49
  treatment vs. control group 84
  see also pain; relaxation; sleep
physical limitations 51, 61, 118, 126, 131–2, 138, 142, 147, 150, 162, 187
POMS (Profile of Mood States)
  description of 217–8
  statistical results 255–8
  summary of results 95–7
positivity 160, 167, 169
post-traumatic stress disorder, MBSR treatment of 23
practice
  daily 83, 115, 121, 168–9, 201–2
  formal 200–3
  informal 200–3
  of mindfulness 29–34
  personal 20, 202–3
praying 132, 148
present moment, being in 110–2, 117–20, 123–5, 129–31, 135–6, 143, 147–8, 154–5, 167, 185, 187, 202
procedure 76–80
Processing Speed Index (WAIS III)
  statistical results 275–6
  summary of results 104–5
psoriasis, MBSR treatment of 23
PSS (Perceived Stress Scale)
  description of 216–7
  statistical results 259
  summary of results 97–8
psychological symptoms
  assessment of 95–8
  effect of MBSR program on 188–90
  improvement in 144, 159–60
  see also anxiety; depression; mood
purpose of life 51–3, 114, 120, 164, 180–2, 198
PWBS (Psychological Well-Being Scale)
  description of 216

statistical results 251–4
summary of results 94–5

qualitative data, treatment of 226–7
qualitative research methods 69–72, 229–30
qualitative results, individual depictions 109–52
quality of life
  assessment of 98–100
  mixed-method results 173–6
quantitative data
  limitations of 66
  statistical tests used 81–2, 211–23
  summary of results 107–8
  treatment of 225–6
  see also statistical results
quantitative research methods 72–4, 229–30

reality, Buddhism and 35
relaxation 113, 118–9, 125, 138, 144, 148, 161
religion
  Catholic upbringing 130
  Catholic values 139
  of participants 84
  spirituality and 24
  see also faith
reperceiving 30–1, 61, 143
research questions 65, 71, 183, 228
researcher, involvement of 69–72
right mindfulness 37
roots (in Buddhism) 35

SCS (Self-Compassion Scale)
  description of 213–4
  statistical results 240–4
  summary of results 88–90
self
  accepting 157
  being with 142, 156, 196
  quest for 45, 113–4
self-compassion 89, 107, 173, 184–7
  see also SCS (Self-Compassion Scale)
self-dialogue 70
self-regulation of attention 29–31

self-transcendence 48, 61–2
serenity 119, 125, 131, 137, 144, 148, 160
SHCI (Subjective Health Complaint Inventory)
  description of 219–20
  statistical results 265
  summary of results 100–1
silent sessions 182
skills, integral 67
sleep, improvement in 113, 119, 125, 148–9, 162
slowing down 68–9, 117, 124–5, 129, 135, 156
social changes (in aging) 44
social interactions
  effect of MBSR program on 192–4
  improvement in 115, 131, 137–8, 142, 148, 158, 166–7
  link to positive health 192–4
  mixed-method results 173–6
spiritual eldering 46–7
spirituality
  and aging 45–9, 52–3
  assessment of 74, 102–3
  at heart of existence 175
  definitions of 24
  development of 120–1, 132, 143–4, 151, 163–6, 180–2
  effect of MBSR program on 195–200
  and MBSR 25–6
  and mindfulness 24–6
  mixed-method results 173–6
  and physical health 49
statistical results
  DPS (Death Perspective Scales) 266–9
  EQ (Experiences Questionnaire) 245–7
  FFMQ (Five Facet Mindfulness Questionnaire) 235–9
  glossary of terms 279–81
  MAAS (Mindfulness Awareness Attention Scale) 231–4
  memory 277–8

PANAS (Positive and Negative Affect Schedule) 249–50
POMS (Profile of Mood States) 255–8
Processing Speed Index (WAIS III) 275–6
PSS (Perceived Stress Scale) 259
PWBS (Psychological Well-Being Scale) 251–4
SCS (Self-Compassion Scale) 240–4
SHCI (Subjective Health Complaint Inventory) 265
SWBQ (Spiritual Well-Being Questionnaire) 270–2
SWLS (Satisfaction With Life Scale) 249
WHOQOL-100 (World Health Organization Quality of Life-100) 263–4
WHOQOL-BREF (World Health Organization Quality of Life BREF) 260–2
Working Memory Index (WAIS III) 273–4
stereotyping, of older adults 50–1, 62
strength (psychological) 112
substance abuse, MBSR treatment of 25–6
suffering
 acceptance of 125, 158
 in Buddhist philosophy 36–7, 54
 finding meaning in 57, 113, 119, 126–7, 149–50, 157, 165
SWBQ (Spiritual Well-Being Questionnaire)
 description of 220–1
 statistical results 270–2
 summary of results 102–3
SWLS (Satisfaction With Life Scale)
 description of 214–5
 statistical results 249
 summary of results 92–3

tacit knowing 70
TMT (Trail Making Test)
 description 222–3
 summary of results 106–7
transcendence
 "gerotranscendence" 47
 self-transcendence 48
transformation 114, 126, 150, 163, 165, 178, 187
transpersonal psychology 19–20, 48–9, 208
transpersonal self 114, 127, 164, 196
treatment group/control group differences 83–4
Truths, Four Noble (Buddhist) 35–7, 54

ultimate reality 35
"unfinished business" 47
universality 69, 114, 120, 123, 127, 133, 139, 151, 164, 196

validity 211, 229–30
values clarification 30
verbal description limitations 129, 207

WAIS III (Wechsler Adult Intelligence Scale III)
 description of 222
 summary of results 103–5
well-being
 assessment of 73, 91–5
 effect of MBSR program on 188–90
 mixed-method results 173–6
 see also physical health; psychological symptoms
Western cultures
 Buddhism influence in 56
 death and dying in 53–4
 older adults in 49–50
WHOQOL-100 (World Health Organization Quality of Life-100)
 description of 218–9
 statistical results 263–4
 summary of results 99–100
WHOQOL-BREF (World Health Organization Quality of Life BREF)
 description of 219
 statistical results 260–2
 summary of results 98–9
wisdom 53, 163, 179–80, 197, 199
 see also late-life development
Working Memory Index (WAIS III)
 statistical results 273–4
 summary of results 103–4

yoga 75, 77–8, 138, 182, 184, 191–2, 201, 205, 209

Zen Hospice Project, San Francisco 56

Author Index

Aldwin, C. M. 18
Alexander, C. N. 29
Allen, J. 23
Allen, N. A. 23
Allen, N. B. 29
Alves, N. C. 73, 100, 220
Anderson, N. D. 66–7, 216
Andresen, J. 24
Armstrong, T. 45
Arnhoff, F. N. 50
Aronson, H. B. 39
Ashman, O. 50
Astin, J. 200

Baddeley, A. 74, 103
Baer, R. A. 24, 34, 73, 85, 186, 189, 200–1, 205, 212, 216–7
Baldwin, R. 61
Baltes, M. M. 42
Baltes, P. B. 42
Barbosa, E. 214
Barks, C. 197
Barnhofer, T. 205
Barreto, H. 74, 103
Barros-Oliveira, J. 73, 101, 220
Batchelor, S. 35
Baylis, N. 18
Bédard, M. 23, 183, 189
Begley, S. 63
Berg, C. A. 193
Best, J. L. 23
Bhikkhu, B. 35, 55
Biegel, G. M. 186, 217
Birnie, K. 186, 189, 213
Birren, J. E. 42, 180
Bishop, S. R. 29, 31, 34, 187
Blackledge, J. T. 33
Boddhi, B. 35
Bond, J. 43, 44
Bonner, G. 22–3
Bowen, S. 25
Braud, W. 65–7

Brazier, C. 24, 35–6, 196, 199
Brennan, A. 45, 58, 196–7
Breteler, M. M. 44
Brewi, J. 45, 58, 196–7
Bridges, L. J. 32
Brown, K. W. 22–3, 30–2, 34, 73, 85, 183, 186, 189, 211–2
Buchalterm E. N. 28
Bucknell, R. 22
Budge, M. M. 27
Burney, R. 23
Burns, A. 61
Butler, R. N. 42, 50
Byock, I. R. 56–7

Cahn, B. R. 21
Campos, J. J. 32
Camras, L. 32
Canavarro, M. C. 74, 98, 100, 102, 191, 218
Caplan, M. 19
Carlson, L. E. 21–3, 183, 186, 189, 190, 202, 212, 218
Carmody, J. 25, 63, 186, 189, 200–1, 212, 214, 216–7
Cassel, C. K. 54
Cavaco, S. 223
Cekic, M. 40, 194
Chambers, R. 23, 29, 31, 33–4, 36, 40, 62, 183, 189, 194, 222
Chandler, E. N. 49
Chew-Graham, C. A. 61
Chodzko-Zajko, W. 191, 195
Churchill, L. 217
Clark, R. 27, 69, 73, 215
Cohen, S. 44, 73, 95, 190, 216
Colaizzi, P. 109, 226
Coleman, P. 41, 43, 48
Cordon, S. 30

Corless, I. B. 53
Craik, F. I. M. 62, 194
Crane, C. 205
Crawford, S. 217
Creswell, J. D. 22, 66–7, 72, 173, 227, 229
Cumming, E. 42

Darowski, E. S. 62, 194
Davidson, R. 23, 40–1, 183, 190, 200
Davis, M. C. 62, 190
Davis, S. 29
De Almeida, P. L. 73
De Groot, J. C. 44
de Vibe, M. 219–20
DeBeni, R. 62, 194
Deberry, S. 29
Deci, E. L. 188
Denham, S. A. 32
Depaola, S. J. 58
Depraz, N. 30
Didonna, F. 17, 22–3, 26, 65, 183
Diener, E. 73, 91, 188, 214–5
Dillon, M. 24, 49
Dimidjian, S. 205
Douglass, B. G. 69
Droppleman, L. F. 217
Dunne, J. D. 40

Ekman, P. 22, 36, 39, 196
Ellison, C. G. 25
Epstein, M. 37
Eriksen, H. R. 73, 100, 190, 219
Erikson, E. 18, 47
Erikson, J. M. 58, 180, 196, 199
Ernst, S. 17, 26, 184, 189, 190
Eyetsemitan, F. E. 50–1
Eysenck, M. W. 74, 103

Feldman, G. 33, 189
Fenner, P. 32
Fernández-Ballesteros, R. 42
Ferreira, C. 74
Field, M. J. 54
Figueiras, M. J. 73, 100, 220
Finch, J. F. 193
Fisher, J. W. 102, 220
Fletcher, K. 23
Follette, V. M. 23
Fontinha, J. M. G. M. 213
Fortner, B. V. 57–9
Fowler, J. W. 48
Frankel, C. B. 32
Frankl, V. 52, 57, 180, 198
Freitas, S. 74, 221
Fresco, D. M. 73, 90, 185, 187, 214

Galinha, I. C. 73, 92, 216
Galvin-Nadeau, M. 23
Garland, E. 41
Garland, S. N. 23, 183, 189–90, 218
Gaylord, S. 41
George, L. K. 25
Germino, B. B. 53
Gesser, G. 57–8
Giles, H. 49–51
Goldenberg, D. L. 23
Goleman, D. J. 21–2, 194
Golub, S. A. 48, 50–1, 63
Gomez, R. 102, 220
Gouveia, M. J. 74, 102, 221
Greco, C. M. 17, 27
Greenland, S. K. 205
Gregório, S. 212–3
Grossman, P. 26
Groth-Marnat, G. 57
Gruenewald, T. L. 44, 50, 190, 193, 197
Gullone, E. 29

Hallett, C. B. 23, 183
Hanlon, S. 28, 189
Hansson, R. 58–9, 199
Harris, M. 72
Hart, W. 37
Hartelius, G. 19
Harvey, I. S. 49
Hayes, S. C. 32–3, 189
Heffernan, D. 195
Henry, W. H. 42
Hill, P. C. 24
Ho, D. Y. 49

Hoppes, K. 205
Huppert, F. A. 18

Ihlebaek, C. 73
Imara, M. 56

Jacobs, B. 219
Jager, C. A. 27
Jewell, A. 44, 190
Jordan, T. 31
Jung, C. G. 46, 180, 196, 199
Jyoti, N. 60

Kabat-Zinn, J. 17, 22–3, 31–3, 62, 183–4, 190, 204
Kachhawa, P. S. 57
Kahn, R. L. 42
Kamarck, T. 73
Kang, C. 22
Kaplan, K. H. 23
Keane, M. T. 103
Kelleher, K. 45
Keller, J. W. 57
Kemeny, M. E. 44, 50, 190, 193, 197
Kempermann, G. 40
Kenerne, B. 18
Keynes, C. L. M. 73, 92, 188, 216
Khong, B. S. L. 37, 40
Kiester, M. 195
King, U. 42
Koenig, H. G. 49
Kornfield, J. 178
Krasner, M. 34
Krishnamurti, J. 21, 31, 69, 177
Kristeller, J. L. 23, 183
Kübler-Ross, E. 53–4, 57
Kuijpers, K. F. 186, 212, 219
Kumar, A. 57
Kumar, S. 59, 60, 199

Laing, R. D. 203
Lajoie, D. H. 19
Langer, E. J. 48–51, 63, 195
Lantz, M. S. 28, 189
Larson, D. B. 25, 49
Lazar, S. W. 40–1, 62, 194
Leigh, J. 25
Leon, H. 50
Levinson, D. J. 48, 58
Levy, B. R. 49–50
Lewis, M. I. 42

Lher, U. 42
Lichtenberg, P. A. 195
Lief, J. L. 62
Likourezos, A. 28, 190
Lindberg, D. A. 28, 189
Linehan, M. M. 205
Lipworth, L. 23
Lo, B. C. Y. 23
Löckenhoff, C. E. 50
Long, J. B. 55–6, 60
Loor, M. 217
Lopez, O. L. 195
Lorge, I. 50
Lorion, R. P. 58
Lotfy, M. 73
Lutz, A. 40
Lykins, E. L. B. 24

McBee, L. 17–8, 28, 44, 60, 184, 190, 205
McCann, R. M. 50
McCullough, M. E. 49
McDowd, J. M. 62, 194
McFadden, S. H. 19
McGlashan, A. 68
Mckenzie, C. S. 215
Mckenzie, E. R. 49
MacKenzie, M. J. 25, 63, 196
MacKinlay, E. 43–4, 51–3, 180, 190, 198–9
McMordie, W. R. 57
McNair, D. M. 217
Madnawat, A. V. S. 57
Marlatt, G. A. 25
Marques, T. 73–4, 95, 217
Martins, C. 67–8, 153
Masuda, A. 33
Meisenhelder, J. B. 49
Merleau-Ponty, M. 191
Mermelstein, R. 73
Mertens, D. M. 211
Metzer, R. 53
Miller, J. J. 23, 62, 183
Mills, N. 23
Mind and Life Institute 22
Missine, L. 52, 180, 182, 198
Moberg, D. O. 24, 49
Moody, H. R. 43, 199
Moore, C. A. 35, 54–5
Moreira, A. R. 74
Morone, N. E. 17, 27–8, 184, 187, 190
Moscovici, S. 49
Mota-Cardoso, R. 217
Moustakas, C. 69–70
Moye, J. 28, 189

Mullin, G. 53
Murphy, R. 23, 183

Nagel, L. 219
Nasreddine, A. S. 75
Neale, N. I. 36–8, 199
Neff, K. D. 73, 88, 213
Neimeyer, R. A. 57–8
Neto, F. 73, 101, 220
Newhill, C. E. 189
Novak, P. 53
Nyanaponika, T. 21
Nyklicek, I. 186, 212, 219

O'Connell, K. 73
Oken, B. S. 192
Olendzki, A. 21–2
Orzech, K. M. 185, 214
Ostir, G. V. 44

Pagnoni, G. 40, 194
Pais Ribeiro, J. L. 73–4, 92, 95, 216–7
Palladino, P. 62, 194
Pargament, K. I. 24
Park, C. L. 18
Patton, J. F. 45
Pavot, W. 215
Peace, S. 43
Pinto-Gouveia, J. 212–3
Piotrowski, C. 57
Pittman, M. 53
Plante, T. G. 25
Polanyi, M. 70
Polich, J. 21
Poulin, P. A. 215
Powell, L. H. 25
Pressman, S. D. 44, 190
Prewitt, S. H. 17, 27, 184, 187

Rabbitt, P. 44
Radhakrishnan, S. 35, 54–5
Ram Dass 49, 60
Ramel, W. 34
Rardin, M. A. 19
Reed, P. G. 48–9, 180, 196, 199
Reinhard, K. E. 29
Reker, G. T. 57
Rizvi, S. L. 205
Robba, S. 43, 47, 199
Rook, K. S. 192, 193
Rosenzweig, S. 218
Rowe, J. W. 42

Rusting, R. L. 44
Ruumet, H. 48
Ryan, R. M. 22–3, 73, 85, 183, 188, 211
Rybarczyk, B. 58
Ryff, C. 73, 92, 188, 216

Salva, V. 210
Santos, R. C. 73
Schachter-Shalomi, Z. 43, 46–7, 180, 196–7, 199
Schaie, K. W. 42
Schumaker, J. F. 57
Schwartz, G. E. 22–3, 30, 187
Scott, J. 58
Seeman, T. E. 193
Segal, Z. V. 29, 33, 205
Seidman-Carlson, R. 215
Selby, J. 24, 196
Shacham, S. 73, 95, 217
Shah, C. S. 41
Shahabi, L. 25
Shapiro, D. H. 30
Shapiro, S. L. 19, 21–2, 30–1, 185–7, 202, 212–3, 216–7
Shauna, S. 202
Sherman, A. C. 25, 74
Sherry, D. 57
Shiomura, K. 50
Shirazi, B. 227
Siegel, D. J. 25, 40–1
Silva, M. E. D. 73–4, 92, 216
Simões, A. 73, 91
Simões, M. R. 74, 221
Singh, K. D. 56–7
Skevington, S. M. 73, 98, 218–9
Smith, A. 17–8, 26, 29, 44, 61–2, 184, 189–90
Smith, H. 53
Sogyal Rinpoche 21, 54–6
Speca, M. 186, 200, 218
Spilka, B. 73, 220
Spiro, A. 18
Spreen, O. 74
Steele, C. M. 50
Strada, E. 54–6
Strauss, E. 74, 103, 222
Stroebe, M. S. 58–9, 199
Strosahl, K. 32
Sunderland, T. 42
Sung, K. 49
Svensson, C. M. 180

Teasdale, J. D. 29, 33–4, 187
Tellegen, A. 73, 215
Thera, N. 34, 37–9, 190
Thoresen, C. E. 25
Thygesen, E. 220
Tombaugh, T. N. 223
Toms, J. 67
Toms, M. 67
Torbjorn, M. 219–20
Tornstam, L. 19, 45, 47, 179, 196, 199
Treadway, M. T. 62, 194
Turner, K. 187, 189

Ursin, H. 73
U.S. Centers for Disease Control Prevention 18, 42

Varela, F. J. 30, 54
Vaughan, F. 19, 61, 69
Vaz Serra, A. 73, 98, 219
Verbraak, A. 47
Viana, M. F. 73, 95, 217
Vijay, A. 23

Wagner, K. D. 58
Walsh, R. 19, 24
Warren, W. G. 57
Washburn, M. 48
Watson, D. 73, 92, 188, 215
Weiner, D. K 17, 27
Welch, D. 205, 210
Welwood, J. 33, 36, 189
Westreich, L. 28, 190
WHOQOL Group 74, 191
Wilber, K. 48
Williams, J. M. G. 29
Wilson, K. G. 32
Wink, P. 24, 49, 58
Wolever, R. Q. 23
Wong, P. T. P. 57
Woods, S. L. 203
Wulff, D. M. 24

Yaffe, K. 191, 195
Yalom, I. 56

Printed in Great Britain
by Amazon